Overcoming Challenges to Gender Equality in the Workplace

Leadership and Innovation

OVERCOMING CHALLENGES
TO GENDER EQUALITY
IN THE WORKPLACE
Leadership and Innovation

Edited by **Patricia M. Flynn,**
Kathryn Haynes and **Maureen A. Kilgour**

Routledge
Taylor & Francis Group

LONDON AND NEW YORK

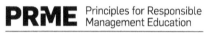 **PRME** Principles for Responsible
Management Education

**Greenleaf Publishing/PRME Book Series –
For Responsibility in Management Education**

First published 2016 by Greenleaf Publishing Limited

Published 2017 by Routledge
2 Park Square, Milton Park, Abingdon, Oxon OX14 4RN
711 Third Avenue, New York, NY 10017, USA

Routledge is an imprint of the Taylor & Francis Group, an informa business

Cover by Sadie Gornall-Jones.

British Library Cataloguing in Publication Data:
A catalogue record for this book is available from the British Library.

ISBN-13: 978-1-78353-546-0 [pbk]
ISBN-13: 978-1-78353-267-4 [hbk]

Contents

The Women's Empowerment Principles

Source: www.weprinciples.org/Site/PrincipleOverview

Equality means business

The Women's Empowerment Principles are a set of principles for business offering guidance on how to empower women in the workplace, marketplace and community. They are the result of a collaboration between the United Nations Entity for Gender Equality and the Empowerment of Women (UN Women) and the United Nations Global Compact and are adapted from the Calvert Women's Principles®. The development of the Women's Empowerment Principles included an international multi-stakeholder consultation process, which began in March 2009 and culminated in their launch on International Women's Day in March 2010.

Subtitled Equality Means Business, the principles emphasize the business case for corporate action to promote gender equality and women's empowerment and are informed by real-life business practices and input gathered from across the globe. The Women's Empowerment Principles seek to point the way to best practice by elaborating the gender dimension of corporate responsibility, the UN Global Compact and the role of business in sustainable development. As well as being a useful guide for business, the principles seek to inform other stakeholders, including governments, in their engagement with business.

- Principle 1: Establish high-level corporate leadership for gender equality
- Principle 2: Treat all women and men fairly at work—respect and support human rights and non-discrimination
- Principle 3: Ensure the health, safety and well-being of all women and men workers
- Principle 4: Promote education, training and professional development for women
- Principle 5: Implement enterprise development, supply chain and marketing practices that empower women
- Principle 6: Promote equality through community initiatives and advocacy
- Principle 7: Measure and publicly report on progress to achieve gender equality

The Six Principles of PRME

Source: www.unprme.org/about-prme/the-six-principles.php

As institutions of higher education involved in the development of current and future managers we declare our willingness to progress in the implementation, within our institution, of the following Principles, starting with those that are more relevant to our capacities and mission. We will report on progress to all our stakeholders and exchange effective practices related to these principles with other academic institutions:

Principle 1 | Purpose: We will develop the capabilities of students to be future generators of sustainable value for business and society at large and to work for an inclusive and sustainable global economy.

Principle 2 | Values: We will incorporate into our academic activities and curricula the values of global social responsibility as portrayed in international initiatives such as the United Nations Global Compact.

Principle 3 | Method: We will create educational frameworks, materials, processes and environments that enable effective learning experiences for responsible leadership.

Principle 4 | Research: We will engage in conceptual and empirical research that advances our understanding about the role, dynamics and impact of corporations in the creation of sustainable social, environmental and economic value.

Principle 5 | Partnership: We will interact with managers of business corporations to extend our knowledge of their challenges in meeting social and environmental responsibilities and to explore jointly effective approaches to meeting these challenges.

Principle 6 | Dialogue: We will facilitate and support dialog and debate among educators, students, business, government, consumers, media, civil society organizations and other interested groups and stakeholders on critical issues related to global social responsibility and sustainability.

We understand that our own organizational practices should serve as example of the values and attitudes we convey to our students.

Introduction
Reducing gender inequality in the workplace through leadership and innovation

Maureen A. Kilgour
University of Winnipeg, Canada

Kathryn Haynes
University of Hull, UK

Patricia M. Flynn
Bentley University, USA

Gender inequality has a long history in business schools and in the workplace and traditions are hard to change. But change they must.

This book on gender equality in the workplace is the second of two on Gender Equality as a Challenge for Business and Management Education in the Greenleaf Publishing/PRME (Principles for Responsible Management Education) book series. These edited volumes are outcomes of the work of the PRME Working Group on Gender Equality. The first book, *Integrating Gender Equality in Business and Management Education: Lessons Learned and Challenges Remaining,* published in 2015, identified the key issues underlying gender inequality in management education and why these must be addressed. With conceptual and research-based chapters, as well as case studies and innovations across disciplinary, institutional, international and pedagogical perspectives, that book provides guidance to faculty on how to integrate issues of gender equality into their teaching and research. More generally, it demonstrates to educational leaders how PRME can be used to create more equitable and inclusive environments that, in turn, can help mitigate the under-representation of women in management and leadership positions in the business world. It effectively makes the case that gender issues must be part of the discussion on sustainability and social justice.

This volume addresses the challenges of achieving gender equality in the workplace. It is written for practitioners, policy-makers and academics, and for businesses, institutions and organizations. It supports the goal of gender equality in businesses and organizations, provides examples of the many ways in which gender equality in the workplace is being addressed, and demonstrates how to deal with and overcome related challenges.

Launched in 2007, PRME is the UN Global Compact's initiative to transform management education, research and thought leadership globally by providing the Principles for Responsible Management Education framework, developing learning communities and promoting awareness about the United Nations' Sustainable Development Goals. The Women's Empowerment Principles (WEPs) were launched in 2010 by the UN Global Compact and by UN Women (formerly UNIFEM) with the goal of helping "the private sector focus on key elements integral to promoting gender equality in the workplace, marketplace and community." In 2011, the PRME Working Group on Gender Equality was formed, with a mission to bring together academics, employers and the business community to provide support and resources for integrating gender issues and awareness into management education and the business world. The PRME Working Group on Gender Equality supports the UN WEPs in many ways, including by integrating a gender perspective into management education, through outreach activities such as this book series, and by calling for attention to be paid to gender throughout all business operations.

There are many reasons for businesses and organizations to address gender inequality. Gender equality is a fundamental human right, and a social justice perspective is sufficient for providing the rationale to address gender and other inequalities. However, the business case for promoting gender equality is compelling. A growing body of research demonstrates benefits that often accompany gender diversity in the workplace (see, for example, Catalyst, 2011; Boatman *et al.*, 2011; Credit Suisse Research Institute, 2012; Hunt *et al.*, 2015). At the corporate board level, for example, legislated gender quotas and voluntary targets are on the rise, especially in Europe. These have often resulted in significant increases in the percentage of women directors on corporate boards. There is substantial evidence that these changes can improve corporate performance (ILO, 2015; Women on Boards *et al.*, 2015). At the other end of the global supply chain, the 2013 Rana Plaza factory collapse in Bangladesh focused the world's attention on textile and clothing global brands and the inequality faced by women in developing economies. Initiatives that followed that tragedy, such as the multi-stakeholder Bangladesh Fire and Building Safety Accord show that business and organizations are willing to play a significant role in working towards gender equality for the most vulnerable women workers. Despite a recent increase in positive corporate initiatives to address gender inequality, often through corporate social responsibility (CSR) programmes and policies, substantial gender gaps remain across the spectrum of occupations. And gender gaps get larger the higher up the skill level and career path one goes. Among S&P 500 firms, for example, women still constitute less than 5% of the CEOs and fewer than 20% of the directors (Catalyst, 2016).

This book addresses issues of gender equality across a wide range of businesses, organizations and cultural environments worldwide. It seeks to provide inspiration and incentives for businesses to address gender inequality throughout their organizations and beyond, including in the communities in which they operate. The range of industries and work situations covered in this volume reflects the nature of women's work and the challenges of gender equality across regions and countries. What links all of these chapters is the reality of working women's lives, challenges and experiences, and the importance of innovation, leadership and organizational commitment to gender equality.

The volume provides conceptual and research rationales as to why responsible businesses and organizations must address the issue of gender equality in the workplace. It also provides case studies of companies that have overcome challenges to gender equality in the workplace; first-hand accounts of leaders and pioneers in tackling gender issues at work; factors beyond the workplace that can help foster greater gender equality at work; and long-standing traditions being challenged to promote gender equality in the workplace.

Organization of the book

The chapters in this book are organized into four parts related to overcoming challenges to gender equality in the workplace.

Part I. Case studies of companies that have overcome challenges to gender equality in the workplace

Part I provides case studies of companies, spanning diverse economic and cultural conditions, which have overcome challenges in the workplace to enhance gender equality. Based on a study of a successful high-tech company in Belgium, Roos and Zanoni (Chapter 1) explore the policies, practices and narratives leading to creation of more equal professional opportunities for women and men. The authors conclude with lessons for other companies, especially newly formed organizations, for overcoming challenges to gender inequality. In Chapter 2, Finnegan and White explore ways in which Cargill, a US-based large-scale business operating in the agricultural sector in Zambia, uses the workplace to foster women's economic empowerment. Incorporating a range of approaches including charitable or philanthropic intervention, CSR activities and creating shared value (CSV) perspectives, the authors demonstrate practices employers can implement to help women overcome barriers and inequalities within and beyond the workplace. Chapter 3 demonstrates the transformational role that lawyers can play in fostering gender equality in the workplace. Focusing on the Fortune 100 US pharmaceutical company Pfizer, Inc., Cecchi-Dimeglio shows how the General Counsel can be a highly successful change agent for gender diversity in a large organization. The chapter concludes with lessons, best practices and guiding principles for General Counsels and legal departments in promoting gender equality in the workplace.

Part II. First-hand accounts of leaders and pioneers tackling gender inequality at work

Part II of the book gets personal. In Chapter 4, CEO and founder Gay Gaddis demonstrates how she led the transformation of T3, the largest woman-owned independent advertising agency in the United States, into a family-friendly workplace. She shows how T3 and Under, the company's innovative on-site childcare programme, provides employees who are parents with the means and opportunity to continue working full-time during the first few months of their babies' lives. The chapter explains the programme's successes as well as failures, and the economic and emotional impacts it has had on all involved. It also demonstrates the critical role of organizational leadership in fostering gender equality in the workplace. Related to the theme of work–life balance for working women, Watton and Stables (Chapter 5) show how their three-year hybrid job-sharing experience in higher education resulted in benefits for their employer as well as themselves, not only providing senior management opportunities on a part-time basis, but also fostering leadership development for these women. The authors hope that, by encouraging other women to consider job sharing as one way to achieve better work–life balance or as an alternative to temporarily leaving the workforce, the number of women in senior positions will increase. In Chapter 6, Reverend Rebecca Roberts takes us along on her personal adventure as the first full-time female priest in charge of a Church of England parish. After summarizing the literature on the concept of the physical body as presented in distributed leadership and social identity theories, the author shows that women's bodies continue to be sexualized and their leadership roles questioned purely as their representation as "other". The chapter concludes with recommendations on how to promote females as leaders and to establish policies and training to counteract sexism.

Part III. Factors beyond the workplace that can foster greater gender equality at work

Part III demonstrates that addressing gender equality in the workplace often requires collaboration and leadership beyond the management team and walls of a company, as the roots of gender inequality are found in society at large. The UN Global Compact and other corporate responsibility initiatives use the concept of the "sphere of influence" to highlight the importance of businesses looking beyond their own organizations to address underlying causes of gender inequality within the spheres in which they operate. In addition, CSR practices and theories draw attention to the importance of cross-sector partnerships, where firms are encouraged to work with stakeholders and governments in order to better affect change. The UN WEPs encourage businesses and organizations to work with a variety of social partners to tackle gender inequality. This section provides innovative examples of how this can be accomplished.

In Chapter 7, Johnstone-Louis highlights the fact that four of six identified contributors to gender inequality in the coffee industry exist outside of the workplace: issues related to women's time, physical mobility, control over assets, and personal safety. The chapter details the experiences of the non-profit International Women's Coffee Alliance (IWCA) as it seeks to advance gender equality across the global coffee supply chain. Lessons learned from the IWCA, which are relevant well beyond the coffee industry, are provided. Grant-Smith, Osborne and Marinelli (Chapter 8) also look beyond the workplace to show how women's access, or lack thereof, to safe, secure and efficient transport can impact their workforce participation. The authors identify a mix of transport and non-transport initiatives from selected OECD nations aimed at reducing barriers to workforce participation and improving women's transport mobility to the benefit of individuals, families, organizations and society. Wibberley, Jones, Bennett and Hollinrake (Chapter 9) next address how domestic violence can hamper performance, attendance and career development at the workplace. The authors explain how trade unions in the United Kingdom have helped both victims, who are predominantly women, and organizations to better handle those affected by such abuse. This is another issue in which the gender inequality experience outside of the workplace can impact women workers and performance in the workplace. It further demonstrates the importance of including a range of different social partners to tackle significant and systemic issues in society at large. In the final chapter in Part III, Norris and Carter-Rogers (Chapter 10) encourage organizations to use service-learning programmes in educational settings as models for what can be achieved in the workplace. These programmes in educational environments have played a role in reducing stereotypes, increasing empathy and raising students' awareness of the importance of diversity. The authors suggest that firms that adopt service-learning for their employees will reap similar benefits, and thus promote organizational cultures that favour gender equality, in addition to increased empathy among co-workers.

Part IV. Long-standing traditions being challenged to promote gender equality in the workplace

Part IV discusses recent changes in long-standing traditions that play a role in the perpetuation of gender inequality in the workplace. First, Gleich (Chapter 11) discusses the demise of the two-tiered system that has characterized the US military for decades. As of January 2016, no military position in the United States is closed to women based on their gender, although women are required to demonstrate "appropriate and identical" levels of physical fitness as men for various positions.

The author discusses the roles that policy changes, cultural barriers and resistance have played in society's understanding of women's roles in the US military and raises important questions in the quest for gender equality, in such institutions. Howaidy (Chapter 12) then tackles the issue of women on corporate boards and both military and religious traditional forces in the changing power structure in Egypt. The author highlights the "key steps and small wins" of the Women on Boards initiative in a country without a legislated mandate to expand the number of women corporate directors. She concludes with recommendations to improve gender equality on boards in Egypt, identifying programmes and policies likely to be relevant in other emerging economies as well. Closing Part IV, Shukla (Chapter 13) demonstrates the benefits of collaboration and partnerships as a business school and a bank in rural India join forces to prepare women to successfully run microenterprises. The Mann Deshi Udyogini provides skills training while the Mann Deshi Bank offers financing with the goal of empowering women in a society that has often treated them as second-class citizens. The chapter provides numerous examples of women whose lives have been transformed by the initiatives of these institutions.

Concluding comments

The book concludes with a chapter that highlights the key messages and lessons learned across a range of industries and cultures.

We hope that you will be inspired by these examples of leadership and innovation in promoting gender equality in the workplace. We wish you well in your own efforts to eliminate gender inequalities wherever they exist.

References

Boatman, J., Wellings, R.S. with Neal, S. (2011). *Women Work: The Business Benefits of Closing the Gender Gap*. Global Leadership Forecast, Pittsburgh, PA: Development Dimensions International.

Catalyst (2011). *The Bottom Line: Corporate Performance and Women's Representation on Boards, 2004–2008*. New York: Catalyst.

Catalyst (2016, February 3). *Pyramid: Women in S&P 500 Companies*. New York: Catalyst.

Credit Suisse Research Institute (2012). *Gender Diversity and Corporate Performance*. Zurich, Switzerland: Credit Suisse AG.

Hunt, V., Layton, D. & Prince, S. (2015). *Why Diversity Matters*. London: McKinsey & Company Insights and Publications.

International Labour Organization (2015). *Women on Boards, Building the Female Talent Pipeline*. Geneva: ILO.

Women on Boards, KPMG & Cranfield University (2015). *Improving the Gender Balance on British Boards, Women on Boards Davies Review, Five Year Summary, October 2015*.

Part I
Case studies of companies that have overcome challenges to gender equality in the workplace

1

Disrupting gendered dichotomies
Gender equality in a high-tech Belgian company

Hannelore Roos and Patrizia Zanoni
UHasselt, Belgium

This chapter aims to draw together theoretical lessons on how to effectively foster gender equality at work. Based on the qualitative case study of a Belgian high-tech company employing a considerable number of women throughout the organizational hierarchy, we identify a constellation of policies, practices and narratives which dilute three classical hierarchized gendered dichotomies at work: (1) male/female identities, (2) individualism/collectivism, and (3) private/public (Ely and Meyerson, 2000). Our analysis suggests that gender equality along these dichotomies is respectively fostered by narratives and practices of: (1) masculine and feminine competences as distinct, equally valuable and acquirable by all, (2) innovative work as a collective achievement, and (3) far-reaching work flexibility. Despite the absence of a formalized gender policy, the emergence of masculine, heroic professional identities is discouraged, creating more equal professional opportunities for women and men, resulting in gender equality.

The persistent, albeit uneven (Cain and Leahey, 2014), exclusion of women in male-dominated, knowledge-intensive industries and occupations, including engineering, IT and science, has been documented by a vast body of literature (Charles and Grusky, 2004; Goodall, 2010; Kirkup *et al.*, 2010; Walby, 2011b; Van Hove *et al.*, 2011;

Busch and Holst, 2011; Ellingsæter, 2013). Women remain heavily under-represented in these industries, as they are less likely than men to enter them and more likely to exit early (Beninger, 2014; Hewlett *et al.*, 2008). Moreover, women that are employed in high-tech companies report having negative professional experiences, and feeling like "outsiders" (Peterson, 2007) and tend to be concentrated in the lower echelons, performing generic, labour-intensive jobs (Huffman *et al.*, 2010).

A variety of mechanisms have been identified to explain gender inequality in male-dominated work environments. Research has shown how apparently neutral and meritocratic human resource (HR) practices, ranging from selection to evaluations, are predicated on dominant notions of gender which devalue women and the skills associated with them, negatively affecting their careers (Rees and Garnsey, 2003; Martin, 1996). Similarly, other studies have unveiled how the notion of an ideal worker both reflects and reproduces hegemonic masculinities in terms of authority, careerism, competitiveness, individualism and technology skills (Connell and Messerschmidt, 2005). These male norms permeate organizations, making it particularly hard for women to be considered valuable employees in the workplace (Bastalich *et al.*, 2007). Women's exclusion is thus conceptualized as the effect of a hidden "gender subtext" (Smith, 1988, 1990; Acker, 1998), a set of concealed power based processes (re)producing gender distinctions to the disadvantage of women in organizations (Benschop and Doorewaard, 1998).

Uncovering and changing institutions reproducing gender inequality remain major topics of concern for gender scholars and practitioners alike (Ainsworth *et al.*, 2010; Benschop and Verloo, 2011). The literature on gender equality traditionally distinguishes three distinct models for the advancement of women: (1) special programmes "fixing" women by offering them the skills they lack to perform at par with men; (2) programmes which stress women's difference from men yet "value the feminine"; and (3) programmes fostering equal opportunities by reducing gender bias in structures and processes and through compensatory measures for women (Rees, 1998, 2005; Walby, 2011a; Ely and Meyerson, 2000; Meyerson and Kolb, 2000). Each of these approaches has been distinctively critiqued for its ineffectiveness in inducing profound, structural organizational change necessary to achieve gender equality (Ely and Meyerson, 2000; Ainsworth *et al.*, 2010). Specifically, it has been argued that they leave the latent gender subtext of organizations intact (Benschop and Doorewaard, 1998; Janssens and Zanoni, 2014; Zanoni *et al.*, 2010) and that, during the implementation of gender change strategies, underlying mechanisms such as social cognitions, ideas on social justice, experiences of threat or the lack of demonstrated utility or direct benefits of gender equality tend to be insufficiently addressed (Kottke and Agars, 2005).

In this chapter, we identify social practices fostering gender equality by drawing on a case study of a high-tech company that has achieved significant progress towards gender equality throughout the organizational hierarchy. Founded in the late 1980s by a married couple, an engineer and a translator by training, SensorInc (pseudonym) is a Belgian multinational company listed on the Euronext Brussels stock exchange. With premises in Belgium, Germany, France, Swiss, Ukraine, Bulgaria, Japan, China,

Hong Kong, the Philippines and the USA, the company is a world player in automotive sensors employing 889 workers in total, 33% of whom are women. Although only 10% of the 273 engineers are female, 29% of the 194 staff members in leadership positions are women (e.g. management roles, as team leader or chief). In the Belgian headquarters, 38% of the 161 employees and 45% of the 58 managers are women.

Since its public listing in 1997, SensorInc's board of directors has been composed of three women and three men. This gender balance is exceptional in the Belgian context, where female directors were a rarity before the introduction of a legal quota in 2011 (11% on the Bel20 index; European Commission, 2015) and where the proportion of female executives lies below the European average (Straub, 2007). SensorInc's alternative approach is grounded in the business case for diversity, publicly communicating that "a diverse and inclusive staff inspires creativity and innovation, enabling the SensorInc vision" (Press release, March 7, 2012). The company has a strong business orientation as expressed in its mission statement which stresses values such as customer orientation, leadership and profitability as well as interpersonal values of enjoyment, a sustainable work–life balance, respect for diversity, mutual trust and equality of opportunities. As a team-based organization it is characterized by a flat organizational structure to enhance knowledge-intensive project work, communication and collaboration.

The main data sources are 36 semi-structured interviews conducted in the Belgian headquarters with the CEO, all the members of the board and 30 employees, including eight men and eight women in management positions (e.g. team lead, financial planning and analysis manger, site and HR manager, portfolio manager, or global supply chain manager). Access to respondents was facilitated by the CEO, who introduced us to the board members and the HR department. The latter compiled a gender-balanced list of employees across various departments, from which we could randomly select respondents. In approaching potential interviewees, we informed them about the goal of the study and granted full anonymity and confidentiality. The interviews probed into the professional background of the respondents, the organizational culture and working environment, their social networks and human resource practices. All interviews took place at the premises of the company during office hours, were recorded and transcribed verbatim. To complement the interview data, we collected relevant internal documents and publicly available year reports and media articles on the company.

SensorInc's social practices disrupting the gender subtext

To interpret the policies, practices and narratives we observed, we draw on a fourth, alternative approach to gender advanced by Ely and Meyerson (2000). This approach rests on an understanding of gender as "a complex set of social relations enacted across a range of social practices that exist both within and outside of formal organizations" and "through which the categories male and female, masculine and feminine, derive meaning and shape experience" (Ely and Meyerson, 2000, pp. 113-114). Despite their gender-neutral appearance, institutionalized social practices in organizations—including formal policies and procedures; informal work practices, norms, and patterns of work; language, and other symbolic expressions; and informal patterns of everyday social interaction (Acker, 1990)—tend to reflect and support men's experiences and male norms (Martin, 1996), reproducing a gendered social order in which men and particular forms of masculinity predominate.

Ely and Meyerson (2000) hold that such social order rests on three foundational, pervasive dichotomies between masculinity/femininity, individual/collective and public/private, which operate as key mechanisms for the unequal allocation of resources, information, and opportunities between men and women in organizations. Hereunder, we outline these dichotomies and discuss how SensorInc disrupts them, respectively, through a strong narrative and practices of masculine and feminine competences as distinct, equally valuable and acquirable by all, innovative work as a collective achievement, and far-reaching work flexibility. Although these social practices are not part of a formal, designated gender policy but rather aim to enhance performance and innovation in a high-tech workplace, they foster gender equality.

Disrupting the male–female dichotomy through the equal valuing of competences

A first gendered dichotomy refers to the understanding of male and female identities as mutually exclusive, hierarchically ordered categories rooted in individuals' biological sex (West and Zimmerman, 1987). To the extent that female identity and roles are devalued by organizations, women who behave according to stereotypical female roles will be professionally disadvantaged. SensorInc disrupted this opposition through HR practices ranging from recruitment to evaluation, training and promotion. The company clearly distinguished between "female business skills" and "male technical skills", yet simultaneously also revalued the former as essential to the company's growth and success and expected individuals to invest in acquiring novel skills complementing their own (gendered) ones through training.

Many respondents, both male and female, upheld common stereotypical ideas about male and female competences. Women were seen to be more caring and social, and good at multitasking, organizing and taking the broader context into account to find compromises. Men were seen as more result-oriented and technical, but also as more conflict-driven and narrow-minded:

> Men are more involved in technical occupations, while women are specialized in soft skills, the administration and organization. They are also good in management. We, men, are more focused on the technical and are good in technical problem-solving (man, Senior System Administrator).

These gender representations were supported by the occupational segregation of men and women in the company, reflecting the low share of women in high-tech higher educational tracks. Female-dominated departments were human resources, operations, global sales and marketing communication, while male-dominated ones were the SensorInc business units, global development and finance.

At the same time, respondents commonly stressed that these different sets of skills are both essential to the company:

> A company has not only a technical side, but forms a human entity that needs to be managed and guided. So you need both types of competences otherwise you will not achieve business results. Initially, a company can drive on its technical core competences, but it will not be able to grow. The more we expand, the more we experience the need for other, complementary competences to make a company successful (man, Facilities Manager).

The idea of the difference and complementarity between men and women was also clearly central in the company's hiring practice, which systematically aimed at gender balance in personnel throughout departments:

> Yes, we look at gender when we recruit. When we notice that certain departments are becoming homogenous, we try to look for candidates of the opposite sex. When two candidates of opposite sexes show the same level of competences and commitment, we take gender into consideration in the final decision to create a better gender balance in our departments. In our HR department for example we would opt for a male candidate, while we would give preference to a female engineer to obtain a healthy mix. Merit remains the foremost quality but when you have equal profiles… You create a different atmosphere, a different dynamic, which is interesting (man, Consolidation Coordinator).

While these narratives undoubtedly reproduced stereotypical understandings of women and men rather than challenging them, different from the classical feminine/masculine identity dichotomy, gender differences were presented as equally valuable and gender heterogeneity in equality as an organizational asset.

Moreover, the essentialistic understanding of men and women was tempered by a strong personnel development policy which expected that employees continuously learned new skills, expanding their own abilities through training and coaching:

> Different competences are stimulated, that depends on the role of each employee. Everybody has a position profile which entails the technical competences of the job but also the business culture that should be mastered. The company supports the employees on those two levels to be able to integrate both the technical competences and the business skills. We do that in different ways, by sending people to conferences, workshops and seminars, by letting people read certain books and offer them trainings, customized to each individual (man, Facilities Manager).

Importantly, this policy softened gender stereotypes by casting "male" and "female" skills as "learnable" by anyone and normalizing the expectation that individuals put in efforts to do so. To further integrate complementary knowledge and skills, the company organized courses and created formal and informal spaces and opportunities for cross-departmental exchange. Also, personnel development was supported by the use of 360 degree appraisals enabling individuals to collect feedback from employees in various positions and on a broad range of skills.

Taken together, these organizational practices appear to disrupt the classical feminine/masculine identity dichotomy by essentializing male and female competences, equally valuing such competences by inscribing them into the business case for diversity, and enforcing a norm of "learning employees" who, to develop themselves professionally, are expected to continuously acquire new skills, including those associated with the other gender. Contrary to what is often the case, at SensorInc, not only men's performance of feminine skills, but also women's performance of male skills is recognized and valued (Katila and Eriksson, 2013; Peterson, 2007).

Disrupting the individualism–collectivism dichotomy through collaborative work practices

A second, hierarchically ordered gendered opposition advanced by Ely and Meyerson (2000) is between an individualistic, male orientation and a collectivistic, female orientation. Historically dominated by men, and despite the celebratory discourses of flat, team-centred organizations, a "masculine" strong, assertive, heroic individual is often still seen as indispensable for business success, while "feminine", team-oriented and supportive workers are less crucial and thus more dispensable for organizations (Gagnon and Collinson, 2014). SensorInc disrupted this second dichotomy through a team-centred organizational structure with a short chain of command and a strong open organizational culture fostering a narrative of collectivism and cooperation.

Business objectives are formulated at both the team level and across departments. In this way, teamwork rather than competition is stimulated. Respondents often elaborated on the collectivist working culture in which successes are seen as the result of collaboration to achieve common goals, and on how a focus on the projects and clients leave little room for blame games:

> When something goes wrong, it is rarely the fault of one individual. We can discuss procedures to make these better and more efficient, but especially during crises we have to work together. That is the only thing what counts: finding solutions for our clients (man, Team Lead).

> You have engineers who are very good in designing, but might have very bad management skills. Success lies in the mix of women and men, of engineers and non-engineers… We have to do everything in order to provide valid answers to our clients. We have to save our face in front of our clients. Our common SensorInc face (woman, Key Account Manager).

This open culture is supported by the material organization of the work space through open offices facilitating communication:

> The concept of open offices is something that was here from the very beginning. Cubicles are something from the previous century. They hamper communication. You don't have to exaggerate, discretion is also important. You should not just put everybody together on one floor and all problems would be solved. No, every day we try to find a balance. There are also disadvantages such as noise, but we try to organize it as such that who needs privacy can have their own space for making phone calls for example, depending on the kind of job. But the basis of our infrastructure is to create an open culture, an open mindset. This way of working suits me well (man, Facilities Manager).

To enhance cross-departmental interaction, a management committee is further charged with organizing round-table brainstorming sessions, trainings and joint presentations.

Also distinctive of SensorInc is an open and informal, "no bosses culture" in which all organizational members, including the founders of the company and the CEO, are addressed by their first name. This practice is meant to enable employees to relate and connect independent of rank, fostering a collective sense of working towards the same objectives, of which respondents are highly appreciative:

> I really like the culture here. It fits my personality. It is very open and transparent. They expect a lot of input and personal commitment from the employees, but they also take our input into consideration. They pay attention to life-work balance, people's development and give constructive feedback. So I feel I can be open and honest. There are not implicit layers of power. Everybody can talk directly to everybody. There is no room for show, people see through that. Yes, that is my cup of tea, substance over form, like I use to call it. People look here for added value and look at your performances and results, not at how long you have been hanging around at the office. The content is of priority here (woman, Finance Manager).

Interpersonal relations and creativity are further stimulated by providing the means and space for bottom-up networking and by organizing network events to thank the employees. All interviewees mentioned the Enjoyment Committee, whose task is to plan and organize leisure activities and staff parties. Also during office hours there are opportunities to meet colleagues from other departments in a casual and informal way. For example, the initiative "Dutch at work" brings non-native Dutch-speaking employees together to practice Dutch. Or during the monthly birthday lunches, employees can meet others who were born in the same month over a pizza. This informal work environment is a strategy created by the management to keep the turnover rate low, in order to retain expertise and experience.

SensorInc disrupts the classical gendered individualism/collectivism dichotomy by fostering a leadership style centred on non-authoritarian relations and collectivism, supported by an open, informal organizational culture and a team-based structure. This is in line with knowledge-intensive firms, which are often characterized by project-based management, a flat structure, decentralized decision-making processes and a highly autonomous workforce (Legault, 2005). Together, these practices are effective in fostering gender equality throughout the company, as they promote "post-heroic leadership" (Fletcher, 2004) and validate "feminine" ways of organizing (Smith-Doerr, 2004).

Disrupting the private–public dichotomy through work flexibility

Finally, a third opposition points to a hierarchically ordered, gendered division of labour between men and women in the public and the private spheres of life. As men's work is associated with the public sphere, men come to embody the ideal worker who prioritizes paid work and, unencumbered by care responsibilities, is able to meet unbound time demands. Women are conversely conceived as primary care givers and thus their commitment to paid work as ancillary, fragile and constrained by care. At SensorInc, this opposition was disrupted by far-reaching formal and informal flexibility arrangements, supported by HR policies which avoided career penalties for using such flexibility to combine one's work with non-professional roles (Leslie *et al.*, 2012).

Many male and female respondents mentioned agreeing flexible working hours and teleworking with their managers. They recounted how they had to deal with travel demands and pressing deadlines but also benefited from the flexibility to organize their work efficiently and to minimize work–personal life conflicts:

> When there is a traffic jam, than I call my boss that it is better to work from home than wasting time in traffic. He allows me to do that, but it is not an official SensorInc policy. Whatever makes sense is the baseline. Since they expect flexibility from us, they have a certain degree of flexibility towards us as well (man, Product Line Manager).

The narrative of autonomy, freedom and self-steering is supported in practice by the absence of a time-clock or any other tracking of people's working hours. This policy creates room for men as well as women to better combine work with care, family life and leisure. A respondent leading a team of engineers told us:

> Flexibility is a very important matter at SensorInc. When you work here, attending a parent meeting at school or picking up the children from school is not a problem. You can easily interrupt your work. We also have a male colleague who is divorced and when it is his turn to look after the children, he doesn't travel. He plans his travel in the even weeks when he is alone and works hard when the children are not with him. When he has the custody of the children, he stops earlier to pick them up. He compensates that completely later on. We as a team know that and take this into account. This is an ideal system for us and for him (man, Test Team Lead).

These excerpts reflect a culture in which employees express their commitment not by spending long hours at the office, but rather by showing self-management capabilities in organizing their own work in relation to the company's goals. These practices are supported by official policies wherein employees' assessments are based on their performances, independent from how they organize their work.

The company's flexibility also translates into a career policy that envisions internal mobility among others to achieve a better "fit" between one's work and family role at specific phases in one's life. Both male and female employees testify how they benefit from intra-company transfers and job rotating opportunities:

> I don't have parents who can support me in taking care of the children to pick them up from school. My parents-in-law are no support either as they are living abroad and my husband works in shifts. So my personal situation impacts my level of flexibility towards my job. I can work full-time, yes, but I try to limit my travel load. Until I started my own family, I was almost continuously abroad. But now, as a mother, my family is my priority and my superiors accept that (woman, Global EPMO Manager).

> You can work from home from time to time or take up your parental leave. When your position requires face time, then you can discuss the possibility to temporarily shift to another role within the company. There is a lot of flexibility towards internal mobility. You can move from the business unit to human relations for example. There are many possibilities (woman, Product Portfolio Manager).

Internal mobility is not only considered an asset in terms of knowledge management, it is also proactively deployed as a way to value employees' commitment without putting undue pressure on the boundaries between private and professional life. This enables employees to better balance work and life, enhancing their work motivation.

Whereas many companies offer work–life arrangements yet leave work organization and careers unaltered, leading to disproportionate career penalties for employees—largely women—who make use of them, SensorInc has chosen to adopt flexibility as a core principle of organizing. Flexibility counterbalances a demanding work culture by creating space for the emergence of alternative, tailor-made career trajectories which have an equalizing effect on women's and men's careers. SensorInc offers and supports M-shaped career paths rather than linear ones, a policy which requires and stimulates employees' "mental" flexibility, or their ability and willingness to learn and step into new work roles.

Although flexible work arrangements are not void of risks, as they have been related to work intensification (Kelliher and Anderson, 2009), the structural flexibility implemented at SensorInc in both the day-to-day organization of work and in careers appears to effectively diffuse traditional boundaries between idealized images of masculine workers who show commitment by being available anytime, anywhere, and of women as being constrained by their reproductive role. The dilution of gendered stereotypes in the workplace likely reflects the slow yet clear evolution towards a more equal gender division of labour (Vanderleyden and Callens, 2015), among others fostered by gender mainstreaming and gender neutrality in policy making, including legislation which, for example, has resulted in joint physical custody[1] as the default arrangement after divorce since 2006 (Sodermans *et al.*, 2013).

---

1 Belgium introduced joint legal custody in 1995, and in 2006, joint physical custody became the default judicial recommendation. Joint physical custody or "shared residence" means that after divorce, the children live alternately with their mother and father (Sodermans *et al.*, 2013).

Discussion and conclusion

SensorInc achieves significant progress towards gender equality by implementing a coherent set of practices and narratives which redefine valuable competences, work and leadership styles and the boundaries between work and private life. Although a formalized gender policy is absent, the company effectively disrupts three key dichotomies of masculinity/femininity, individual/collective and public/private which have historically favoured male ascendancy in Western workplaces (Ely and Meyerson, 2000). Common notions of "masculinity" and "femininity" remain a strong organizational gender subtext; however, crucially, these notions no longer operate as an axis of power in the organization. Rather, gendered skills are equalized and recast as complementary organizational assets by inscription in the business case for gender diversity (cf. Ely and Thomas, 2001). Their maximal deployment is ensured through a team organization of work and structural, far-reaching work flexibility arrangements for all employees. These practices create a work context in which employees are both enabled and expected to self-manage their work while co-ordinating with others, continuously develop their knowledge and skills, and perform at best.

In this sense, SensorInc offers an example of a workplace in line with Ely and Meyerson's (2000) "alternative" approach to gender equality, which also enhances organizational effectiveness in that it elicits employees' high commitment while at once leveraging the value in gender diversity. This approach echoes (neo-)liberal forms of feminism (Fraser, 2013; Rottenberg, 2014) aligning gender equality with capitalistic organizing and entrepreneurial employees' subjectivities. Differently from this type of feminism, however, responsibility for equality is not fully individualized, as SensorInc proactively shapes practices and narratives conducive to women's equal participation in the organization and its success.

Although the observed practices and narratives could be linked to the disruption of unequal gendered dichotomies advanced in the literature, a single-case research design does not allow us to identify under which conditions these practices and narratives are likely to emerge. In what follows, we reflect on features of SensorInc which might have played a role in its ability to achieve and sustain gender equality. First, as mentioned in the case background, SensorInc was organized through equality-fostering practices and narratives from its foundation. This condition is unlikely to be a small detail in attempts to explain its success, as the organizational literature eloquently shows the pitfalls of change processes, which are often hindered by intense manifest or latent conflict, resentment and resistance, and backlash effects undermining equality (Konrad and Linnehan, 1995; Kidder *et al.*, 2004; Rudman and Phelan, 2008). Accordingly, this case might be more informative of how gender equality can be created in new companies rather than changing existing ones.

Second, the substantial number of women in top management in SensorInc is likely to be an important condition for its ability to foster gender equality. The gender literature consistently highlights the importance of critical mass for women to avoid the negative effects of tokenism, affect decision-making processes, and co-shape management and leadership styles (Chesterman *et al.*, 2005; Kanter, 1977; Torchia *et al.*, 2011). The presence of women in (top) leadership positions, including a female CEO, is further important for its role modelling effects. Third, the growth SensorInc has known since its origins might be a necessary condition for some of the implemented equality-fostering practices. The virtuous circle created by the observed set of practices and narratives seems predicated on a continued ability of both employer and employees to meet high mutual expectations. For instance, internal mobility, which is central to the flexibility policy of the company, is facilitated by growth-driven job creation. To the extent that business growth is an essential condition of gender equality, equality might be subject to business conjuncture more than we could capture in our analysis.

References

Acker, J. (1990). Hierarchies, jobs, bodies: A theory of gendered organizations. *Gender & Society*, 4(2), 139-158.

Acker, J. (1998). The future of "gender and organizations": Connections and boundaries. *Gender, Work & Organization*, 5(4), 195-206.

Ainsworth, S., Knox, A., & O'Flynn, J. (2010). A blinding lack of progress: Management rhetoric and affirmative action. *Gender, Work & Organization*, 17(6), 658-678.

Bastalich, W., Franzway, S., Gill, J., Mills, J. & Sharp, R. (2007). 'Disrupting masculinities: Women engineers and engineering workplace culture. *Australian Feminist Studies*, 22(54), 385-400.

Beninger, A. (2014). *High Potentials in Tech-Intensive Industries: The Gender Divide in Business Roles*. New York: Catalyst. Retrieved from http://www.catalyst.org/system/files/high_potentials_in_tech-intensive_industries_the_gender_divide_in_business_roles_0.pdf.

Benschop, Y., & Doorewaard, H. (1998). 'Six of one and half a dozen of the other: The gender subtext of Taylorism and team-based work. *Gender, Work & Organization*, 5(1), 5-18.

Benschop, Y., & Verloo, M. (2011). Gender change, organizational change, and gender equality strategies. In E. Jeanes, D. Knights & P. Martin (Eds.), *Handbook of Gender, Work, and Organization* (pp. 277-290). Chichester, UK: John Wiley & Sons.

Busch, A., & Holst, E. (2011). *Gender-Specific Occupational Segregation, Glass Ceiling Effects, and Earnings in Managerial Positions: Results of a Fixed Effects Model*. Berlin: German Institute for Economic Research. Retrieved from http://www.diw.de/documents/publikationen/73/diw_01.c.368341.de/diw_sp0357.pdf.

Cain, C., & Leahey, E. (2014). Cultural correlates of gender integration in science. *Gender, Work & Organization*, 21(6), 516-530.

Charles, M., & Grusky, D. (2004). *Occupational Ghettos: The Worldwide Segregation of Women and Men (Vol. 200)*. Stanford, CA: Stanford University Press.

Chesterman, C., Ross-Smith, A. & Peters, M. (2005). The gendered impact on organizations of a critical mass of women in senior management. *Policy and Society*, 24(4), 69-91.

Connell, R., & Messerschmidt, J. (2005). Hegemonic masculinity: Rethinking the concept. *Gender & Society*, 19(6), 829-859.

Ellingsæter, A. (2013). Scandinavian welfare states and gender (de) segregation: Recent trends and processes. *Economic and Industrial Democracy*, 34(3), 501-518.

Ely, R., & Meyerson, D. (2000). Theories of gender in organizations: A new approach to organizational analysis and change. *Research in Organizational Behavior*, 22, 103-151.

Ely, R. & Thomas, D. (2001). Cultural diversity at work: The effects of diversity perspectives on work group processes and outcomes. *Administrative Science Quarterly*, 46, 229-273.

European Commission (2015). Board members. Brussels: European Commission. Retrieved from http://ec.europa.eu/justice/gender-equality/gender-decision-making/database/business-finance/supervisory-board-board-directors/index_en.htm.

Fletcher, J. (2004). The paradox of postheroic leadership: An essay on gender, power, and transformational change. *Leadership Quarterly*, 15, 647-661.

Fraser, N. (2013). *Fortunes of Feminism: From State-managed Capitalism to Neoliberal Crisis*. London: Verso Books.

Gagnon, S. & Collinson, D. (2014). Rethinking global leadership development programmes: The inter-related significance of power, context and identity. *Organization Studies*, 35(5), 645-670.

Goodall, A. (2010). Sister's winning formula. *Times Higher Education*, 1967, 34-39.

Hewlett, S., Luce, C., Servon, L., Sherbin, L., Shiller, P., Sosnovich, E., & Sumberg, K. (2008). *The Athena Factor: Reversing the Brain Drain in Science, Engineering, and Technology*. Boston, MA: Harvard Business Publishing.

Huffman, M., Cohen, P. & Pearlman, J. (2010). 'Engendering change: organizational dynamics and workplace gender desegregation, 1975–2005. *Administrative Science Quarterly*, 55(2), 255-277.

Janssens, M. & Zanoni, P. (2014). Alternative diversity management: Organizational practices fostering ethnic equality at work. *Scandinavian Journal of Management*, 30(3), 317-331.

Kanter, R. (1977). 'Some effects of proportions on group life: Skewed sex ratios and responses to token women. *American Journal of Sociology*, 82(5), 965-990.

Katila, S., & Eriksson, P. (2013). He is a firm, strong-minded and empowering leader, but is she? Gendered positioning of female and male CEOs. *Gender, Work & Organization*, 20(1), 71-84.

Kelliher, C., & Anderson, D. (2009). Doing more with less? Flexible working practices and the intensification of work. *Human Relations*, 63(1), 83-106.

Kidder, D., Lankau, M., Chrobot-Mason, D., Mollica, K. & Friedman, R. (2004). Backlash toward diversity initiatives: Examining the impact of diversity program justification, personal and group outcomes. *International Journal of Conflict Management*, 15(1), 77-102.

Kirkup, G., Zalevski, A., Maruyama, T. & Batool, I. (2010). *Women and Men in Science, Engineering and Technology: The UK Statistics Guide 2010*. Bradford: UK Resources Centre for Women in Science and Technology.

Konrad, A.M., & Linnehan, F. (1995). 'Formalized HRM structures: Coordinating equal employment opportunity or concealing organizational practices? *Academy of Management Journal*, 38(3), 787-820.

Kottke, J., & Agars, M. (2005). Understanding the processes that facilitate and hinder efforts to advance women in organizations. *Career Development International*, 10(3), 190-202.

Legault, M. (2005). Differential gender effects of project management and management by project on skilled professionals. In K.S. Devine & J. Grenier (Eds.), *Reformulating Industrial Relations in Liberal Market Economies* (pp. 105-124). Concord, Ontario: Cira & Captus Press.

Leslie, L., Manchester, C., Park, T. & Mehng, S. (2012). Flexible work practices: A source of career premiums or penalties? *Academy of Management Journal*, 55(6), 1407-1428.

Martin, P. (1996). Gendering and evaluating dynamics: Men, masculinities, and managements. In D. Collinson & J. Hearn (Eds.), *Men as Managers, Managers as Men: Critical Perspectives on Men, Masculinities and Managements* (pp. 186-210). London: Sage.

Meyerson, D. E., & Kolb, D. M. (2000). Moving out of the "armchair": Developing a framework to bridge the gap between feminist theory and practice. *Organization*, 7(4), 553-571.

Peterson, H. (2007). Gendered work ideals in Swedish IT firms: Valued and not valued workers. *Gender, Work & Organization*, 14(4), 333-348.

Rees, B. & Garnsey, E. (2003). Analysing competence: Gender and identity at work. *Gender, Work & Organization*, 10(5), 551-578.

Rees, T. (1998). *Mainstreaming Equality in the European Union*. London: Routledge.

Rees, T. (2005). Reflections on the uneven development of gender mainstreaming in Europe. *International Feminist Journal of Politics*, 7(4), 555-574.

Rottenberg, C. (2014). The rise of neoliberal feminism. *Cultural Studies*, 28(3), 418-437.

Rudman, L., & Phelan, J. (2008). Backlash effects for disconfirming gender stereotypes in organizations. *Research in Organizational Behavior*, 28, 61-79.

Smith, D. (1988). *The Everyday World as Problematic: A Feminist Sociology*. Milton Keynes, UK: Open University Press.

Smith, D. (1990). *The Conceptual Practices of Power: A Feminist Sociology of Knowledge*. Boston, MA: Northeastern University Press.

Smith-Doerr, L. (2004). *Women's Work: Gender Equality vs. Hierarchy in the Life Sciences* (Boulder, CO: Lynne Rienner Publishers.

Sodermans, A.K., Matthijs, K., & Swicegood, G. (2013). Characteristics of joint physical custody families in Flanders. *Demographic Research*, 28, 821-848.

Straub, C. (2007). A comparative analysis of the use of work-life balance practices in Europe: Do practices enhance females' career advancement? *Women in Management Review*, 22(4), 289-304.

Torchia, M., Calabró, A. & Huse, M. (2011). Women directors on corporate boards: From tokenism to critical mass. *Journal of Business Ethics*, 102(2), 299-317.

Van Hove, H., Reymenants, G. & Bailly, N. (2011). *Vrouwen en mannen in België: genderstatistieken en genderindicatoren 2011*. Brussels: Instituut voor de Gelijkheid van Vrouwen en Mannen.

Vanderleyden, L. &n Callens, M. (eds.) (2015). *Arbeid en Gezin: Een paar apart* [Work and Family: A distant couple]. Brussels: Studiedienst van de Vlaamse Regering. Retrieved from https://www.vlaanderen.be/nl/publicaties/detail/arbeid-en-gezin-een-paar-apart-1.

Walby, S. (2011a). *The Future of Feminism*. Cambridge, UK: Polity.

Walby, S. (2011b). Is the knowledge society gendered? *Gender, Work & Organization*, 18(1), 1-29.

West, C. & Zimmerman, D. (1987). Doing gender. *Gender & Society*, 1(2), 125-151.

Zanoni, P., Janssens, M., Benschop, Y. & Nkomo, S. (2010). Unpacking diversity, grasping inequality: Rethinking difference through critical perspectives. *Organization*, 17, 9-29.

Hannelore Roos works as a postdoctoral researcher at the Faculty of Business Economics, UHasselt where she is embedded in the research group SEIN—Identity, Diversity & Inequality Research. She is affiliated as a Research Fellow with the Interculturalism, Migration and Minorities Research Centre, KU Leuven.

Patrizia Zanoni is professor in Organization Studies and the director of SEIN—Identity, Diversity & Inequality Research, the Faculty of Business Economics, UHasselt, and a Research Fellow with the Research Center of Organisation Studies, KU Leuven.

2

Linking women and the private sector
A win–win approach from agribusiness in Zambia

Gerry Finnegan
International Development Consultant, UK

Pamela White
FCG International, Finland

This chapter presents a case study on the Zambian operations of Cargill, a multinational corporation that has been actively linking women and private sector agribusiness in Zambia. The company's approaches have elements of corporate social responsibility (CSR), but they go further in creating shared value (CSV) and developing win–win situations both for the company and for the women. The company's strategies are largely consistent with human rights-based approaches and contribute to enhancing women's rights and women's economic empowerment. By promoting women's clubs for small-scale cotton farmers, Cargill supports women with: training in farming techniques; advice on access to credit; encouragement to diversify; and strategies for strengthening of their organization and leadership skills. The women produce more and better cotton and improve their incomes; the company benefits from having reliable supplies of cotton.

The World Bank Nordic Trust Fund financed the Finnish Consulting Group (FCG) to conduct research on the theme of "Incentivizing the market: linking women and the private sector—a human rights-based approach". The study was led by the co-authors of this chapter and carried out in Zambia during 2013–14 with a particular focus on the approaches taken by the private agribusiness sector in linking with their female staff and contractors (White *et al.*, 2015).

The World Bank has traditionally worked through governments and public–private partnerships (PPPs) in implementing its development agenda. However, increasingly the Bank has been looking to the private sector as an important driver of development issues.

This chapter presents a case study of Cargill, a US-based, large-scale business operating in the agriculture sector in Zambia.[1] Research was conducted to examine ways in which the company engaged with women as part of its business—women as small-scale and subsistence farmers and entrepreneurs; women as full-time, part-time and seasonal workers; and women as members of their local community. The case study development took place in the context of global, African and Zambia-specific approaches to, and lessons from, corporate social responsibility (CSR) and creating shared value (CSV) perspectives. In this chapter, we will briefly introduce key concepts used, and present our findings and conclusions on Cargill.

The World Economic Forum (WEF) defines CSR as:

> The contributions a company makes to society through its core business activities, its social investment and philanthropy programs, and its engagement in public policy. The manner in which a company manages its economic, social and environmental relationships, as well as those with different stakeholders, in particular shareholders, employees, customers, business partners, governments and communities determines its impact (as cited in Jamali *et al.*, 2015).

---

1 The case study was developed to help address gaps in the literature on the combination of women's empowerment and gender equality, private sector agriculture and human rights-based approaches (HRBA). The core team conducted 25 individual interviews with Cargill staff (both in administration and labourers in the plant), management and farmers; and six focus group meetings with farmers, with between 5 and 28 members (mixed, men alone and women alone). In addition, enumerators interviewed 5 employees and 15 farmers (all women). The questionnaire used was developed based on ideas gathered during the literature review and on the framework of the study.

However, numerous definitions of CSR can be found in the literature.[2] Many international corporations have signed up to various international CSR instruments, including the UN Global Compact.[3]

In the context of women's empowerment, some 800 companies have endorsed the Women's Empowerment Principles.[4] In recent years, the World Bank Group, including the International Finance Corporation (IFC), has produced a range of conceptual tools and practical guides on the economic empowerment of women, and many of these companies apply these principles as part of their CSR policies and orientation (e.g. IFC, 2013).

Creating shared value (CSV) has been defined as:

> policies and operating practices that enhance the competitiveness of a company while simultaneously advancing the economic and social conditions of the communities in which it operates. Shared value creation focuses on identifying and expanding the connections between societal and economic progress (Porter and Kramer 2011).

CSV is considered to be a win–win business case rather than philanthropy, reparations or part of public relations. It is not a wealth redistribution approach, but rather aims to expand the total pool of economic and social value. CSV is integral to a company's profitability and competitiveness position (Porter and Kramer, 2011). CSV is also consistent with other business models such as the triple bottom

2 CSR, according to the United Nations Industrial Development Organization (UNIDO) has been defined as "a management concept whereby companies integrate social and environmental concerns in their business operations and interactions with their stakeholders. CSR is generally understood as being the way through which a company achieves a balance of economic, environmental and social imperatives ('Triple-Bottom-Line- Approach'), while at the same time addressing the expectations of shareholders and stakeholders." Retrieved from http://www.unido.org/what-we-do/advancing-economic-competitiveness/competitive-trade-capacities-and-corporate-responsibility/csr/what-is-csr.html

The UNIDO publication *Corporate Social Responsibility: Implications for Small and Medium Enterprises in Developing Countries* (2002) states that CSR is variously defined as "the continuing commitment by business to behave ethically and contribute to economic development while improving the quality of life of the workforce and their families as well as of the local community and society at large" (World Business Council for Sustainable Development); "Being socially responsibly means not only fulfilling legal obligations, but also going beyond compliance and investing more into human capital, the environment and relations with stakeholders" (European Commission); "Operating a business in a manner that meets or exceeds the ethical, legal, commercial and public expectations that society has of business" (Business for Social Responsibility).

3 The ten principles of the UN Global Compact, https://www.unglobalcompact.org/what-is-gc/mission/principles

4 As developed by the UN Global Compact in association with UNIFEM (now UNWomen); http://www.unwomen.org/en/partnerships/businesses-and-foundations/womens-empowerment-principles - accessed 17 February 2015.

line and bottom of the pyramid although, as indicated above, CSV offers a more integrated and sustainable approach to a company's longer-term profitability and competitiveness.

Human rights-based approaches (HRBA) integrate the norms, principles, standards and goals of the international human rights system into the plans and processes of development. Activities are linked to national and international legal responsibilities, and HRBA operates through identified rights-holders and duty bearers. (Kirkemann *et al.*, 2007). HRBA, which embrace women's rights, pay more attention to the marginalized and poor, empowering them to demand their rights, rather than be passive recipients of assistance. While CSV is based more on a win–win situation for both company and community, it does not necessarily address human rights or gender equality issues.

This case study incorporates the "Protect, Respect and Remedy" framework on the issue of human rights and transnational corporations, a framework produced by the United Nations (UN) Secretary-General's Special Representative John Ruggie (Business and Human Rights Resource Centre, 2008). This provides a useful context for a corporate response to human rights, and proposes that companies undertake "due diligence" to manage the risk of human rights harm with a view to avoiding it—often referred to as "Do no harm". Specific corporate actions may include: workplace human rights policies, impact assessments, and integration of the approach to human rights throughout a company. Ruggie also proposed that companies can assist in providing access to appropriate remedies by establishing their own effective grievance mechanism. The UN Human Rights Council (2011) adopted a revised set of Guiding Principles on Business and Human Rights in June 2011 (see also United Nations Human Rights Office of the High Commissioner, 2011).

The researchers consider that there is a spectrum of approaches applied by the private sector in Zambia, ranging from pure philanthropy, CSR, and CSV, to needs- and rights-based approaches. Within the four companies (including Cargill) initially studied for the World Bank research, some of their activities were seen as philanthropic, while others are more focused on a win–win approach, or even HRBA (such as the strict application of occupational health and safety rules). In order to analyse the approaches of the four companies, a framework was constructed, comparing CSR, CSV and HRBA concepts across six domains critical to women's lives: government, workplace, marketplace, environment, community, and home (White *et al.*, 2015). The activities of Cargill were particularly interesting to the researchers, and merited further investigation. In total, this involved two rounds of consultations with Cargill staff at its Lusaka headquarters; two visits to its Eastern Province offices in Chipata for interviews with local management, female office staff and female factory workers; as well as field visits to five villages from which Cargill sourced its cotton supplies. In addition, a more global perspective on Cargill's operations and approaches was gained from reviewing its website and in-house magazine.

Cargill in Zambia

This case study deals with the cotton operations of Cargill in the Eastern Province of Zambia, including the company's relationship with outsourced cotton producers, as well as with its management and workers in its cotton ginnery.

Cargill began its cotton operations in Zambia in 2006, and opened a grain and oilseed trading office in Lusaka in 2008. As of March 2014, Cargill had 1,030 employees in Zambia, 858 men and 172 women.[5] Cargill's website states that it includes a corporate responsibility approach to both the production and the processing elements of its value chain and, as will be shown below, its activities embrace elements of both CSR and CSV. Cargill has defined its approach as follows: "Cargill is committed to operating responsibly across the agriculture, food, industrial and financial markets we serve as we pursue our goal of being the global leader in nourishing people".[6] This fits into the CSR approach of "operating responsibly" in its business operations.

The researchers found that Cargill's policies on workplace safety and health, succession planning and ethical principles are a positive aspect of the company's operations, and contribute to decent working conditions for both women and men as employees and contracted labourers. It was noted that workplace safety was particularly strong and visible. The company's ethical standards are well promoted within the workplace and were spontaneously mentioned by many of those interviewed—women and men, permanent and casual employees, as well as labourers and management. For instance, one woman referred to "the initial training and then constant reinforcement, including in the annual assessments. It is a living document—not just something put up on the wall". We found considerable evidence that the ethical standards are being reinforced regularly and applied in practice.

The provision of five months of maternity leave is above normal for Zambia, where the statutory provision is for 120 days.[7] A transport allowance is paid to all workers. Both labourers and supervisors reported that most of Cargill's seasonal casual staff return to the company year after year. This pattern of workers returning would appear to be good both for Cargill and the workers, as it is easier for the company to engage experienced labourers with whom it has a history, and the seasonal workers can rely on reasonably remunerated (in comparison with similar labouring jobs) and decent employment opportunities annually.

There is also considerable evidence of Cargill giving prominence to the role of women as managers and workers throughout its operations. As an illustration of this point, the company's global in-house magazine has given a lot of attention to

5 Cargill website, www.cargill.com/worldwide/zambia/index.jsp, accessed 10 June 2014.
6 Cargill website, http://www.cargill.com/corporate-responsibility/index.jsp, accessed 15 April 2016.
7 See Mywage.org/Zambia, http://www.mywage.org/zambia/main/decent-work/maternity and-work/maternity-leave, accessed 04 August 2015.

the role that women play in the company both in Zambia and in its global operations (Cargill, 2013). Cargill's country director for Zambia is a woman,[8] and several of the female employees interviewed noted that having women in top management roles was inspirational and motivating. The company has had many cases of women rising through the ranks, from lower labouring roles to supervisory positions. Several of these women were interviewed during our field research. Career support is offered in some cases, particularly for women taking study leave or to cover the cost of examinations.

There is an active trade union presence at the ginnery (the National Commercial and Industrial Workers' Union) and an elected representative committee. The casual labourers are not union members; however they elect their own committee to negotiate with management. The company requests that workers elect equal numbers of women and men to these committees (though this is a recommendation rather than a requirement, as it is up to the workers themselves to decide). According to the interviews with staff (randomly chosen) and management, Cargill actively promotes participation, representation and transparency in all decision-making.

Cotton schools to assist smallholders

Cotton is largely grown by outgrower farmers, many of whom are women. In order to improve productivity and crop quality, Cargill introduced informal "cotton schools" where farmers could be trained in crop management, use of fertilizers and related skills. These schools are places where the farmers are trained in techniques aimed at improving productivity and quality. The schools range from open demonstration fields to sheds and more formal structures where the training takes place.

However, through its own research Cargill learned that men generally controlled and dominated the cotton schools, of which there are 2,023 affiliated with Cargill throughout its Zambia operations.[9] Yet the research also showed that it was women who were mainly participating in cotton farming, and thus there was a significant mismatch between the men learning the cotton skills, and the (largely) untrained women working in the fields. There were several gender-related reasons for this situation: the schools were often held at the depot, located at a distance from the village and family home, and therefore it was inconvenient for the women to attend while also looking after children and doing domestic chores as well as their farming activities. Related to this, the women experienced "time poverty" as a result of which they were unable to find the time to travel to and participate in the training (Abdourahman, 2010), and husbands did not like the idea of their wives attending training with lots of men.

---

8 Lezanne van Zyl, Country Director for Zambia, was interviewed on several occasions in gathering case study material.
9 As reported in September 2013.

Women's clubs and links to cotton schools

This situation largely resulted from the traditional cultures and accepted gender norms, and in order to rectify the skills imbalance Cargill promoted the creation of "women's clubs". Once the women were members of these clubs, the clubs were able to affiliate with the cotton schools and training was organized for women in locations much closer to home, thus enabling them to acquire valuable cotton-growing skills. Men are also able to be members of the women's clubs, but they cannot take leadership roles. The creation of the women's clubs and the links to the cotton schools were culturally acceptable ways for the women to learn the skills required to improve quality, quantity and productivity, at a time and place that better suited them. The training was delivered specifically for women and provided on-site in the village, rather than at a distant depot, thus making it much easier for women to participate. The training covered good farming practices for various crops (cotton and maize): for example, preparation of fields, use of manure/fertilizers, planting, weeding, spraying chemicals, harvesting, and conservation farming.

Once the women's clubs are linked to the cotton schools, their members are able to seek help and advice from the schools. From the time the first women's clubs started in 2010, the number of clubs increased to 599 in 2012, and reached 800 on Cargill's books in 2013—although only 381 of these actively dealt with Cargill in the 2013–14 season. The women's clubs have 20–25 members, with the smallest having around 15 members (Cargill has a total of 106,000 farmers listed as suppliers).[10] The company encourages the women's clubs to also belong to cooperatives in order to increase their negotiating power and have access to government-subsidized inputs under the Fertilizer Input Support Programme. According to senior management, there is a clear benefit for Cargill in working with women farmers, as to date there have been no defaulting women farmers (as borrowers) and the company's records show that women are better at debt servicing than men.[11]

The evidence demonstrates the impact of the women's club-cum-cotton school links on women's farming activities. In 2009 18% of all contracts issued by Cargill were directly to women farmers; in 2013 34–35% of contracts were issued to women. This increase was in addition to the reported improvement in productivity and crop outputs resulting from the women's training. There is no marked difference in the scale or content of the contracts issued to women and men—each farmer receives around 300 Kwacha (approximately £30) pre-financing per hectare. Most women understood the content of their contract with Cargill, and those who were not literate had them explained by other women. Furthermore, as Cargill does not make cash payments to third parties, if the contract is in the name of the woman she is the only person entitled to receive payment, and this is an important safeguard for the women farmers. All the women interviewed reported that they

---

10 Statistics provided by Cargill management during field investigations.
11 Interview with Cargill's Country Director for Zambia, Lezanne van Zyl.

receive their payment in cash, and they appreciated the reliability and promptness of payments from Cargill immediately after the crop was delivered. This is unlike the case for government maize purchases, for which it was reported that payment is delayed. Many of those interviewed commented that it was important that the women received payment directly and can use it for household needs, as men often go and drink beer when they receive payment for their own contracts—or when they had collected payments for their wives' crops.

Women's economic empowerment

Cargill's Projects Manager, Mr Emmanuel Mbewe,[12] indicated that Cargill plans to document the changes in people's lives as outcomes from the cotton growing and the company was in discussion with a US-based academic centre to conduct this assessment. The co-authors were also aware of USAID's Feed the Future programme which is aimed at empowering women in Eastern Province, where Cargill mainly operates. Under this programme a sophisticated mechanism, the Women's Empowerment in Agriculture Index (WEAI), has been created to measure the impact of agricultural activities on women's empowerment, and a simplified version of this Index is under preparation (Alkire *et al.*, 2014). Collectively, measures such as this and those of Cargill will help to monitor and evaluate supportive actions more systematically, as well as measure the impacts on gender relations and women's empowerment.

Those women farmers interviewed reported the benefits they derive from attending a cotton school as follows:

- Gaining access to soft loans
- Increasing their level of self-confidence
- Increasing diversity of crops and thus reducing the reliance on cotton
- Generating increases in income at the household level, and as a result the greater ability to:
- Send their children to school
- Buy more food for the household
- Increase their stock of personal assets, e.g. buy bicycles, livestock (cows)
- Improve their housing, e.g. by buying iron sheets for roofing
- Buy household goods, such as pots and furniture, as well as clothes for themselves and children

12 Based on several interviews with co-authors 2013–14.

- Buy fertilizer to improve the quality of their farm outputs

- Build new homes (as seen in a number of cases)

- Undertake additional income-generating activities, such as rearing chickens, growing vegetables and selling them in the village, as well as bee-keeping in some communities

- Build their self-confidence and develop leadership roles

Group discussions were conducted with separate or mixed groups of women and men (the smallest being a group of five men, and the largest being a group of 27 women and one man), and semi-structured interviews with 18 individual women (three interviews by the core team and 15 by the enumerators). From these field sources, it was clear that farming households are very positive about the support given to women through the cotton schools' support for the women's clubs—including support coming from the husbands—and this helps to empower the women at the community and family levels. Involvement in the clubs also contributes to the women having a greater say in the management of the household and use of household assets. It was evident from the interviews that through their involvement in the women's clubs, many women had a greater involvement in community activities, and the clubs became engaged in addressing a range of community issues such as alcohol abuse and gender-based domestic violence.

In addition to promoting women's empowerment through its support for the women's clubs, Cargill has contributed to improvements in household nutrition, and HIV and AIDS awareness raising activities. Cargill is involved in building and supporting a range of community and social facilities, such as building and fitting out schools, improving water supply and sanitary facilities, and providing solar batteries. Some of these activities can be categorized as Cargill's CSR approach in building community support and loyalty, with the additional spin-off of good public relations. Other support activities can be seen as a means of CSV, as the company's investments in developing local human resources are important in creating loyalty among the workers, farmers and consumers for its future operations.

Finance and credit

Access to finance is an important element of women's economic empowerment. As noted above, Cargill operates in such a way that payments for sales of cotton are made directly to the contract-holder, and payments cannot be made to third parties. Thus women's income is more secure when it is paid directly into their hands rather than collected on their behalf by their husbands. This represents real progress in terms of women's empowerment.

While land may be readily available in some villages, in others it appears that only a few people control the allocation of land and this has favoured men. As a further benefit from the activities of women's groups, some groups have been able to negotiate and obtain land from traditional chiefs or village headmen.

As access to credit is a major impediment faced by all farmers, in a recent development Cargill has been promoting the creation of micro-banks in several villages where it works with large numbers of smallholders. Cargill's support for these micro-banks will allow both women and men to have bank accounts and help them to protect their savings, rather than hiding money at home.

In addition, the company provides input costs (for seed and fertilizer) in the form of a loan, and many of those interviewed regarded Cargill as a preferred partner as it has a reputation for paying promptly.

Problems facing smallholders and Cargill

The relationships between Cargill and its smallholders and the Government of Zambia are not always smooth and positive. Global cotton prices remain a real risk for cotton farmers, and market fluctuations suggest to some parties, including government, that Cargill is not paying farmers enough for their crops. Since 2010 global cotton prices have had a distorting impact on farmers' interest in growing cotton, starting from the very high prices in 2010, followed by a significant fall in price over 2011–2012, thus making many farmers question their commitment to cotton. Some farmers thought they were being cheated as they did not fully understand the link between global markets and local prices. Although prices have stabilized and showed moderate increases in 2013, they remain below the 2010 peak. Zambian cotton production was 270,000 metric tonnes in 2010–11, but this fell to 95,000 tonnes in 2013–14, mainly because of world price fluctuations. In the 2013–14 season Cargill procured some 25,000 tonnes of cotton (or 26% of national production). In 2012, newspapers reported clashes between farmers and Cargill regarding the low prices, with farmers actually burning their cotton (*Times of Zambia*, 2012).

It is not easy for everyone to understand that in a free market there is the possibility of high prices, but also the risk of low prices and consequent losses. As a large company, Cargill has some flexibility to cushion the impact of such price fluctuations on the local farmers and it encourages farmers to maintain diversity by growing several crops, both for commercial markets as well as for household consumption and food security. Cargill helps farmers to diversify into maize and soya, since the company's input programme enables farmers to grow a range of crops, and in this way the company helps the farmers mitigate some of their risk. This approach aims to provide a greater level of security and stability in the face of variable weather and unpredictable market prices. This situation also seems to provide benefits for Cargill. One of the Cargill field operations managers reported "last year when production was down, the other companies only reached 60% of their targets, but we were still able to reach 90%, as the farmers like to sell to us."

The women farmers interviewed frequently mentioned the falling prices for cotton—most complaining that for the most recent season the price was very low, and they hardly made a profit. The most significant environmental problem mentioned by the farmers was the poor soil quality which requires fertilizer application. This can be an important factor for success or failure, and small-scale women farmers are less likely to be able to access and acquire the appropriate fertilizer. Cargill has started to provide fertilizer as part of the credit support to farmers (including the women farmers) who have a good track record, and this should lead to improvements in crop production. Over 65,000 Cargill-sponsored farmers received fertilizer for the 2014 growing season. "Farmers have seen an increase in yields of more than 30 per cent over the past three years in the region where our fertilizers and approaches were applied", said Lezanne van Zyl.[13]

General problems included the lack of credit availability—although Cargill is starting to work with this—and this seems to be a particular difficulty faced by most women. Furthermore, the lack of tools for use in the field, such as hoes, sprays and ploughs, limits the productivity and profitability of the farmers' efforts. Resulting from this, many interviewees complained of the lack of money to pay for hired labour, as the non-availability of ploughs means there is a lot of work to be done by manual labour.

Agricultural chemical use is an environmental risk in cotton production and Cargill aims to minimize its use. The company encourages farmers to move to "softer" chemicals, but these inputs are more expensive. Cargill aims to counteract the impact of the chemicals on bees and honey production, and it is promoting beekeeping as a pilot scheme with income-generating potential among several women's groups.

Cargill's farming operations in Zambia had been the subject of criticism from the Minister of Finance at an international agriculture forum in Abu Dhabi (5 February 2014). Agriculture Minister Bob Sichinga said that:

> "with all due respect, there is no way Cargill can be part of a solution (for agriculture in Africa)." The Minister took issue with the unlisted U.S. firm, one of the world's biggest agricultural commodities companies, paying farmers in Zambia low prices for their cotton crop (*Reuters News*, 2014).

Such was the fallout from this criticism of Cargill that the company's senior management began to question how this research and case study material were going to be used, but in due course full cooperation was restored.

Philanthropy, CSR and CSV

Cargill uses a range of approaches in its operations. We identified charitable or philanthropic interventions (such as support for chicken farming by women's groups); CSR activities (including provision of overalls for labourers, water and sanitation and renewable energy, or education activities); CSV, where we identified the

13 In an interview with co-authors, March 2014.

provision of above-average maternity leave, and the work in building relationships with women farmers; and rights-based approaches such as Cargill's strict occupational health and safety observance (even if management would not necessarily describe them as rights-based). By empowering women, Cargill is working to create a stronger and more loyal sourcing base, providing support to active and healthier women to enable them to earn additional and more secure incomes. In turn, this enables Cargill to strengthen a sustainable source of suppliers. In the short term this can have an immediate impact on crop quality and quantity resulting from training women to reduce or eliminate bad practices and adopt better and more productive farming techniques. In the longer term, the women farmers will want to continue their relationship with Cargill and remain as suppliers to the company, as they are able to see real benefits. In the past many of the women thought of cotton as a "man's crop", but now they are confident about successfully engaging in cotton production.

Conclusion

At the country level, Cargill's Zambian operations benefit from its head office's core focus on rights and social responsibility and the company's broad ethos. Management in Zambia has been encouraged to work with women and to implement rights-based policies and actions essential for women's economic empowerment. Cargill meets many of the criteria for providing core elements of decent work[14] (rights at work, social protection, representation and voice, and decent employment opportunities)—an integral part of any rights-based approach to women's empowerment. Cargill also complies with Zambian labour laws and applies various elements of CSR and CSV.

Cargill recognizes many of the major barriers that are restricting women's participation in agribusiness and takes actions to address them. Among the gender-related constraints, women typically experience difficulties in accessing the core factors of production, acquiring skills training and benefiting from decent work conditions (World Bank, 2011). Cargill is working with women to help them overcome many of these barriers and inequalities. As a result of its own activities, Cargill has seen that women work well together and can support each other in their groups. Repeatedly the field staff and management commented that women are trustworthy, reliable and unlikely to default on loans.

Cargill has adopted a number of practices to address common challenges and constraints. These include:

• Improving women's access to finance, land and farming inputs

14 As defined by the International Labour Organization, www.ilo.org

- Connecting smallholders to commercial markets, as well as to relevant government departments
- Introducing additional income-generating opportunities (such as beekeeping and chicken-raising)
- Providing training and skills for women, as well as building leadership skills
- Addressing women's household burdens and time poverty (e.g. through support for school-building and digging boreholes to source water locally)
- Providing decent work for female and male employees
- Recognizing and rewarding women's and men's work and effort equally.

Cargill and other case study companies included in the World Bank report (White *et al.*, 2015) could voluntarily undertake to pay higher cotton prices or salaries; however they are profit-oriented businesses working within the global market economy, and are reliant on favourable world prices to stay profitable. In addition, the government could do more to require companies to provide better working conditions and comply with national laws, rather than having to depend upon voluntary compliance. However, the government's lack of resources and insufficient field staff make this problematic. This study demonstrates that companies can go about their business profitably, respect the rights of workers and create conditions that are beneficial and sustainable for employer, employee and supplier alike. Companies are only likely to do this if there is a benefit for their bottom line, and ultimately for their shareholders' interests. These strong messages from the case study point to actual and potential win–win situations experienced by "linking women and the private sector", and these benefit both the women and the company.

References

Abdourahman, O.I. (2010). Time poverty: A contributor to women's poverty? *Journal Statistique Africain*, 11, November 2010. Retrieved from http://www.afdb.org/fileadmin/uploads/afdb/Documents/Publications/Time%20Poverty%20A%20Contributor%20to%20Womens%20Poverty.pdf

Alkire, S., Meinzen-Dick, R.S. & Quisumbing, R.S. (2014). *Measuring Progress Toward Empowerment: Women's Empowerment in Agriculture Index—Baseline Report*. Washington, DC: Feed the Future.

Business and Human Rights Resource Centre (2008). *UN "Protect, Respect and Remedy" Framework and Guiding Principles*. Retrieved from http://business-humanrights.org/en/un-secretary-generals-special-representative-on-business-human-rights/un-protect-respect-and-remedy-framework-and-guiding-principles

Cargill (2013, July/August). Cargill News: Special Edition—Africa Rising (in-house magazine for Cargill employees globally) 78(1). Minneapolis, MN: Cargill Corporate Affairs.

International Finance Corporation (IFC) (2013). *Investing in Women's Employment: Good for Business, Good for Development.* Washington, DC: World Bank Publications. Retrieved from http://www.ifc.org/wps/wcm/connect/5f6e5580416bb016bfb1bf9e780 15671/InvestinginWomensEmployment.pdf?MOD=AJPERES

Jamali, D., Karam, C. & Blowfield, M. (2015). *Development-Oriented Corporate Social Responsibility: Volume 1.* Sheffield, UK: Greenleaf Publishing.

Kirkemann Boesen, J., & Martin, T. (2007). *Applying A Rights-Based Approach: An Inspirational Guide for Civil Society.* Copenhagen: Danish Institute for Human Rights.

Porter, M.E. and Kramer, M.R. (2011). Creating shared value. *Harvard Business Review,* January-February 2011.

Reuters News (2014, February 5). "Paternal" western firms can't solve Africa's farming problems, says Zambia. *Reuters News.*

Times of Zambia (2012, July 1). Cotton war: Irate farmers burn cotton belonging to Cargill cotton Zambia. *Lusaka Times.* Retrieved from https://www.lusakatimes.com/2012/07/01/cotton-war-irate-farmers-burn-cotton-belonging-cargill-cotton-zambia/

UN Human Rights Council (2011). *UN Protect, Respect and Remedy Framework and the UN Global Compact: Guiding Principles on Business and Human Rights,* endorsed on 16 June 2011. Retrieved from https://www.unglobalcompact.org/news/130-06-17-2011

United Nations Human Rights Office of the High Commissioner (2011). *Guiding Principles on Business and Human Rights: Implementing the United Nations "Protect, Respect and Remedy" Framework.* New York: United Nations. Retrieved from http://www.ohchr.org/Documents/Publications/GuidingPrinciplesBusinessHR_EN.pdf

United Nations Industrial Development Organization (UNIDO) (2002). *Corporate Social Responsibility: Implications for Small and Medium Enterprises in Developing Countries.* Vienna: UNIDO. Retrieved from http://www.unido.org/fileadmin/user_media/Services/PSD/CSR/CSR_-_Implications_for_SMEs_in_Developing_Countries.pdf

World Bank (2011). *World Development Report 2012: Gender Equality and Development.* Washington, DC: World Bank.

White, P., Finnegan, G., Pehu, E., Poutiainen, P. & Vyzaki, M. (2015, June). *Linking Women with Agribusiness in Zambia.* World Bank Group Report Number 97510-ZM. Washington, DC: World Bank. Retrieved from http://www-wds.worldbank.org/external/default/WDS-ContentServer/WDSP/IB/2015/08/19/090224b083081f19/2_0/Rendered/PDF/Linking-0women00an0rights0approaches.pdf

Gerry Finnegan is a consultant in international development. He was an International Labour Organization (ILO) official from 1998 to 2010. While with ILO he worked extensively on entrepreneurship, women's entrepreneurship development and gender equality. Prior to the ILO he lectured in Marketing (Ulster University) and Accounting (College of Business Studies, Belfast).

Pamela White is a generalist, working with gender and human rights, rural development, water and sanitation issues. She works with a consulting company in Finland (FCG International) and carries out short-term consultancies globally. She is also currently working on a PhD in Development Studies at the University of Helsinki.

Pursuing diversity in the legal market
A case study of Pfizer General Counsel Amy Schulman*

Paola Cecchi-Dimeglio
Harvard Law School, Center for the Legal Profession, USA

This study focuses on how a female general counsel can impact the legal market and beyond in pursing diversity, gender equality and leadership development. The subject of study is Pfizer Inc. (Pfizer) General Counsel Amy Schulman and her legal department at the American Fortune 100 pharmaceutical firm. Pfizer, and Amy Schulman in particular, were selected for several reasons. These include Pfizer's well-documented record and recognition in the areas of gender equality and diversity, accessibility, and comprehensive institutional structure, and Amy Schulman's track record and personal commitment to actively pursuing diversity. This chapter examines some of the specific actions guided by the leadership of Amy Schulman at Pfizer that have influenced gender equality and women's leadership development within and outside the organization. These findings bring insights into

* The author is especially grateful for the helpful comments, guidance, help and support of David Wilkins, Iris Bohnet, Hannah Riley Bowles, Kathleen McGinn, Robert Mnookin, Tanina Rostain, Gillian Hadfield, Scott Cummings, Deborah Kolb, Carole Silver, Richard Susskind and Derek Davis. The author also wishes to thank for their helpful comments the participants attending the presentation of this paper at the Law and Society Conference in Seattle (2015) and at the Women and Public Policy Program at Harvard Kennedy School (2015).

> how (female) general counsels can help in closing the gender gap and in developing the leaders of tomorrow. The case study and its findings offer valuable lessons that provide insights well beyond Pfizer, delivering practical contributions and implications for pursing diversity in the legal profession.

Globally, there has been an increased focus on women's role in the economy, in both the public and the private sector. In the United States, women currently comprise 50.8% of the population and constitute nearly 50% of the country's workforce (US BLS, 2014). This number, however, is not reflected in the percentage of women with positions in senior management, indicating a troubling lack of women in positions of leadership. Women are under-represented in top leadership positions across the board and often face disadvantages, including salary shortfalls, when they do occupy these roles (Eagly and Carli, 2007; Ely *et al.*, 2011).

This problem extends to, and is in fact heightened, in the legal profession. There has been much discussion in the legal profession about women's under-representation in positions of leadership, and the compensation differences between women and men (ABA, 2013, 2014). Despite a roughly equal number of women enrolled in law schools nationwide, the legal profession still has significantly fewer women in leadership roles at law firms and in-house legal departments (Cecchi-Dimeglio, 2014, 2015; Rhode, 2010, 2012). In 2013, only 19.9% of law firm partners and 21.6% of Fortune 500 general counsels were women (ABA, 2014). In addition to being under-represented at the top, women attorneys in those roles earn significantly lower salaries than their male counterparts (Neil, 2013). For example, in 2013 women attorneys in law firms earned 78.9% of what male attorneys earned in the same position (ABA, 2013, 2014). In in-house positions, women general counsels (GC) and chief legal officers (CLO) earn roughly 79% of what men earn, and male general counsels also earned roughly 40% higher bonuses than female general counsels (ABA, 2014; Neil, 2013). The legal profession is seeking solutions to remediate these issues (ABA, 2013, 2014).

Lawyers, including in-house legal counsel, are becoming key actors that influence how business and legal practices evolve at both domestic and international levels (Higgott *et al.* 2000). They not only create value for their principals as negotiators, drafters, and implementers of (international) contracts, but also help establish authoritative rules for social and business relationships (Mnookin *et al.*, 2000). As such, lawyers are playing a significant role in finding a balance between public and private interests in both domestic and international transactions, including in the area of gender equality, diversity and inclusion (Cecchi-Dimeglio, 2014). General counsels and legal departments are at the centre of both the law and its practice, especially in carrying out corporate social responsibility policies and actions related to gender equality, diversity and inclusion.

One can say general counsels have an Archimedean point of view (Dubey and Kripalani, 2013, p. 114). The position of general counsel provides a vantage point through its teams of lawyers as negotiators and drafters of contracts as well through its role in setting policies and practices. The general counsel exerts the force needed to govern the legal, social and political concerns of the organization. Because of their pivotal role in organizations, they hold immense power to shape norms relating to gender (Whelan and Ziv, 2013). Indeed, there is no institutional actor within a corporation that encapsulates all the constraints of organizational rule makers and enforcers as thoroughly as the general counsel (Cecchi-Dimeglio, 2015).

Although considerable research has been carried out into the mechanisms of gender equality, diversity and inclusion, the study of the role of the general counsel and the impact of their leadership in this area, is still in its infancy. Thus, this chapter contributes to several strands of literature. First, it highlights some specific actions that the general counsel and in-house department can undertake to influence gender equality and leadership development within their organization and with external stakeholders. Second, the chapter contributes to the debate on the legal and social forces pressuring or encouraging corporations to appoint a larger proportion of women across leadership positions including as a general counsel.

This chapter uses a case study to illustrate how the general counsel and its legal department at Pfizer have influenced gender equality and leadership development outside the bare bones of legal compliance—the organizational efforts to ensure they comply with minimum regulatory standards. To address this question, this chapter reviews the related literature on the role of lawyers in the evolution of business practices, including gender equality, diversity issues, and leadership development. It then explores the actions that Pfizer's General Counsel Amy Schulman and Pfizer's legal department have undertaken to influence gender equality, diversity and leadership. From this review, a set of insights and lessons is derived which may help in-house lawyers recognize and seize the opportunities that having women in leadership roles brings to organizations.

This research is located at the intersection of three broad bodies of literature: theories of the legal profession, theories of gender and diversity, and theories of leadership.

The lawyer's role as an agent of change

Governance structures are changing as a result of globalization and this includes the role lawyers and general counsels play in the business sector (Cummings, 2013; Prakash and Hart, 1999). Although empirical findings are limited, available evidence suggests that the influence of in-house counsel and legal departments has grown as the significance of legal considerations has escalated in the strategic planning process (DeMott, 2006; Liggio, 1997, 2002; Daly, 1997; Chayes and Chayes, 1985). Therefore, they fulfil both formal and informal functions using both traditional and non-traditional lawyering roles while influencing how business practices evolve at both domestic and international levels (Wilkins and Papa, 2013; Duggin, 2007; Higgott et al., 2000).

In the same vein, the way in which entities deal with legal issues including gender equality, diversity and inclusion is critical to their survival and success especially in the corporate arena. Company goals and efforts are generally managed within individual business units, but the legal team, under the leadership of the general counsel, coordinates and facilitates them globally. Fostering gender equality, diversity and inclusion requires more than simply formulating a set of gender goals at a societal, institutional and organization level (Rake, 2008; Rees, 2006). It demands a clear strategy and the successful implementation of that strategy to realize those goals (Rai, 2004).[1] Otherwise, developing activities aimed at empowering women and attracting and retaining high-potential female talent will be met with practical obstacles that impede and minimize the impact of programmes and activities at both an organizational level and a societal level (UN Women, 2011; Duflo, 2012; Beaman *et al.*, 2009). Gender and leadership scholars agree that whether the set gender, diversity and inclusion goals will translate into tangible outcomes on the ground depends on a number of factors (Sturm, 2010, 2011; Rees, 2002, 2006). Such factors include the procedures and programmes in place in an organization, and the involvement of key departments and senior management in supporting and implementing such procedures and programmes (Beveridge *et al.*, 2000).

The general counsel and his or her team are pivotal nodes in a network of organizations. A typical example in the setting of a global company is the core role of the general counsel in their organizational efforts to ensure that the various subsidiaries as well as the suppliers comply with minimum regulatory standards at both the global and the national level (compliance). General counsels are significantly embedded in the inter-organizational network, and may be critical to many systems that keep the organization overall functioning effectively including in programmes and policies aiming at enhancing women in leadership roles and reducing the salary shortfall for women within an organization and with external stakeholders (Soohan *et al.*, 2012).

General counsels are closely involved in development and implementation of and compliance with a corporation's (internal) policies and practices including in gender equality, diversity and inclusion matters. Overall, they contribute resources such as information and knowledge to their board, their organization, and to any

1 The goal of gender equality can be achieved through gender mainstreaming (a process or strategy that, if implemented successfully, leads to equality and empowerment of women) (Grosser, 2009; Grosser and Moon, 2008; Grosser *et al.*, 2008). Gender mainstreaming is defined as the process of assessing the implications for women and men of any planned action, including legislation, policies or programmes, in all areas and at all levels and offering specific activities aiming at empowering women (Beveridge *et al.*, 2000; Rubery, 1998). It is a strategy for making women's as well as men's concerns and experiences an integral dimension of the design, implementation, monitoring and evaluation of policies and programmes in all political, economic and societal spheres so that women and men benefit equally and inequality is not perpetuated (UN Economic and Social Council, 1997, p. 28).

other third party with whom they interact on behalf of the organization. In sum, they are important linchpins in creating a cohesive group among the different stakeholders (Westphal and Zajac, 1995; Windolf, 1998) as they encapsulate all the constraints of organizational rule makers and enforcers.

General counsels' and in-house lawyers' influence on gender and leadership issues

The influence of lawyers in new areas of business practice, including gender, diversity and leadership development, is inevitable. For instance, Professor Richard Susskind in his seminal book, *End of Lawyers?*, discusses the need for legal professionals—including lawyers and in-house counsel—to adapt to the modernizing world (Susskind, 2008). To continue to claim their role in society, lawyers need skills that reach beyond their knowledge of the legal framework, as well as to embrace opportunities to expand their influence beyond strict legal compliance and in new areas (Cecchi-Dimeglio and Kamminga, 2014). This is a reflection of the fact that

> [i]n a business world that is growing smaller with the globalization of industries, and in a society where consumer decisions are made primarily by women, lawyers and in-house lawyers cannot afford to build a legal team that fails to reflect the diversity of the broader society (ABA, 2013, p. 5).

In sum, the power to close the gender gap lies in part with law firms as well as in-house legal departments' efforts both in terms of the number of women in leadership positions and in terms of salary equality (NAMWOLF, 2012; Rhode, 2012).

Indeed, there is a noticeable trend that has been observed in recent years, where general counsels and in-house corporate legal departments have increasingly used their power to influence diversity and leadership development both within their own team and with their outside partners, such as suppliers and external law firms (Lalla, 2010). For instance, general counsels and in-house departments collaborate on a regular basis with external law firms to help carry out legal matters on behalf of the organization. The effort of diversity and inclusion at the external law firms that are working with them on various matters is important to general counsels.

A spectrum of methods is used by in-house general counsels to monitor the diversity efforts of their outside counsel. For example, Shell Oil gathers extensive information on potential law firms' diversity policies before hiring outside counsel. Other companies have policies in place that aim to "reduce a law firm's ability to have women do sales pitches and presentations" but then remove them from the assignment once the business is secured (Ginsburg, 2005; ABA, 2013, p. 5). Some require law firms to submit an engagement letter specifying the firm's policy on diversity, or track the number of hours billed by minority lawyers relative to the total of hours billed by a firm, or include diversity related feedback in the company's annual performance evaluation of the outside firm. Others reward law firms for their diversity initiatives on a "pay for performance" basis (ABA, 2013, p. 5-1).

All in all, various techniques are used to strengthen gender equality and support diversity by in-house counsels and legal departments with their external partners. However, these methods appear to be of variable effectiveness and so far no single method has clearly been adopted as the leading approach.

Purpose, research question and methodology

This chapter evaluates the extent to which a general counsel and the legal department can influence gender equality and leadership, going beyond the bare bones of legal compliance. It is based on a case study of the work of Amy Schulman and her legal team at Pfizer Inc. (Pfizer). The focus is on the actions and complex sets of processes, rules, tools and systems used by the general counsel and the legal department to adopt, implement and monitor an integrated approach to influence gender equality and enhance leadership opportunities and positions for women within the organization and at third parties.

Methodology
Why a case study

The case study method was chosen for several reasons. First, in the last two decades scholars across disciplines have recognized the value, the richness and the persuasive power of case studies in theory building (Siggelkow, 2007; Weick, 2007; Suddaby, 2006). Second, "the real value" of the case study approach is to "offer the opportunity to explain why certain outcomes might happen—more than just finding out what those outcomes are" (Denscombe, 2003, p. 31). Furthermore, an overwhelming number of social science, management and empirical scholars have recognized that theories that are based upon cases are often regarded as the "most interesting" research (Bartunek *et al.*, 2006). Finally, evidence of the value placed on case studies among academics in the field of management, is that the most highly cited pieces in the *Academic Management Journal*, with an impact disproportionate to their numbers (Eisenhardt, 1989; Gersick, 1988), are case studies (Eisenhardt and Graebner, 2007; Bartunek *et al.*, 2006).

Overall, while choosing an organization that is considered to provide "best practices" may lead to somewhat unique findings, it can offer valuable lessons and a framework that is expandable well beyond the organization itself as well as provide guidelines for "best practices" useful to other organizations.

Why Pfizer and Amy Schulman?

Several reasons have driven the choice of taking Pfizer, an American Fortune 100 pharmaceutical firm, its general counsel Amy Schulman and her legal department as objects of study. Important in the selection of a case is how much a researcher can learn, as well as the ability to position the case in a broader perspective (Stake, 2000). First, this company is a prime example of an organization that has pioneered investment in gender equality. Pfizer devotes much attention to its corporate social responsibility and the gender sensitivity of its policies and programmes, as well as to its internal organizational structure, procedures, culture, and human resources. Gender equality plays a major role in the overall business strategy at Pfizer and is a pillar for achieving its mission of "working together for a healthier world" (Pfizer, 2011: 6). These investments have paid off.[2] For more than five consecutive years, Pfizer has been included in the global Top 20 Best Companies for Leadership and was among the noteworthy companies named by Diversity Inc. It has also been named one of the best 100 companies for working mothers, and listed in the top 50 best corporations for executive women (Working Mother, 2010; *Diversity Magazine, 2008*), among other awards. Its commitment to gender equality also translates into leadership at the highest levels. For instance, the composition of its board of directors grew its female presence from 19% to 33% and the composition of its executive leadership included more than 31% women from 2009 to 2013 (Pfizer, 2009, 2010, 2011, 2012, 2013).

Second, Pfizer is regarded by diversity and gender equality organizations assessing Fortune Top 100 companies as exemplary in its gender equity practices. Among the most noticeable policies, Pfizer offers: 1) paid maternity and paternity leave (up to 12 paid weeks); 2) a phased return programme after maternity and paternity leave; 3) adoption leave; 4) an elder care case management programme, which connects employees with a consultant who helps them address issues associated with caring for aging relatives; 5) mentoring circles and a global council for women; 6) tuition aid of up to $10,000 annually, as well as educational leave of absence of up to a year, including health benefits; 7) flexible working time; and 8) on-site childcare places and childcare services (Pfizer 2009, 2010, 2011, 2012, 2013).

Furthermore, Pfizer integrates diversity and inclusion in its organization effectively. When implementing strategies, it encompasses a large spectrum of stakeholders, ranging from employees to customers to suppliers, and it involves societal groups by initiating various community actions. The experiences at Pfizer provide valuable insights into the role that various departments play in developing and implementing the gender mainstreaming strategy, and how this strategy can be advanced on a global level and within different diverse communities.

Third, the involvement of key departments and individuals in strengthening the cause of gender equality internally as well as externally seems to have been an

---

2 For the full list of Pfizer's accolades, see http://www.pfizer.com/about/accolades/accolades

important factor in creating gender equality, diversity and leadership opportunity at Pfizer and beyond. For instance, in late 2008, under the guidance of its Global Women's Council (GWC), Pfizer developed an integrated diversity and inclusion (D&I) strategy. This D&I strategy includes colleagues, customers, suppliers and the communities where Pfizer employees work and live. As a result, Pfizer clearly committed itself to be a leader in the diversity and inclusion space.

Fourth, Amy Schulman's leadership appears to be a worthy example of an innovative female general counsel holding a leadership position and simultaneously being at the forefront of gender equality and diversity matters both within her own organization and with external stakeholders.

> Ms. Schulman's business acumen, commitment to clients, skill as a legal advocate and efforts to advance women have earned her accolades from leading publications and organizations. In 2013 *Fortune* magazine named her one of the "50 Most Powerful Women in Business." That same year, *The American Lawyer* named her one of the "Top 50 Innovators," and *The National Law Journal* named her one of "The 100 Most Influential Lawyers in America." The American Bar Association honored her with the Margaret Brent Women Lawyers of Achievement award in 2012. She was one of 10 "leading lights" featured in *The Financial Times* 2011 U.S. Innovative Lawyers report. In 2009 *Forbes* magazine included her on its list of "The World's Most Powerful Women." (Pfizer, 2012)

In sum, the choice of Pfizer and its general counsel as a case study lies in its well-documented record and recognition in the areas of gender equality and diversity, accessibility, and comprehensive institutional structure as well as Amy Schulman's track record and personal commitment to actively pursuing diversity.

Data collection

Amy Schulman's actions to close the gender gap

An interpretive design has been adopted for this research, following Suddaby and Greenwood's (2009) advice to analyse facets of inside-outside phenomena. I used a content analysis method to examine transcripts of publicly available speeches, interviews and scholarly articles to examine the actions Amy Schulman undertook to influence gender equality, diversity and leadership opportunities for younger talent. This allows us to better understand the actions that have had an impact beyond Pfizer.[3]

---

3 Content analysis is a research technique widely used in the social sciences that allows the objective and quantitative study of qualitative data.

Method

To examine the actions Amy Schulman and her legal department have taken to influence gender equality, diversity and leadership opportunities for younger talent, the research adopted a content analysis method. "Content analysis is any technique … for making inferences … by objectively and systematically identifying specified characteristics of messages" (Holsti, 1969, p. 25). It is an appropriate process when the investigator's data are limited to documentary evidence (Krippendorf, 1980, p. 10). Content analysis permitted the researcher to identify the characteristics of the general counsel's leadership in the area of gender equality and diversity as well as the actions, policies and programmes undertaken by the general counsel focusing on diversity and inclusion efforts at Pfizer.

I utilized the Factiva and HeinOnline databases to analyse interviews, speeches and scholarly articles.[4] Both databases provide the capability to search for content by date range and key words.[5] For this research, the period in which Amy Schulman was the general counsel at Pfizer Inc. was chosen for analysis (23 June 2008 to 20 December 2013). For the publicly available speeches and interviews, I limited the search to a set of three important business publications (*Financial Times*, *Wall Street Journal*, and *New York Times*) and five important legal flagship publications for lawyers, chief legal officers, general counsels and in-house counsel (*Corporate Counsel Magazine*, *Inside Counsel*, *National Law Journal*, *The American Lawyer*, and *The ABA Journal* (formerly *American Bar Association Journal*)).

The measure of terms selected for creating our independent variables (leadership, gender equality and diversity, and policies and programmes) were derived from extant literature in both leadership and law and gender. A review of literature pertaining to the measurement of these terms suggested that a large number of measures might possibly be appropriate (Fiedler, 1967; Bowers and Seashore, 1966).

4 The Factivia subscription news and business intelligence service was chosen as the core source of textual data for this research. Factivia is a database of over 8,000 business and news publications. It provides extensive coverage of a wide variety of newspapers and other news sources for the US and other countries. Sources are in 22 languages, date back as far as 1969, and include trade journals, newswires (Dow Jones, Reuters, and others), media programmes, and company and stock reports. HeinOnline is a digital collection of legal and law-related materials organized into modules called libraries. HeinOnline is a fully searchable, image-based database of over 2,000 legal journals and other resources related to legal history. The sources of information available on the Factivia and HeinOnline databases are qualified to be a reliable and reputable source of information to carry on textual searches. The focus target on general counsel and the legal sector is well covered by both sources.

5 An additional function provided by Factivia and HeinOnline that is important for this research is the provision of a regularly maintained intelligent taxonomy. The taxonomy capabilities provide key terms describing the content they are providing. These terms provide "concept" matching capabilities whereby relevant articles can be easily identified without necessarily containing exact textual matches.

The following terms have been used to create the leadership variable: leader, cooperative, collaborative and collaboration, innovator and pioneer. The following terms have been used to create the gender equality and diversity variables: champions and women issues, gender equality and diversity, advocate for women and men, closing the gender gap. The following terms have been used to create the policies and programmes variables: gender equality and diversity policies and programmes, diversity and inclusion policies and programmes, leadership development programmes and actions.

The total number of articles collected across these sources containing the name of the company (Pfizer) and general counsel (Amy Schulman) and/or Pfizer legal department resulted in a population of 203 articles. I controlled for time, frequency and sources and I also included a dummy variable controlling for whether several terms identified as our independent variables appeared in the same articles.

Findings

Both as a general counsel and as an executive sponsor of Pfizer's GWC, Amy Schulman took actions towards closing the gender gap and developing leaders of tomorrow both in the legal community and well beyond.

Amy Schulman's leadership: her actions towards closing the gender gap as a general counsel

First, Schulman as a general counsel appears to take actions that reflect "her values" including to be "a thoughtful and pervasive role-model for others" willing to challenge the status quo and taking people out of their comfort zones (Hill *et al.*, 2014a; Burks, 2012; Post, 2012). One of her assistant general counsels noted: "She has changed the culture quite a bit... She's a very dynamic leader, and she's not afraid to challenge people to do things differently. I think she wanted to take people out of their comfort zones" (Park, 2009, citing Heidi Chen, a Vice President and Assistant General Counsel for Pfizer). Schulman's leadership also appears to be driven by her abilities to enjoy her work beyond the scope of her task. As she noted: "the willingness to challenge and reinvent yourself and to say that fun matters, is the biggest driver" (Schulman, 2010). Finally, Schulman's introspection abilities probably enhanced her qualities as a leader, as she says, "[I] want to hear feedback openly. I tend to be very straightforward. I know how to laugh at myself. I'm not afraid of criticism. My door is always open" (Bryant, 2011). In sum, Schulman's motivation, self-awareness and self-regulation allowed her to clearly express the values, attitudes and behaviours she believed in, including challenging the status quo to improve the organization and society more broadly (Brewer and Gardner, 1996; Brewer and Weber, 1994).

In this vein, Schulman's leadership demonstrates that her legal department had a decisive role to play at Pfizer, not only in the revolutionary changes that businesses encounter such as in scientific, technological and regulatory matters, but also in gender equality and diversity matters. Moreover, Schulman is willing to address and act on these changes. For instance, speaking about the problem of inequality between men and women in the legal field and other professions, she noted: "We need to have the courage to *insist* on calling out pernicious false choices and refuse to remain hostage to unconscious biases" (Post, 2012). It appears that she is willing to "spend some of her political capital and voice to ensure women have a seat at the table that we are entitled to" (Burks, 2012; Hewlett and Rashid, 2010). She leveraged her political power and high-profile position on behalf of other women to change the way the leadership viewed its obligation to develop women and diverse talent (Burks, 2012). In sum, "her willingness to take the risk as a general counsel" including in the area of gender equality and leadership development for a diverse pool of talent, makes her a "model to others how to behave in new and often unnatural ways" (Hill *et al.*, 2014a, b).

The Pfizer Legal Alliance (PLA) is a perfect illustration of her ability to challenge the status quo, and demonstrate to others how changing business practices can benefit everyone, including enhancing a diverse pool of talent and leaders. PLA is a network of 19 of the company's external law firms that work with Pfizer. While the PLA is mainly known in the legal world to have created a structure of flat fees instead of the traditional billable hour model between Pfizer and external law firms, the PLA programme went well beyond the fees structure (Hill *et al.*, 2014a, b). Schulman saw in this programme the opportunity to impact gender equality, diversity and leadership development in the external firms Pfizer works with, as well as opportunities to inspire others about the practice of law. She noted "the genuine passion and enthusiasm I feel about the general practice of law—I want to reignite that in younger colleagues" (Burks, 2012). Some notable examples of the PLA work on gender equality are discussed below.

Junior Associate Program. The Junior Associate Program was developed to strengthen the professional development of high-potential law school graduates through hands-on exposure to Pfizer legal matters. It consists of hiring high-potential lawyers right out of law school, which is not the norm in the legal profession, especially in the in-house corporate world. Junior Associates rotated assignments between Pfizer and one of the law firm members of the PLA. The Junior Associates in their third year were given the choice to join Pfizer or one of the member firms of the PLA (Hill *et al.*, 2014a, b).

Lead, Engage, Advance, and Develop (LEAD) Program. The LEAD Program is a diversity and inclusion initiative as part of the PLA firms and at Pfizer itself. It provides personalized development opportunities for rising minority lawyers. The ultimate goal of the programme is to build the skills and profile of diverse associates at Pfizer PLA law firms. Schulman's idea behind the programme is that by sponsoring these high potential associates she can give them the support they need to reach the next level in their careers. This Pfizer LEAD Program is clearly aligned with the PLA's structure and culture of collaboration. It further provides a broader range of professional opportunities and sponsorship that would not have been available in a more traditional one-on-one client–firm relationship. The programme leverages the culture of teamwork and cross-firm relationships to develop future leaders.

Associate Roundtable. The Associate Roundtable brings together on a regular basis star associates from each member firm to discuss and further build their legal and social skills. The group has become a strong social network in which the associates can cross-refer matters and give younger attorneys opportunities for growth and development. Each Roundtable member is paired with a Pfizer mentor, who identifies opportunities for the associates to do more high profile work. The idea behind these programmes is to develop high potential associates, especially women and minority attorneys, and give them the support they need to reach the next level in their careers and to be a successful leader.

Amy Schulman's leadership: her actions towards closing the gender gap as executive sponsor of the Pfizer's GWC

Second, Schulman's role as an executive sponsor of Pfizer's GWC contributed towards closing the gender gap in developing female leaders inside and outside Pfizer. The Pfizer's GWC is a group comprising senior-level female and male colleagues from across the organization that focuses on women's talent and pipeline management. The mission of the Council is to increase the number of senior women business leaders through recruitment, advancement, engagement and retention, while working to eliminate potential barriers to advancement. Pfizer's GWC initiated and sponsored various programmes to shape the company's efforts to increase diversity and expand opportunities for both women and men. Schulman's role in the Council is reported to have "led Pfizer into a significant increase of women in senior level jobs from 2009 to 2011" (Pfizer 2012; Shrestha 2011, Pfizer, 2009, 2010, 2011).[6] Schulman describes her role as follows:

> I have long been a champion for women in the profession and that hasn't changed now that I have this seat (referring at both Senior Vice President and General Counsel of Pfizer Inc.). I am one of the executive sponsors of Pfizer's robust diversity and inclusion effort, and I chair the women's component of that effort. We have measurable and accountable goals, and we're working with our outside firms to ensure that they understand the centrality of diversity at Pfizer. This is a big priority for me and continues to be a focus of my attention (Schulmann, 2010).[7]

---

6 The author gained access to the data as part of her three-year empirical study at Pfizer, Inc. Unfortunately, for confidentiality reasons these data cannot be shared in this article. The public data on the growth of female board members from 19% to 33% between 2009 and 2013 is however indicative of the significant increase in female senior leadership at Pfizer.

7 Amy Schulman interview, 17 March 2010.

Three noticeable examples initiated and guided by the Global Women's Council should be mentioned here to illustrate Schulman's impacts in closing the gender gap and developing leaders, both of which received a lot of attention from the media.

The first example is the Raise Your Hand initiative, which builds the next generation of Pfizer's women leaders by increasing their business acumen. On the one hand, it allows colleagues to share stories about flexible working arrangements and mentoring from the perspectives of both manager and colleague. On the other hand, it boosts women's confidence through small mentoring circles, specialized business courses and activities that enhance leadership and executive presence. By sharing their experiences and learnings, Pfizer increased women's participation in employee resource groups, and accessing mentorship opportunities.

Second, the pilot programme in India had the overall goal of creating and developing a high performance community through the development of women's talent. To do so the programme focuses on the following:

- Ensuring top female talent feels valued and supported

- Strengthening connections among Pfizer's high-performing women and their women customers

- Testing an approach potentially useful in other markets (Hewlett and Rashid, 2010)

In this programme, Pfizer first identifies its top ten women in sales and marketing and its ten most important women customers (including physicians in private practice, medical professionals in high profile hospitals, medical technologists, and so forth). Then, the women identified participated in a focus group to discuss their career goals and the professional challenges and opportunities they faced. What emerged was a "narrative of blazing ambition often blocked by cultural barriers" (Hewlett and Rashid, 2010). As a result, Pfizer's GWC initiated various training and programmes available to Pfizer employees and important women customers of Pfizer to help them in overcoming the barriers identified. In other words, it offered leadership development tools to empower them (Hewlett and Rashid, 2010).

Finally, Schulman's role in the GWC led Pfizer to be part of the decisive Step Towards the First Global Certification for Gender Equality in the Workplace. Participating companies are organizations that proactively manage gender diversity and have demonstrated a long-term commitment to improving gender equality in the workplace. As Schulman describes it: "the Gender Equality Project establishes standards that help companies understand the kind of inclusive behaviours that bring out the best in people and organizations" (Alcatel Lucent, 2011).

In summary, Schulman's involvement as a general counsel and as an executive sponsor of Pfizer's GWC contributed to support and to the establishment of various programmes aimed at closing the gender gap and developing leaders. The perception of successful role models, such as Schulman, might support and inspire other companies and general counsels to undertake similar actions while in leadership positions (Rhode and Packel, 2010; Wolbrecht and Campbell, 2007).

Lessons derived

There are many social, economic, and institutional factors that impact the retention and attrition of women in the legal profession, and only some of those factors are within the control of the law firm and in-house lawyers. However, in-house lawyers are well positioned to influence gender equality and leadership developments that may be beneficial to a corporation and to society more generally. They might shape activities and policies extending well beyond ensuring just legal compliance (DeMott, 2006).

In this vein, this study has several key practical contributions and implications. First, we can derive guiding principles of best practices to enhance gender equality and diversity. Second, specific strategy and actions for in-house legal departments can be recommended.

First, the best practices and guiding principles for fostering gender equality and diversity that can be derived are the following:

- Top leadership commitment to gender equality and diversity (Fiedler, 1967)
- A clear communication that a more inclusive and diverse workforce enhances productivity and organizational performance by top-level management throughout the organization and department (Ely and Rhode, 2010)
- Diversity and gender equality goals as part of the organization strategic plan including mechanism controls to foster its actions (e.g. measurement and accountability)
- Succession planning and recruitment identifying a diverse talent pool and developing them into an organization's potential future leaders including with business partners
- Employee involvement and diversity training to foster driving diversity throughout an organization and with external stakeholders

Second, to maximize the effectiveness of the best practices principles in closing the gender gap and fostering leadership development, in-house counsel can strategize, educate, initiate and benchmark their organization and their outside legal service providers in the area of gender equality and diversity. The corporation's core values of diversity and inclusion will be mirrored. Together corporate clients and lawyers can create real and meaningful opportunities for women and leadership within the legal profession and beyond. By using their political and economic powers to level the playing field for women, in-house counsel can play a key role in shattering the glass ceiling for women. For instance, the legal department supports the creation of a diversity committee within the legal department supporting the initiative of the D&I committee within the organization if one exists. In-house counsel can foster and help companies develop guidelines mirroring the company's diversity expectations and state why having a diverse pool of partners is important to the company.

The external efforts of the company to support gender diversity should complement the internal efforts. The general counsel and legal department can require outside firms and suppliers to provide detailed diversity and gender equality measures while reporting annually. This effort can be overseen by the law department's diversity committee and could help to develop a diversity scorecard or report for discussion with outside partners. Additionally, in-house counsels can create mechanisms to develop a diverse pool of lawyers while working on company matters. Both the companies and the law firm can jointly implement programmes for mentoring and networking activities. Also, the company can collaborate with the outside firm to identify and train talent in areas that meet the company's needs.

In-house lawyers can support policies to advance gender diversity such as the creation of a diversity committee within the legal department but also take a leadership role in this area. Likewise, the company can also benchmark external partners, by not only implementing and monitoring mechanisms to collect data on an annual basis (e.g. for associates working on the company matters) but also by establishing economic mechanisms to incentivize the behaviour wanted. For instance, the company could offer a "Pay for performance" bonus approach to enhance diversity. In this case, we could imagine that a firm would be eligible for a specific percentage bonus on all legal fees if specific criteria such as a year-over-year specified increase in hours worked by diverse attorneys on the company's matters, or a specified percentage increase in the diversity of its attorneys. Similarly, the company can also utilize the social norms mechanisms to incentivize firms to advance diversity and inclusion. For instance, the company could implement an annual award recognizing outside counsel firms that made the most significant contribution in this area. Another possibility could be to create a roster to match a diverse law firm that is smaller, with one of the company's large firms to jointly work on matters for which a smaller and diverse law firm would not be considered. In other words, the company acts as a platform to enhance opportunities. Finally, the company should be willing to sanction firms if diversity standards are not met, including severing the relationship with the existing legal service provider if progress is not made.

Conclusion

The gender gap is particularly acute in the legal world, where fundamental change is needed to address and ameliorate long-standing disparities in compensation and inclusion of women in top management and leadership positions. General counsels and in-house counsels can play a key role in organizing how corporations and firms work together to help close the gender gap.

General counsels can help in making the business case for ensuring that a critical mass of senior women and diverse lawyers are part of their own team as well as part of the team of third parties providing services to the organization. Corporate clients represent a tremendous power to bring meaningful change for women in the legal profession overall. They are extraordinarily well positioned to provide outside firms with examples of best practices that will lead to greater equality in compensation, advancement and leadership opportunities for women.

Finally, additional field research may further increase our understanding of how diversity in the legal profession may be established. The case study is a first step but it is not without limitations. Despite the clear strengths of this type of study, field studies with a larger sample may offer a richer understanding of context going beyond our case study. I do, however, consider that this case study lays the foundations for other works in the field. In particular, this study provides clear supporting anecdotal evidence regarding the influence of a general counsel and the legal department on gender equality and leadership effort.

Bibliography

Alcatel Lucent (2011, January 28). The Gender Equality Project provides multinational companies with standardized method for achieving gender equality. Press release retrieved from http://www.alcatel-lucent.com/press/2011/002325

American Bar Association (ABA) (2013). *Power of the Purse: How General Counsel Can Impact Pay Equity for Women Lawyers.* Chicago, IL: American Bar Association.

American Bar Association Commission on Women (2014). *A Current Glance at Women in the Law.* Retrieved from http://www.americanbar.org/content/dam/aba/marketing/women/current_glance_statistics_july2014.authcheckdam.pdf

Bartunek, J. M., Rynes, S., & Ireland, R. D. (2006). What makes management research interesting, and why does it matter? *Academy of Management Journal*, 49, 9-15.

Beaman, L., Chattopadhyay, R., Duflo, E., Pande, R. & Topalova, P. (2009). Powerful women: does exposure reduce bias? *Quarterly Journal of Economics*, 124(4), 1497-1540.

Beveridge, F., Nott, S., & Stephen, K. (2000). Mainstreaming and the engendering of policy-making: a means to an end? (Special Issue). *Journal of European Public Policy*, 7(3), 385-405.

Bowers, D. G., & Seashore, S. E. (1966). Predicting organizational effectiveness with a four factor theory of leadership. *Administrative Science Quarterly*, 11(2), 238-263.

Brewer, M. B., & Gardner, W. (1996). Who is this "we"? Levels of collective identity and self representations. *Journal of Personality and Social Psychology*, 71, 83-93.

Brewer, M. B., & Weber, J. G. (1994). Self-evaluation effects on interpersonal versus intergroup social comparison. *Journal of Personality and Social Psychology*, 66, 268-275.

Bryant, A. (2011, December 10). A blueprint for leadership: show, don't tell. *New York Times.* Retrieved from http://www.nytimes.com/2011/12/11/business/amy-schulman-of-pfizer-on-demonstrating-leadership.html?_r=0.

Burks, R. (2012, August 15). Risk taker is honored by the American Bar Association for helping women in law succeed, businesswire. Retrieved from http://www.businesswire.com/news/home/20120815005200/en/'Risk-Taker'-Honored-American-Bar-Association-Helping#.VSAqp0ITMuh

Cecchi-Dimeglio, P. (2014). *Legal Education and Gender Equality: Where are We? Women up! 2, A transatlantic gender dialogue.* Brussels: Foundation for European Progressive Studies, pp. 85-97.

Cecchi-Dimeglio, P. (2015). Legal education and gender equality. In Patricia M. Flynn, Kathryn Haynes and Maureen A. Kilgour (eds.), *Integrating Gender Equality into Business and Management Education.* PRME initiative. Sheffield, UK: Greenleaf Publishing.

Cecchi-Dimeglio, P. & Kamminga, P. (2014). The changes in legal infrastructure: empirical analysis of the status and dynamics influencing the development of innovative practice. *Journal of the Legal Profession*, 38(2), 191-230.

Chayes, A. & Chayes, A.H. (1985). Corporate counsel and the elite law firm. *Stanford Law Review*, 37, 277-321.

Cummings, S.L. (2013). Empirical studies of law and social change: what is the field – what are the questions? *Wisconsin Law Review*, 1, 171-204.

Daly, M.C. (1997). The cultural, ethical and legal challenges in lawyering for a global organization: the role of the general counsel. *Emory Law Journal*, 46, 1057-1102.

DeMott, D.A. (2006). The discreet roles of general counsel. *Fordham Law Review*, 955-978.

Denscombe, M. (2003). *The Good Research Guide for Small Scale Social Research Projects* (2nd ed.). Buckingham, UK: Open University Press.

Diversity Magazine (2008). Diversity Leader Award: Profiles. Retrieved from http://www.diversityjournal.com/

Dubey, P. and Kripalani, E. (2013). *The Generalist Counsel: How Leading General Counsel are Shaping Tomorrow's.* New York: Oxford University Press.

Duflo, E. (2012). Women's empowerment and economic development. *Journal of Economic Literature*, 50(4), 1051-1079.

Duggin, S. (2007). The pivotal role of general counsel on promoting corporate integrity and professional responsibility. *St Louis University Law Journal*, 51, 989-1100.

Eagly, A.H., & Carli, L.C. (2007). *Through the Labyrinth: The Truth about how Women become Leaders.* Boston, MA: Harvard Business School Press.

Eisenhardt, K.M. (1989). Building theories from case study research. *Academy of Management Review*, 14, 532-550.

Eisenhardt, K. M. & Graebner, M. E. (2007). Theory building from cases: opportunities and challenges. *Academy of Management Journal*, 50(1), 25-32.

Ely, R. J., & Rhode, D. (2010). *Women and Leadership: Defining the Challenges.* Cambridge, MA: Harvard Business Press Chapter.

Ely, R. J., Ibarra, H., & Kolb, D. (2011). Taking gender into account: Theory and design for women's leadership development programs. *Academy of Management Learning and Education*, 10(3), 474-493.

Fiedler, F.E. (1967). *A Theory of Leadership Effectiveness.* New York: McGraw-Hill.

Gersick, C. J. G. (1988). Time and transition in work teams: toward a new model of group development. *Academy of Management Journal*, 31, 9-41.

Ginsburg, R.S. (2005). Diversity Makes Cents: The Business Case for Diversity. Retrieved from http://www.royginsburg.com/published-articles/diversity-makes-cents-business-case-diversity/

Grosser, K. (2009). CSR and gender equality: women as stakeholders and the EU Sustainability Strategy. *Business Ethics: A European Review*, 18, 290-307.

Grosser, K., & Moon, J. (2008). Developments in company reporting on workplace gender equality? A corporate social responsibility perspective. *Accounting Forum*, 32, 179-198.

Grosser, K., Adams, C., & Moon, J. (2008). *Equal Opportunity for Women in The Workplace: A Study of Corporate Disclosure*. Research Report. London: Association of Chartered and Certified Accountants.

Hewlett, S.A., & Rashid, R. (2010, May). The globe: the battle for female talent in emerging markets. *Harvard Business Review*. Retrieved from http://www.persiangendernetwork. org/upload/HBR_Battle_4_Female_Talent_in_Emerging_Markets.pdf

Higgott, R.A., Underhill, G. R.D., & Bieler, A. (2000). *Nonstate Actors and Authority in the Global System*. London: Routledge.

Hill, L.A., Brandeau, G., Truelove, E., & Lineback, K. (2014a). *Line Back Collective Genius: The Art and Practice of Leading Innovation*. Boston, MA: Harvard Business Review Press.

Hill, L.A., Lineback, K., Brandeau, G. & Truelove, E. (2014b). *Be a Great Boss: The Hill Collection*. Boston, MA: Harvard Business Review Press.

Holsti, O.R. (1969). *Content Analysis for the Social Sciences and Humanities*. Reading, MA: Addison-Wesley.

Krippendorff, K. (1980). *Content Analysis: An Introduction to Its Methodology*. Newbury Park, CA: Sage.

Lalla, T., (2010, July 10). The importance of diversity in corporate legal departments. *Inside Counsel*. Retrieved from http://www.insidecounsel.com/2010/07/01/ the-importance-of-diversity-in-corporate-legal-departments

Liggio, C. D. (1997). The changing role of corporate counsel. *Emory Law Journal*, 46, 1201-1251.

Liggio, C. D. (2002). A look at the role of corporate counsel: back to the future – or is it the past? *Arizona Law Review*, 44, 621-652.

Mnookin, R.H., Peppet, S.R., & Tulumello, A.S. (2000). *Beyond Winning: Negotiating to Create Value in Deals and Disputes*. Cambridge, MA: The Belknap Press.

National Association of Minority & Women Owned Law Firms (NAMWOLF) (2012). The Inclusion Initiative: Leading companies with a commitment of nearly $139 million to work with minority and women owned law firms. Retrieved from http://c.ymcdn.com/ sites/www.namwolf.org/resource/resmgr/docs/inclusion_initiative.pdf

Neil, M. (2013, September 10). Top in-house lawyers get paid a lot less when female, survey says. ABA Journal. Retrieved from http://www.abajournal.com/news/article/ top_in-house_lawyers_get_paid_a_lot_less_when_female_survey_says

Park, M.Y. (2009, November). Pfizer's Legal Sentry. *Corporate Counsel*. Retrieved from http:// www.superlawyers.com/new-york-metro/article/Pfizers-Legal-Sentry/b4bbb7da-24e9- 436f-96d3-9655ee09e70b.html

Pfizer (2011). *Annual Review 2011*. Retrieved from http://www.pfizer.com/files/investors/ financial_reports/annual_reports/2011/downloads/pfizer_11ar_entire_site.pdf

Pfizer, (2012). Leadership. Retrieved from http://www.pfizer.com/files/investors/financial_ reports/annual_reports/2012/leadership-team.html

Pfizer (2009, 2010, 2011, 2012, 2013). Pfizer financial reports. Retrieved from http://www. pfizer.com/investors/financial_reports/financial_reports

Post, A. (2012). The Margaret Brent Women Lawyers of Achievement Award celebrates women who have paved the way for other women in law. *Inside Counsel*. Retrieved from http://www.insidecounsel.com/2012/08/16/ pfizer-gc-amy-schulman-wins-womens-achievement-awa.

Prakash, A., and Hart, J. A., (1999). *Globalization and Governance*. London: Routledge.

Rai, S. (2004). Gendering global governance. *International Feminist Journal of Politics*, 6(4), 579-601.

Rake, K. (2008). *Women and The Future Workplace: A Blueprint For Change*. A Fawcett Society think piece for the launch of the Gender Equality Forum. London: The Fawcett Society.

Rees, T. (2002). The politics of "mainstreaming" gender equality. In E. E. A. Breitenbach (ed.), *The Changing Politics of Gender Equality in Britain*. New York: Palgrave.

Rees, T. (2006). Promoting equality in the private and public sectors. In D. Perrons (ed.), *Gender Division and Working Time in the New Economy: Public policy and changing patterns of work in Europe and North America*. Cheltenham, UK: Edward Elgar.

Rhode, D.L. (2010). Lawyers and leadership. *Professional Lawyer*, 20(3), 1-17.

Rhode, D.L. (2012). Developing leadership. *Santa Clara Law Review*, 52(3), 689–724.

Rhode, D.L., & Packel, A., (2010). *Leadership: Law, Policy, and Management*. Amsterdam, NL: Wolters Kluwer.

Rubery, J. (1998). *Gender Mainstreaming in European Employment Policy, A Report by the European Commission's Group of Experts on Gender and Employment in the Framework of the Fourth Action Programme for Equal Opportunities for Women and Men*. Brussels: European Commission.

Schulman, A. (2010). Pfizer's Amy Schulman on what women need to succeed in their careers. Knowledge@Wharton 10(5). Retrieved from http://knowledge.wharton.upenn.edu/article/pfizers-amy-schulman-on-what-women-need-to-succeed-in-their-careers

Shrestha, B. (2011, October 13). Innovative corporate counsel: Amy Schulman. Law360. Retrieved from http://www.law360.com/articles/277749/innovative-corporate-counsel-amy-schulman.

Siggelkow, N. (2007). Persuasion with case studies. *Academy of Management Journal*, 50, 20-24.

Soohan, K., Kalev, A., & Dobbin, F. (2012). Progressive corporations at work: the case of diversity programs. *Review of Law and Social Change*, 36(2), 171-213.

Stake, R.E. (2000). Case studies. In N.K. Denzin & Y.S. Lincoln (Eds.), *Handbook of Qualitative Research* (pp. 435-454). Thousand Oaks, CA: Sage.

Sturm, S.P. (2010). Activating systemic change toward full participation: the pivotal role of mission-driven institutional intermediaries. *Saint Louis Law Journal*, 54, 1117-1137.

Sturm, S.P. (2011). Reframing the equality agenda. Paper presented at the *Harvard Law School Conference on Evolutions in Anti-Discrimination Law in Europe and North America, Cambridge, MA, 30 April 2011*.

Suddaby, R. (2006). What grounded theory is not. *Academy of Management Journal*, 49, 633-642.

Suddaby, R., & Greenwood, R. (2009). Methodological issues. In D. A. Buchanan & A. Bryman (Eds.), *Researching Institutional Change: The Sage Handbook of Organizational Research Methods* (pp. 177-195). Thousand Oaks, CA: Sage.

Susskind, R.E. (2008). *The End of Lawyers? Rethinking the Nature of Legal Services*. Oxford, UK: Oxford University Press.

United Nations Economic and Social Council (1997). Report of the Economic and Social Council for 1997. A/52/3, 18 September.

UN Women (2011). 2011–2012 Progress of the World's Women: In Pursuit of Justice (New York). Retrieved from http://www.unwomen.org/~/media/headquarters/attachments/sections/library/publications/2011/progressoftheworldswomen-2011-en.pdf

US Bureau of Labor Statistics (US BLS) (2014). Women in the Labor Forces. Retrieved from http://www.bls.gov/opub/reports/womens-databook/archive/women-in-the-labor-force-a-databook-2014.pdf

Weick, K. E. (2007). The generative properties of richness. *Academy of Management Journal*, 50, 14-19.

Westphal, J. D., & Zajac, E. J. (1995). Who shall govern? CEO/board power, demographic similarity, and new director selection. *Administrative Science Quarterly*, 40, 60-83.

Whelan, C.J & Ziv, N. (2013). Law firm ethics in the shadow of corporate social responsibility. *The Georgetown Journal of Legal Ethics*, 26, 153-177.

Wilkins, D. & Papa, M. (2013). The rise of the corporate legal elite in the BRICS: Implications for global governance. *Boston College Law Review*, 54, 1149-1178.

Windolf, P. (1998). Elite networks in Germany and Britain. *Sociology*, 32, 321-353.

Wolbrecht, C. & Campbell, D.E. (2007). Leading by example: female members of parliament as political role models. *American Journal of Political Science*, 51(4), 921-939.

Working Mother (2010). 2010 Working Mother 100 Best Companies. Retrieved from http://www.workingmother.com/tags/2010-working-mother-100-best-companies?page=2

Paola Cecchi-Dimeglio (Magistere-DJCE, LLM, PhD) is the chair of the Executive Leadership Research Initiative for Women and Minorities Attorneys (ELRIWMA) at the Center for the Legal Profession at Harvard Law School (HLS) and a Senior Research Fellow, jointly appointed at HLS (PON) and Harvard Kennedy School (Women and Public Policy Program). Her areas of expertise and research are women, dispute resolution and leadership in the legal profession. She has been nominated Expert-Coordinator for several projects on lawyers, alternative dispute resolution and gender funded by the EU and the UN.

Part II
First-hand accounts of leaders and pioneers tackling gender inequality at work

4

T3 and Under
A workplace childcare programme and a family-friendly workplace

Gay Gaddis

T3, USA

This chapter is about T3 and Under, a programme started in 1995 out of necessity, when four employees all got pregnant about the same time. We found a way to help parents transition back to work after maternity leave that has been a huge success and has involved almost 100 babies. It has transformed my company and how our employees relate to each other. The chapter explains why we did it, how it works, both successes and failures and the economic and emotional impact it has had on all of us. It is not a solution that will work for everyone, but it has worked for us. Most of the participants have been mothers, but we have had several fathers caring for their babies with great success. So it is not a programme just focused on women. It is a programme designed for the difficult back-to-work transition. We have seen many social, financial, business and emotional benefits from T3 and Under. Our hope is that this programme will demonstrate that creative thinking from employers and employees working together can invent new ways to deal with both career and family responsibilities. It has been an amazing personal journey for me and probably the most rewarding thing I've ever done.

The story of T3 and Under

When working for another advertising agency in 1989, I felt strongly that there was a real market opportunity for an agency that did outstanding creative work but also focused on delivering tangible results to clients. I presented a business plan to our management team that recommended we shift our corporate strategy to pursue that idea. Later that day, the president walked down the hall and said he would not support my ideas.

I fumed in my office for about an hour and then walked into his office and resigned. A few weeks later, I was in business for myself executing the business plan I believed had lots of potential. I cashed in my \$16,000 IRA[1] for working capital, hired two employees and we went to work. I was able to restore my IRA in 90 days, avoiding a 10% penalty.

T3 ultimately grew into the largest independent advertising agency owned by a woman in the United States. Today we focus on working with Fortune 500 companies and have over \$300 million in billings. The company employs over 170 people with offices in Austin, New York, Atlanta and San Francisco. We were early into digital advertising and this year we were named by Forrester Research as one of the top five most innovative agencies in the country.

We call ourselves an advertising agency because that is what people understand. But I have always believed we are a marketing solutions company because the right solution for a marketing problem is not always an advertisement. We have produced university-level training programmes, we have staged major events, we have been at the forefront of the mobile revolution and today we are helping traditional brands transform into something we call Useful Brands™.

To foster such a dynamic and creative environment, we always knew that our culture was critical. To this day I can walk into the office and feel the vibe—good or bad. We work hard but we have fun.

Soon after I started T3, I got an unexpected challenge. This was 1995 and over the course of one month, four of my key employees came into my office and told me they were pregnant. With a new business and not enough time to find and train replacements, I had to scramble to find a solution. We were too small to justify a professional daycare programme and I knew that some of the women would not return to work if they had to place their infants in daycare.

So I went to them all and offered them the opportunity to bring their infants to the office after they had completed their maternity leave. Each mother would be responsible for the care of her baby. We simply provided a place for them to care for and feed their babies. That's how our "T3 and Under" programme was born.

---

1 An IRA stands for an Individual Retirement Account set up at a financial institution that allows you to save money for retirement on a tax-deferred basis.

We set ground rules that required the children go into some other programme at around six months. A year later, we had an office that was humming, happy clients and babies everywhere.

The big idea that made it work was that the parents were responsible for their children. We do not provide any caretakers. The parents had to learn to care for their babies in the middle of a productive workday.

Photo 4.1 **Gay Gaddis (on the right) ensures that every infant who participates in the programme receives a pair of red cowboy boots—similar to the pair she received as a child from her parents. Taylor, with her mother Jonette James, is wearing a pair.**

Source: photo courtesy of Gay Gaddis/©Jennie Trower.

Twenty-six years after I started T3 we've had almost 100 babies come through the programme. I've been on the *Today Show* twice, *ABC Nightline* and have had hundreds of articles describing our success including in *The New York Times* and

USA Today. We were recognized at the White House, among others, for our efforts to create a family-friendly workplace.

As of October 2015, the statistics are:

- 92 total children

- 3 sets of twins

- 10 parents with more than one child

- 12 dads

- 1 grandparent (on occasion)

The evolution of T3 and Under

The evolution of the T3 and Under programme has been relatively seamless. The biggest challenge came when we changed the location of T3's Austin office. The company originally resided in five different but adjacent historic buildings in downtown Austin. Most of the offices were designed for one or two people, so a majority of the new parents could keep their children in their offices, although many feared crying and other child-related activities might distract co-workers nearby. The positive side of this physical arrangement was that the houses allowed a cohesive and interactive space for the mothers to get to know the infants. It allowed the mother to feel like her child was an active part of the office.

Today, T3 resides in a large refurbished office building in central Austin and fits all 120+ Austin employees in one location. When the office was built, designers planned a T3 and Under suite that was a bit more private. It has sleeping rooms, changing tables, cribs and play-mats. Parents bring Baby Bjorn carriers and strollers or use the T3 cribs to make it easy to take care of their child. This arrangement provides a quieter environment for the children and also allows the mothers privacy to nurse, and not be concerned about disturbing others during the workday. The trade-off is that it does not encourage as much interactivity between the entire office and the mother as the previous location. We do have a central kitchen and café, so everyone gathers there several times a day.

What we have learned

T3 and Under is not a perfect fit for every parent or child. Over half of the parents who were interviewed did not keep their children in the programme for the entire allotted time. The shortest amount of time that a baby was included in T3 and Under was 2 weeks. Reasons ranged from colicky children who needed extra attention, to having a job that required frequent client meetings and travel. But having children in the programme for less than the full-term did not decrease the parents' praise for the programme. No child has been mandated to leave the programme in its 20-year history.

We have worked hard trying to "make it work" by adapting to individual needs. This has included providing a list of sitters for an executive team member who has frequent client meetings, allowing parents to work from home two days a week and upgrading childcare equipment as necessary.

T3's parental leave policy

Employees are encouraged to report pregnancies as early as possible to help the company to better accommodate planning for their absence and return. If the mother has been with T3:

- At least six months to one year, she will receive two weeks of maternity leave with pay, and have the option to take accrued vacation and sick time

- More than one year, but less than two years, she will receive four weeks with pay plus the options described above

- More than two years, but less than four years, she will receive five weeks with pay plus the options above

- More than 4 years, she will receive six weeks with pay plus the options above

The expectant father, who has been with T3:

- For six months to one year, will receive two weeks paternity leave with pay plus have the option to take accrued vacation and sick time

- For more than a year, will receive two weeks paternity leave with pay, the options above and the remaining leave time without pay[2]

Our parental leave policy helps our team members get through the financial challenges of having a baby, and rewards people who have been with us for a long time.

---

2 In the United States, maternity leave is protected through the Family and Medical Leave Act of 1993 (FMLA). Per the FMLA, companies are not required to provide maternity leave compensation.

Employee benefits of T3 and Under

The T3 and Under programme has evolved over two decades, but the concept of bringing the infants to work has helped T3's employees learn how to balance parenting and a successful career—by actually doing it. We have fostered an open conversation about the realities of work/life balance. And, the amazing thing is that our young mothers have peers at T3 who have taken their babies through the programme; they actually become coaches to address emotional, financial and everyday practical issues facing the new parents.

In preparing to write this chapter, I went back and interviewed mothers and fathers who have participated in the programme. All of them agree that the greatest benefit has been the flexibility it allows new parents.

Most employees are expected to return to work after two or three months. Yet a child at that point of development is just beginning to acknowledge sounds, eat on a schedule and finally, sleep (Facts for Life, 2010). According to T3 and Under mother, Jen Faber, "The job of motherhood had just gotten fun, and I felt like I was going to have to give it up if I went back to work without the baby."

"For me, T3 and Under was all about transition," three-time T3 and Under mother, Allie Hewlett told me.

> Logistically, it isn't easy to totally change your schedule in the blink of an eye. You don't know what it's like having a baby until you have it, especially for the first time mom, you aren't sure what daycare means, how that works, or what it's like to have a nanny. T3 and Under gave me time I wouldn't have had otherwise to figure it out and make the right choice for me and my family without knowing anything in advance.

Having those extra months with their child allows time to bond, to figure out the work/life balance and to continue their career path uninterrupted. Women who do not have options like T3 and Under face wrenching emotional and financial choices. Sheryl Sandberg's findings in her book, *Lean In*, were that 43% of highly qualified women were leaving their careers or "off ramping" for a period of time. Only 74% of professional women will rejoin the workforce in any capacity and only 40% will return to full-time jobs (Sandberg, 2013).

Research shows that women who leave the workplace for a year will see a decrease in earnings by 20% and 30% after two or three years (Knowledge@Wharton, 2014). On a financial level, the rising cost of childcare has added another pressure to the workplace that causes women to not return to a full-time job and widens the gender equality gap (Payne *et al.*, 2011). The average cost for six months of infant care is around $6,000. T3 and Under eases that financial burden and delays childcare expenses until both parents are back at work.

I see bright, capable women struggle with these choices. The emotions are real. The choices are hard. I watch the women who participate in the programme learn how to make it all work together. Staying in the game is particularly important in our field. Technology is ramping up so fast that people who step out of the workforce for as little as six months are at risk of being left behind.

I see the mothers who successfully navigate the programme gain confidence in their ability to multitask. They learn how much more they can do when they have to, and they continue to expand their business expertise, putting them on a path to success and personal accomplishment.

Impact on the babies

We don't always have babies in the office, but we do most of the time. I continue to be surprised how quickly the babies adapt to the routine, the number of people they interact with and the stimulation and learning they are exposed to. They tend to be super well-adjusted, happy kids who each make amazing transformations during the time they are with us.

If you think about it, most children raised before the 1950s were raised by big families in rural environments. Grandparents, aunts, uncles and older siblings were all involved in caring for babies. I believe T3 and Under creates a similar experience for the babies and makes them much more open and well-adjusted.

Often during the workday, a mom will need to take a phone call and there is usually another T3 team member close by willing to walk with the baby. This exposure to warm, loving people makes the babies much more comfortable when travelling or staying with a babysitter or nanny.

More than half of the parents who have gone through the programme agree with me and say that this early socialization made their children's transition into daycare much easier. I can't prove this, but I also believe the babies are healthier when they go into daycare because they have already been exposed to lots of people and other children.

The parents tell me that most of these children do really well in school and are very well socialized. It is truly remarkable how many of them have taken leadership roles in their schools and organizations.

Impact on the parents

Marshall Wright, father of two daughters and T3 and Under participant, commented,

> The close relationships I have developed with my daughters are partly due to the time I was able to spend with them early-on during T3 and Under. I bonded with them more deeply than I would have if I hadn't been able to see them during the day and enjoyed getting to know them one-on-one. We still have a close bond. It also gave me the opportunity to have a closer relationship with my employees in the company, as they saw me as a dad and a co-worker—it was an invaluable experience.

Now, parenting and the T3 and Under programme are both something that employees look forward to participating in as they grow in the company. Executive Producer, Courtney Barry mentioned,

> I was in my early twenties when I first joined T3 and immediately loved taking care of the different children that were in the office at the time. I was looking forward to T3 and Under and always knew that I would participate with my child.

She did with her son, Weston.

Impact on the families

When I started the programme, my goal was to help the company survive four pregnancies and to help the babies and moms make an easier transition. Looking back on this after 20 years, the thing I never imagined was the impact it made on our employees' families.

Photo 4.2 **Gay Gaddis, Kim Martin, and her daughter Haley Martin. Haley Martin was the first baby enrolled in T3 and Under.**
Source: photo courtesy of Gay Gaddis/©Homero Cavazos.

We often have two or three babies at a time in the office. And, children who have been through the office frequently return for short visits. As a result, they become fast friends and playmates. So, guess who gets invited to birthday parties? And guess who gets invited to join a Little League team or meet for a summer picnic?

The children often come back to T3 as they grow up for Halloween trick-or-treating, selling Girl Scout cookies, or even working at the office. Kim Martin's daughter, Haley, returned as a summer intern in the office in 2014 and 2015. Haley was one of the original four children in the programme and enjoyed coming back as a grown up. (Haley completed two years as a high kicker in the Kilgore Rangerettes and is now attending college—if you don't know what the Kilgore Rangerettes are, look it up!)

The goodwill and trust that has developed between these families is amazing. Many, many lifelong friendships have been made. They form big support networks that are much like actual extended families—but it is so much more powerful because these people work together every day.

Impact on our business

One of the things I love to do is to walk new clients through our offices and introduce them to the people who will be working on their business. The office is pretty casual and pretty cool and the clients appreciate that. But inevitably we'll walk by a conference room and there will be a baby in a carrier sound asleep in the middle of a client conference call. The women almost always say, "Gee, I wish I could work here!" Not a bad way to start a relationship.

It is impossible to walk through our office and not walk away with a certainty that T3 is a family-friendly business. And that culture of caring permeates through the way we treat each other, our clients and our business partners. That impression is also important in our recruiting efforts. As we interview new candidates, we don't have to explain our family-friendly policies, they are right there in front of them. And, I know it impacts our retention programme because very few other companies offer a similar benefit.

Our business is a high pressure, high stress environment. We strive to do the most powerful creative work possible and get the best results for our clients. Deadlines and budgets are often tight. Everyone juggles multiple priorities every day. Smiling, sleeping, crawling, drooling babies see to it we don't take ourselves too seriously.

Looking forward

Photo 4.3   **Allie Hewlett (back right) is a three-time T3 and Under mother. Pictured here, her daughter Scout with Andrea Lytton, Sherry Carroll and Carolyn Compas.**

Source: photo courtesy of Gay Gaddis/©Jennie Trower.

In the future, T3 and Under will continue to be an important part of the company—it is ingrained in our culture.

Today, I have the flexibility to spend time working on helping mentor both men and women in finding a good work/life balance. I'm just completing two years of serving as Chair of the Committee of 200—a US women's organization made up of very successful business women across the country who focus on championing women in the workplace. I also speak internationally on many of these issues and mentor other companies who are looking for innovative solutions to these challenges all families face.

I am not a bleeding heart. I have turned a profit each of the 26 years I've been in business. We just wrapped up our 638th consecutive payroll. So I know something about business.

We are understanding of the parents who participate in the programme. But we continue to have the same high expectations of them that we have of everyone else. Work needs to get done and this is not continued maternity/paternity leave. In fact, my experience is that it enhances productivity. We have never had an issue with a returning parent about work performance. I think those parents understand the trust we put in them and they will not let us, or their co-workers, down. And they know that if they help a colleague with a crying baby, that favour will be undoubtedly returned.

I see the timestamp of many of the emails the parents send, and it is not unusual to receive one sent at about 10:30 p.m., wrapping up the last issues of the day at work while the baby gets the last feeding before bed. I know it is not easy. But I know that mom and that baby got to spend their day together. I think that is a fair exchange.

Two last points

This is not a women's issue. This is a family issue. Clearly, the burden of childcare weighs more heavily on women. But we have had 12 fathers successfully participate in the T3 and Under programme. One was a young man whose wife was an expert diesel mechanic who worked on high performance cars. She did not have the option to bring the baby to work. But her husband did and it worked beautifully.

And finally, next time ask me about our dogs at work programme.

References

Facts for Life (2010). *Childhood Development and Early Learning* (4th ed.). New York: United Nations Children's Fund. Retrieved from http://www.factsforlifeglobal.org/03/.

Knowledge@Wharton (2014). *Why Child Care Is the Economy's "Invisible" Driver*. Pennsylvania: University of Pennsylvania. Retrieved from http://knowledge.wharton.upenn.edu/article/economic-impact-of-child-care/.

Payne, S.C., Cook, A. & Diaz, I. (2011). Understanding childcare satisfaction and its effect on workplace outcomes: The convenience factor and the mediating role of work-family conflict. *Journal of Occupational and Organizational Psychology*, 85, 225-244.

Sandberg, S. (2013). *Lean In*. New York: Alfred A. Knopf.

Gay Gaddis is CEO and Founder of T3, the largest woman-owned independent advertising agency in the United States. Founded in 1989, today T3 has four offices and serves innovative creative solutions to Fortune 500 companies. Gay is an active spokesperson and writer for women in business issues. She is a regular contributor to *Forbes*, part of *Fortune*'s Most Powerful Women Insider Network and a frequent guest on Bloomberg Television. Gay is the former chair of the Committee of 200, a women's business organization, the first female Chairman of the Texas Business Leadership Council, sits on the board of publicly traded Monotype Imaging Holdings, Inc. and is an avid painter. Her first solo art show is currently on display at the Curator Gallery in New York. She is the mother of three grown children: Ben, Rebecca and Sam Gaddis.

5

The benefits of job sharing
A practice-based case study

Emma Watton
Lancaster University Management School, UK

Sarah Stables
University of Cumbria, UK

This case study demonstrates the practical application of a successful hybrid job share for two women leaders working in a senior
management role at a higher education institution. Over the three
years of the job share a number of benefits from an employee,
employer and leadership development perspective were discovered. In particular, the job share created opportunities for the
authors to overcome some of the barriers women leaders can face
such as achieving a better work–life balance and having increased
levels of confidence. The authors hope that the multiple benefits
of performing a leadership role through job sharing may encourage more employees and employers to consider job sharing as a
way of increasing the number of women in senior positions.

This case study analyses a three-year hybrid job share experience for two women
leaders working in a senior management position within higher education. Over
the period of the job share a number of benefits from an employee, employer and
leadership development perspective were identified. In particular the job share
enabled the authors to overcome some of the barriers women leaders face. The
multiple benefits of performing a leadership role through job sharing may highlight the opportunity for more employees and employers to consider job sharing
at a senior level as a way of growing and developing leadership capability within
organizations and helping to address some of the challenges of retaining and
increasing the number of women in senior positions.

Context

There have undoubtedly been significant gains for gender and diversity in management over the past two decades, which have been well documented by prominent writers and researchers (Eagly and Carli, 2007; Madsen *et al.*, 2005; Gatrell and Swan, 2008; Stead and Elliott 2009).

Yet, progress remains slow with women remaining under-represented at board and senior levels across most sectors (Eagly and Carli, 2007; Stead and Elliott 2009; Ely *et al.*, 2011). For many women wanting to undertake a senior role, a number of barriers remain commonplace (Sinclair, 2007; Eagly and Sczesny, 2009; Hoyt and Simon, 2011; Kempster and Parry 2014). Northouse (2007) categorizes these barriers into three areas: human capital differences; gender differences and prejudice. He further observes that (2007, p. 278) "gender stereotypes can significantly alter the perception and evaluation of female leaders and directly affect women in or aspiring to leadership roles". Eagly and Carli (2007) propose the use of a labyrinth as a contemporary metaphor that conveys the sense of a leadership journey for women which is often through new ground, with dead ends and set-backs, however, with a way forward being possible.

Within higher education the situation for senior women leaders follows the pattern described above with a shortfall of prepared leaders able to step into senior leadership roles in academia (Madsen, 2012). Although women do advance to leadership roles in universities, "gender imbalance among senior university academics is an acknowledged problem in many countries" (Airini *et al.*, 2011, p. 44).

Airini *et al.* (2011, p. 59) discovered a number of key factors that play a part in this context: work relationships, university environment, invisible rules, proactivity, and personal circumstance.

Evidence now supports some of the positive benefits for individuals, teams and organizations of having more women in leadership roles (Eagly and Carli, 2007; Taylor, 2013). Examples include several studies which show a small increase in the transformational leadership qualities demonstrated by women over men (Eagly and Johnson, 1990; Bass and Avolio, 1994; Eagly *et al.*, 2003). Similarly slight differences in behaviours have been identified (Eagly and Johnson, 1990) with women focusing more on tasks and personal relationships compared with men. Further there is the opportunity for the "feminization" of leadership which affords equal opportunity for both men and women to develop as better leaders through behavioural changes (Jackson and Parry, 2008).

The White House Report (2009), a report focused on women leaders in US higher education institutions identified that successful women leaders working with students, faculty and staff, provide positive experiences that can help change people's perspectives towards women in leadership positions. Further, these women can act as "powerful role models and mentors to younger women starting out on the path to leadership themselves" (p. 16).

For women in leadership positions the decision to have children and/or to take time off for childcare is often challenging. Women with a family often find returning to work problematic with many discovering that they are unable to return to their former role (Northouse, 2007; Daniels, 2011). Davies (2011) suggests that high levels of female attrition are due in part to the lack of flexible working arrangements. Her 2011 study showed that 80% of highly qualified women wished to work part-time. However, many women perceived that by opting to work part-time, they would hamper their career.

The opportunity to retain talented women returning from maternity leave within organizations through either part-time working or job sharing seems attractive from both an employer and employee perspective (Davies, 2011; Taylor, 2013). However, in many cases the implementation of these opportunities is through roles at a lower level, with less responsibility and for less remuneration (Eagly and Carli, 2007; Gatrell and Swan, 2008).

The Job Share Project, a global, collaborative venture between Capability Jane and seven organizations, namely Centrica, Deloitte, DHL, Freshfields Bruckhaus Deringer, Herbert Smith, KPMG and Royal Bank of Scotland (RBS), commissioned a report by Daniels (2011) into making job sharing work at a senior level. The report highlights the feasibility and advantages of job sharing at a senior level. Working Families is a charity and the UK's leading work–life balance organization; in 2007 it produced a report "Hours to Suit" that emphasized the advantage of having two heads over one as well as other benefits such as greater diversity in teams, enhanced productivity, people management innovation and process improvement.

However, evidence from both Working Families and the Job Share Project suggests that although the numbers of applications for job sharing roles has increased over recent years, adoption remains low. Gatrell and Swan (2008) indicate that this low level of adoption can be due to the tokenism from employers in needing to offer family-friendly policies from a legislative perspective but for various reasons finding it hard to implement the policies in practice. Several studies (Eagly and Carli, 2007; Gatrell and Swan, 2008; Taylor, 2013) have shown that for women in management positions, who are able to set up part-time or job shares, continued upward promotional prospects remain limited.

In the next section we will share how the authors successfully initiated a job share at their organization and the benefits this had for employees and employers.

A job share in practice

The authors successfully undertook a three-year hybrid job share while working in a senior management position within higher education. The role was that of Enterprise Manager within the Faculty of Arts, Business and Science at the University of

Cumbria. This role was a professional services position which reported to the Executive Dean and entailed leading a team of 15 staff with an annual income turnover of £3 million.

The University of Cumbria was established in 2007 from the merger of a number of pre-existing higher education (HE) organizations in Cumbria. The University of Cumbria Annual Equality, Diversity and Inclusion Report (2015) indicates that in 2013/2014 the University had 1,096 staff of which 67.7% were women, higher than the UK HE sector average of 54%; 50% of the leadership group of the university is female and within the university executive team the balance is 66% female and 33% male. This profile is unusual within the HE sector which is largely male dominated at senior positions (Ridgley and Rhodes, 2015). Job sharing currently makes up less than 1% of the total number of staff employed. The Higher Education Statistics Agency (HESA) is the official source of data about UK Universities and Higher Education Colleges. Data from the HESA report "Higher Education Statistics for the UK" (August, 2015), which analyses HE sector data for 2013/14, indicates that of the 395,780 staff employed in the sector, 47.2% of full-time staff and 66.9% of part-time staff were female.

The path to the job share

The authors had followed similar career paths before commencing their job share. Both were born in the early 1970s and after school and higher education had joined in the early 1990s private sector industries (financial services and telecommunications) in which senior leadership positions were male dominated. Both authors achieved early career success in their chosen sectors, both operating in a management role by their late 20s. Sinclair (2007, p. 65) indicates that women in male-dominated industries often achieve success by being "hard-working", "clever", "conscientious" and "dutiful" and the authors fitted this profile. The authors then joined the higher education sector in 2002 and 2004, in emerging knowledge exchange initiatives. The business skills they had developed proved valuable in enabling partnerships to be developed between higher education and industry.

During this time the acceptance of flexible working as a business practice was increasingly being driven by numerous factors including enabling technology, legislative changes and societal expectations (Valcour and Hunter, 2005). The technological advances included laptop computing and smart phones, and legislative changes in the UK included the right to request flexible working introduced as part of the Employment Act 2002 and further amended in 2014.

Why job share?

For the authors the reasons were different. Sarah was returning from maternity leave after the birth of her second child and needed to balance the demands of a young family with her career. While Emma who had successfully completed the role for the 14 months of Sarah's maternity leave wanted to maintain a position at a higher grade with a better work/life balance.

The University of Cumbria was initially resistant to a job share in a senior management role that included the line management of a large team. However, after a meeting that included a more complete understanding of the arrangement of the job share, the numerous benefits to the organization as well as to the individuals, and the practical concerns over how it could work, the university agreed. The agreement was initially on a three-month trial period.

Photo 5.1 **The authors undertaking their job share: Sarah Stables and Emma Watton**

The job share was on a "hybrid" basis with the role split to have shared responsibility (80%) and some split responsibilities (20%) based on individual strengths and complementary capabilities and expertise (definition as per Daniels, 2011). Sarah was appointed on a 0.5 full-time equivalent (fte) basis (3 days per week term time only) and Emma was appointed on a 0.6 fte basis. Holidays were organized to ensure that apart from one week at Christmas and one week at Easter, either Sarah or Emma was in work. The job share lasted for 3 years and ended when Emma was offered a full-time academic position at Lancaster University Management School in the Lancaster Leadership Centre. After analysis the main benefits of the authors' job share experience are summarized as follows:

Employee benefits

From an employee perspective we discovered several benefits of the job share. For Sarah, it enabled the continuity of her career; the alternative would have been a part-time role in a lower-paid job. For Emma it enabled her to continue to gain the senior management experience that the role entailed. For both authors it enabled us to have a better balance between our work and home lives. For example Emma provided support to allow Sarah to attend key milestone events such as school sports days; Sarah reciprocated by supporting Emma when she had submission deadlines for her MBA. In addition Emma and Sarah knew that during periods of annual leave one of them was covering the role meaning there was less of a backlog on returning to work.

These benefits link to the human capital differences described by Northouse (2007) and the conflict women face in balancing their work and home roles, particularly with the desire to care for children through part-time employment. Similarly, Sinclair (2007) observes that as their careers progress, being hard-working and single-minded in their achievements becomes stressful and unsustainable for women, especially those with a family. The authors were motivated and committed to perform the role well and ensure the job share was successful; the commitment was to one another as well as to their employer. They had an increased sense of wellbeing and ability to handle stressful situations. Because of these benefits they had a higher rate of productivity and a lower rate of absence. The authors' experience concurs with employee benefits highlighted in the Job Share Project Report (Daniels, 2011) and links to employer benefits in terms of continuity.

Employer benefits

There were several employer benefits. For example, the arrangement fundamentally changed senior managers' and colleagues' perceptions about how a job share could work in practice, particularly at a senior level: for example the Executive Dean had had a negative experience of a job share previously where handover and communication was poor. The job share enabled the retention of two key members of loyal staff, as Sarah would not have been able to undertake the role on full-time basis with two very young children and Emma wanted to work part-time due to personal circumstances. There was always cover during holidays or absence. During the period of the job share the authors voluntarily undertook additional responsibilities to partly cover an unfilled vacancy at the Associate Dean level, for a period of 18 months, saving the organization significant salary costs. The ability to undertake this role can be largely attributed to the success of the job share.

Leadership development

Emma and Sarah discovered multiple benefits from a leadership development perspective which the authors felt enabled them to overcome some of the leadership barriers women face. For example, the authors had increased confidence in their ability to perform a leadership role and were able to observe and learn from one another's leadership practice. They were able to advance their careers and had an increased range of experiences in a shorter time frame, for example experience of working at an Associate Dean level.

The job share ended in 2014 with Emma going on to secure an academic teaching role at Lancaster University Management School; Sarah remained at the University of Cumbria, working flexibly in the same role but not in a job share capacity. Both authors feel that their careers and perhaps perceptions of their worth within their respective organizations have increased as a result of having been part of the job share. Observations on the job share from the Pro Vice Chancellor for Enterprise at the University of Cumbria indicated that she had trust and respect for the authors' professional competence at an individual and joint level and identified both authors as having strong leadership capabilities.

The benefits from a leadership development perspective have synergy with the work of Kempster (2009) on how managers learn to lead in which he describes the importance of tacit learning through participation with leaders observing and learning vicariously from one another. It also addresses the benefits of having a mentor or role model (Hoyt and Johnson, 2011) through a shared, trusted relationship. Further, it links to the suggestion by Sinclair (2007) that women need to validate and identify their own strengths in leadership to be able to progress further in the future. These benefits identified through this case study lead us to our recommendations.

Recommendations

The authors hope this chapter will act as a catalyst for other women who may be considering a job share role to embrace the opportunity as not only a means to achieve a better work–life balance but also as a route through which to grow and develop their leadership potential. Further it is hoped employers will see the multiple benefits for the business in encouraging job sharing at more senior levels within organizations and as a way of retaining or indeed increasing the number of women in senior roles. Emma and Sarah hope it will also help business recognize that job sharing is possible and successful at senior grades, including strategic roles that involve line management. This example is of a job share in higher education; however the Job Share Project report (Daniels, 2011) indicates that this experience is echoed in other fast-paced global companies in a range of sectors.

The infographic shown in Fig. 5.1 summarizes the various considerations and benefits from both an individual and business perspective.

Figure 5.1 **Rise of flexible work in the UK Infographic**

Source: Expert Market (2013), reproduced with permission.

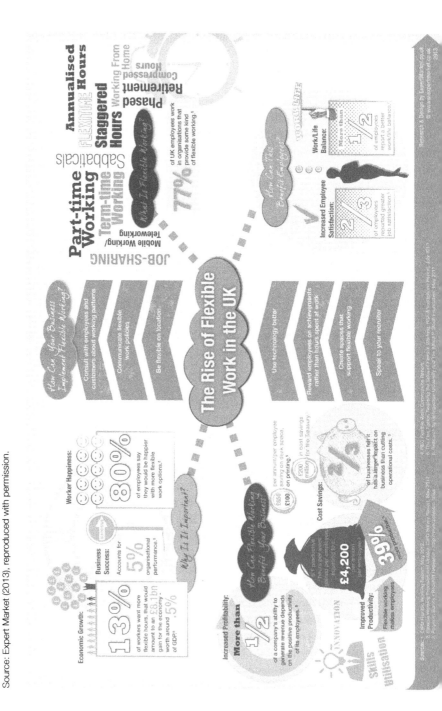

The infographic indicates a number of key benefits including several from a business perspective linked to business productivity. For example the figures state that a Polycom Survey (2012) found that in terms of cost-cutting the adoption of flexible working practices were two-thirds more effective than operational cost-cutting and flexible working practices made employees 39% more productive (in Expert Market, 2013). The figures state that a report produced by RSA and Vodafone (2013) showed that the overall adoption of flexible working would lead to a 5% increase in overall business productivity as summarized by Expert Market (2013). From an individual perspective research carried out by Georgetown University and the Alfred P. Sloan Foundation (2011) showed that 80% of employees report they would be happier with more flexible options (in Expert Market, 2013). Of those employees that adopted flexible work arrangements the report by RSA and Vodafone (2013) highlighted that two-thirds reported greater job satisfaction and productivity as illustrated by Expert Market (2013).

The Agile Futures Forum Report (2013) urges businesses to consider workforce agility (formerly known as flexibility) as key to business growth in the future. The report states that historically agility (flexibility) has been positioned as solely an employee benefit. In the future it urges business leaders to drive forward agility as a strategic business need in an increasingly competitive global market.

The authors would like to propose five steps that they feel would be beneficial for women to consider when seeking to introduce a job share arrangement:

1. Prepare a business case of employer benefits to accompany your application for job sharing. The business case should include benefits that are appropriate for your role, organizational context and sector including relevant reports such as those highlighted above from the Polycom Survey and Agile Futures Forum Report.

2. Consider the practicalities of establishing the job share to ensure the job share will achieve both personal goals and business continuity: for example, hours and days of work; annual leave entitlement; relationship management; and business context.

3. Develop a communications strategy and acknowledge that it is the responsibility of the job share partners to ensure effective communications: for example, an online shared file storage area and joint email account or a process of copying in on emails.

4. Establish a personal contract between the individual job share partners covering the foundations for establishing the job share; preferred ways of working; personal development aspirations and an exit strategy for the job share when these personal goals are met. For example Emma completing her MBA and securing an academic role was an objective of the job share from the outset.

5. Engage, clarify and be transparent about the job share and how it will work on a day to day basis with key stakeholders: for example, peers, direct reports or team members and the line manager for the job share partners.

References

Airini, Collings, S., Conner, L., McPherson, K., Midson, B., & Wilson, C. (2011). Learning to be leaders in higher education: What helps or hinders women's advancement as leaders in universities. *Educational Management Administration & Leadership*, 39(1), 44-62.

Bass, B.M. & Avolio, B.J. (1994). Shatter the glass ceiling: Women may make better managers. *Human Resource Management*, 33(4), 549-560.

Daniels, L. (2011). *Job Sharing at a Senior Level: Making it Work*. The Job Share Project. Retrieved from www.thejobshareproject.com.

Davies, E.M. (2011). *Women on Boards*. UK Government Report. Retrieved from https://www.gov.uk/government/uploads/system/uploads/attachment_data/file/31480/11-745-women-on-boards.pdf.

Eagly, A.H. & Carli, L.L. (2007). *Through the Labyrinth: The Truth about How Women Become Leaders*. Boston, MA: Harvard Business School Publishing.

Eagly, A.H. & Johnson, B. (1990). Gender and leadership style: A meta-analysis. *Psychological Bulletin*, 108, 233-256.

Eagly, A.H. & Sczesny, S. (2009). Stereotypes about women, men and leaders: Have times changed? In Barreto, M., Ryan, M.K. & Schmitt, M.T. (Eds.), *The Glass Ceiling in the 21st Century* (pp. 21-48). Washington, DC: American Psychological Association.

Eagly, A.H., Johannesen-Schmidt, M.C. & Van Engen, M.L. (2003). Transformational, transactional, and laissez-faire leadership styles: A meta-analysis comparing women and men. *Psychological Bulletin*, 129, 569-591.

Ely, R.J., Ibarra, H. & Kolb, D.M. (2011). Taking gender into account: theory and design for women's leadership development programs. *Academy of Management Learning and Education*, 10(3), 474-493.

Expert Market (2013). The rise of flexible work in the UK [Infographic]. Retrieved from http://wallblog.co.uk/2013/09/10/the-rise-of-flexible-working-in-the-uk-info-graphic/

Gatrell, C. & Swan, E. (2008). *Gender and Diversity in Management, a Concise Introduction*. London: Sage.

Hoyt, C.L. & Johnson, S.K. (2011). Gender and leadership development: A case of female leaders. In: Murphy, S.E. & Reichard, R.J. (Eds.) *Early Development and Leadership: Building the Next Generation of Leaders* (pp. 205-228). New York: Routledge.

Hoyt, C.L. & Simon, S.L. (2011). Female leaders: injurious or inspiring role models for women? *Psychology of Women Quarterly*, 35(1), 143-157.

Jackson, B. & Parry, K. (2008). *A Very Short, Fairly Interesting and Reasonably Cheap Book About Studying Leadership*. London: Sage.

Kempster, S. (2009). *How Managers Have Learnt to Lead: Exploring the Development of Leadership Practice*. Basingstoke, UK: Palgrave Macmillan.

Kempster, S. & Parry, K. (2014). Exploring observational learning in leadership development for managers. *Journal of Management Development*, 33(3), 164-181.

Madsen, S.R. (2012). Women and leadership in higher education: Learning and advancement in leadership programs. *Advances in Developing Human Resources*, 14(1), 3-10.

Madsen, S. R., Miller, D. & John, C.R. (2005). Readiness for organizational change: Do organizational commitment and social relationships in the workplace make a difference? *Human Resource Development Quarterly*, 16(2), 213-234.

Northouse, P.G. (2007). *Leadership Theory and Practice* (4th ed.). Thousand Oaks, CA: Sage Publications.

Ridgley, C. & Rhodes, H. (2015). *University of Cumbria Annual Equality, Diversity and Inclusion Report*. Retrieved from http://www.cumbria.ac.uk/Public/LISS/Documents/Equality/EIDAnnualReport201314.pdf

Sinclair, A. (2007). *Leadership for the Disillusioned: Moving Beyond Myths and Heroes to Leading that Liberates*. New South Wales: Allen & Unwin.

Stead, V. & Elliott, C. (2009). *Women's Leadership*. Basingstoke, UK: Palgrave Macmillan.

Taylor, J. (2013). *Gender Diversity in the Healthcare Sector: How Much Progress Have We Made?* London: The Kings Fund. Retrieved from http://www.kingsfund.org.uk/sites/files/kf/media/judy-taylor-gender-diversity-in-the-public-sector-nov13.pdf

The Agile Future Forum (2013). *Understanding the Economic Benefits of Workforce Agility*. Retrieved from http://www.agilefutureforum.co.uk/AFFReport/index.html#p=1.

The White House Project (2009). *The White House Project Report: Benchmarking Women's Leadership*. Retrieved from http://thewhitehouseproject.org/documents/Report.pdf

Valcour, P.M., and Hunter, L.W. (2005). Technology, organizations and work-life integration. In Kossek, E.E. and Lambert, S.J. (Eds.). *Work and Life Integration: Organizational, Cultural, and Individual Perspectives* (pp. 61-84). Mahwah, NJ: Erlbaum.

Working Families (2007). *Hours to Suit: Working Flexibly at Senior and Managerial Levels*. Retrieved from http://www.workingfamilies.org.uk/publications/hours-to-suit-working-flexibly-at-senior-and-managerial-levels/

Emma Watton is Senior Teaching Fellow in the Department of Leadership and Management, Lancaster University Management School. Emma's career started in the financial services industry where she worked for 15 years. She then became a freelance consultant to the financial services industry before moving into higher education 11 years ago. Emma's research interests are in the areas of responsible leadership and women's leadership. Emma is a member of the British Academy of Management and the International Leadership Association.

Sarah Stables is Business Development and Enterprise Lead at the University of Cumbria. Sarah's career started in the telecommunications industry where she was a business development manager in the Europe, Middle East and Asia (EMEA) region for 9 years. She started working in the UK higher education sector 13 years ago. Sarah's research interests are in the areas of women's leadership and job sharing. Sarah is a director of the Association of University Research and Industry Links (AURIL) and a member of the Royal Geographical Society.

6

Embodied leadership

Corporeal experiences of a female Anglican priest

Rebecca Roberts
Church of England

This chapter explores the concept of the physical body in distributed leadership theory and social identity theory. I explore and evaluate the premise that bodies and body performances are a central part of leadership: women's bodies and bodily leadership are perceived differently from those of men and can bring a positive and different model of leadership from a heroic style. The second part of the chapter, in the form of an embodied case study, reinforces the theory of "intersubjectivity" through my own experience. Flesh goes beyond perception; it is the way in which my entire sense of being is created—a person's interaction with the world. I conclude that women's experience of leadership, especially within the church, exemplifies the hiddenness of male bodies in leadership. Women's bodies continue to be sexualized and their leadership roles questioned purely in their representation as "other". Women can provide a different model from heroic leadership style. The Church of England as an organization must encourage images and texts that promote female as leader and develop policies and training that counteract its sexism.

Latest Church of England statistics show that female clergy now account for 23% of full-time parochial clergy and 11% of senior clergy (Archbishops' Council, 2014).[1] In the Salisbury diocese, 25% of full-time clergy are females (Archbishops' Council, 2014).[2] I work as the first female incumbent[3] in Salisbury deanery. I have been an ordained priest for 12 years. One of the biggest challenges I have faced since taking up my current position has been my own embodiment as a woman leading an institution whose organizational policies support sexism and a culture in which male heroic leadership is still the norm.

It is from this context that I explore the concept of corporeality (the physical body) from the perspective of distributive leadership theory and social identity theory. Sinclair (2007) and Ladkin (2010) suggest that bodies and body performances are a central part of leadership and that women's bodies and bodily leadership are perceived differently from those of men. I critique their theories and apply it to my own leadership role and situation as a female Anglican priest.

Heroic and embodied leadership

A recurrent dominant leadership model is the heroic model based on physical strength, winning and individual performance.

Typically, heroic leadership, in comparison to relational leadership, is rooted in the masculine concepts of "the strongest, of competition, of separation, and sub- object" (Steyeart and Van Loiy, 2010, p. 56). Heroic leaders are powerful and dominate their followers to achieve results (Western, 2008). Heroic leadership is also associated with bodily strength and prowess "the capacity to work long hours, travel at short notice, client rituals based around sports such as football or golf" (Sinclair, 2005, p. ix) which again supports a male archetype. Although this heroic model is socially constructed, it is not treated as such.

Sinclair's (2007) critique of the heroic model of leadership is based on the concept of the body of the heroic leader, its perceived strength and impassibility, its hidden male prototype, and attraction. She argues that the heroic model does not acknowledge the hunger for power as a central drive; the power structures within wider society that enable some individuals to rise more naturally and easily into leadership positions; or the unconscious emotional dynamics of the sexual performance and sexual desires that are often played out in leadership roles.

1 Report by the Research and Statistics Department of the Archbishops' Council (2012). Of 349 senior clergy 39 were female. Senior clergy means management roles as Archdeacons and Cathedral Deans, Cathedral clergy and Diocesan and Suffragan bishops. Since this report one female bishop has been appointed. Recent media reports state that 20.3% of Church of England clergy are women and 79.7% men. (Hughes and Ferguson, 2014).
2 Of 192 full-time clergy there are 50 female; of 3 part-time clergy there is 1 female; of 103 non-paid self-supporting clergy 68 are female.
3 Incumbent is a priest in charge of the Parish area.

In a common feminist critique of the dichotomy of rationalism versus experience (Loades, 1990), gendered norms determine how bodies are made visible and judged: men have a body; women are body (Bekkenkamp *et al.*, 1998). "White male leader bodies usually enjoy the privilege of not being 'seen': they are often pictured suited and covered up, and they are rarely publicly assessed for their fitness (physically or otherwise) for the top job" (Sinclair, 2013, p. 27).

Without bodies, leaders can be elevated and rescued from the ailments that affect women who are often reduced to their bodies and gendered roles (Sinclair, 2013) and the heroic leadership mystique is maintained. Leaders' bodies become motifs for flawless command in which the mind is elevated above the body.

Of bodies that are not totally invisible, but deliberately revealed, physical weaknesses are concealed and masculinity and athleticism reinforced (Ladkin and Spiller, 2013; Leimon *et al.*, 2011).[4] "Leadership assumes able bodied men" (Sinclair, 2007, p. 30), and therefore, often, a mythology of physical strength is carefully cultivated. Leadership itself is perceived as an accomplishment of masculinity (Calas and Smircich in Sinclair, 2007). The whole act of leading is dominated by the hidden assumption of masculine conquest and the impregnability of a distanced male (Lamdin, 2012). Even the writing about leadership has been imbued with themes of seduction (Sinclair, 2007). Strongly masculine performances are required for many leadership roles and looking good becomes synonymous with being good. Attractiveness and the physical ability to sustain long hours are seen as part of leadership potential. By their physical size and the space that they "own", men can easily make a greater impact than women (Leimon *et al.* 2011, p. 182). "Leaders are often chosen on seemingly irrelevant characteristics such as height" (Schaller *et al.*, 2014, p. 303).

Gender and sexuality in leadership remain invisible until challenged by the presence of a leader whose body does not meet the gendered cultural specific assumptions: "Bodies are seen, appraised and responded to according to pre-existing cultural norms, institutional practices and gender and racial regimes" (Sinclair, 2007, p. 62).

However, the gender bias of heroic leadership is often questioned by women and is seen as reason for not pursuing leadership roles (Leimon *et al.* 2011, p. 146).[5] Moreover, women can be undermined by negative projections relating to their sexuality: "Promiscuity is viewed differently for each sex: for men it means prowess and for women, shame and weakness. Would Clinton have survived if he were a woman?" (Heifetz *et al.*, 2002, p. 177).

Women de-sexualize themselves and take on the role of daughter, sister or mother figure as this is safer for them to maintain their leadership status. "Dynamics of

---

4 Leimon also notes that athleticism associated with leadership is often spoken of in men's jokes and metaphors used for success in the general narrative of male leadership networks (Leimon *et al.* 2011, p. 145).

5 Studies show that women who do not identify with the paternalistic autocratic heroic leadership styles may consider themselves unlikely to succeed and even less likely to enjoy a leadership position (Leimon *et al.* 2011, p. 146).

appearance... are a product of social and cultural projections, including a deep discomfort with female power and sexuality" (Ladkin and Spiller, 2013, p. 243).

For example: Christina Rankin, chief executive of the Department of Work and Income in New Zealand, recalled that State Services Commissioner, Michael Wintringham, met her in November 2000 to tell her, informally, that her contract would not be renewed and identified three reasons: her overseeing of dramatic change in a controversial department, which had made her a political liability; *her appearance*; and the conference overspend. She typically appeared in short skirts and dangly earrings (Ladkin and Spiller, 2013, p. 258).

In other words, Rankin's appearance was perceived as related to her performance, and deemed as threatening to her peers. Binney *et al.* (2013) suggests that the anxiety caused by the fast pace of change means people seek leaders in whom to place their hope and security, a messiah figure, ideally placed as a scapegoat. Fear creates the heroic leader.

In Girard's mimetic theory (Palaver, 2013, pp. 133-134) based on unconscious dynamics, at the heart of all hierarchical institutions, is a desire to be safe and protected. The group looks for safety in the leader of the institution; the leader becomes an object of envy of the desires of the followers. When the norm is challenged, more anxiety arises and the leader is replaced (Lamdin, 2012).

People attack your style when they don't like the message (Heifetz *et al.*, 2002, pp. 182,197). For women, the attacks on style harbour the projections of societal fears surrounding female power and sexuality. They are more likely to be criticized for trying to "be themselves" in a leader role because "women's authenticity is judged against norms that highlight their bodies and gendered roles in contrast to the disembodied way authenticity is usually calculated for male leaders" (Sinclair, 2013, p. 240). By reducing women to their bodies and associating them with bodily weaknesses they are undermined (Sinclair, 2013). They are punished harshly for being authentic, and these assessments spilled over into assessments that they were "lacking" leadership (Sinclair, 2013, p. 240). "A woman leader's efforts towards authentic leadership, especially when they involve the performance of an embodied sense of self, are not read as authentic. Rather they are seen as disruptive and dangerous to the established patriarchal order" (Ladkin and Spiller, 2013, p. 246).

Those with "different" bodies therefore have to provide enough structure and authority to contain those deeper anxieties, and at the same time, to be aware that structure and authority can produce unreflective dependency and the abdication of responsibility of the followers (Sinclair, 2007, p. 41). The female leader has to work harder to ensure that she contains the projected fears of her followers (Sinclair, 2007). A man would represent the distance, steadiness and the ability to withstand pressures by being well defended—the norm of an assured leader (Hirschorn, 1997).

Van Knippenburg and Hogg (2011) research the power of prototype in the leader–follower relationship. The leader is picked or supported by followers precisely because he or she is most like them and the characteristics, values and norms of the group. If not of this prototype, leaders have to work harder to build relationships. This must take into account visible posture, looks and ways of being in the world. Hogg's (Jackson *et al.*, 2011) studies on the engendered nature of prototype in which undergraduates were placed in a group that was to have either an instrumental norm (male stereotypical) or communal norm (female stereotypical) demonstrate this. A leader was randomly appointed: either male or female.

> Group salience would increase the perceived effectiveness of the male group leaders for those groups that had been assigned instrumental norms and of female leaders for those with a communal norm. It reduced the perception of effectiveness of male leaders for groups with communal norms and females with instrumental norms (Jackson *et al.*, 2011, p. 59).

This research also challenges the conviction that for Generation X and Y[6] power and communication are more influential than gender for their success in leadership (Jackson *et al.*, 2011). In social identity theory the concept of prototype extends to speech, dress, attitude, and interaction styles of groups. Demographic minorities of women, or ethnic minorities, can find it difficult to maintain top leadership positions because they do not match the organizations' societal prototypes well (Jackson *et al.*, 2011).

Often, therefore, women find their desire to be authentic embodied leaders more difficult, as they deal with the emotion of "playing the game". Christine Nixon, former Chief Commissioner of Victoria Police, Australia, quoted in Sinclair (2013, p. 243) acknowledges her intention to be authentic in mind and body.

> I know I can do the job and that I can do it as a woman should—not as a bloke might, and not as someone else might, just as me. I know some women adopt the model of looking like the blokes, but I don't think that's the way for women to progress and so, as a role model, I try to be just me—unashamedly, honestly, me.

This struggle for authenticity in leadership is evident in the Church of England:

> No wonder that some of our more gifted and energetic women priests feel that the only way forward is ambitiously to compete with men in this new "business" model of the Church's organization; yet the loathing that they then accrue to themselves is itself a sign of the Church's false consciousness: men work the system in one way, but it is held against women if they join the new game (Coakley, 2011, p.11).

Because questions around women's leadership are often based on bodily appearance, more careful wardrobe choices, more media training, better stylists and a tighter image management are necessary (Sinclair, 2007, 2013). However, when Julia Gillard, Australia's first female Prime Minister took the opportunity to counterbalance the complaint that she always had carefully scripted and orchestrated

6 Strauss and Howe (1998) analysed generational characteristics in the book *Generations.* Generation X describes Anglo/Americans who were born after 1970; Generation Y were born after 1990.

performances, by talking about her decision to not have children, she was still criticized: "She didn't have much love" (Sinclair, 2013, p. 248).

Similarly, for the first US female vice-presidential candidate, Geraldine Ferraro, her defeat has been attributed to the fact that her gender embodied questions regarding women's ability and perspectives: "What would it mean for a woman to be second in line to the most powerful position in authority in the world? What has sexual revolution done to our families?" (Heifetz *et al.*, 2002, p. 197).

Body language and bodily practice

Body *language* is often used in order to execute a more masterful performance. Both Ladkin and Sinclair note its importance to create a leadership image *and* endorse a means of perception: "encouraging people to be in their bodies more consciously changes their mindset towards themselves and others. It can foster a capacity to read and feel more empathetically what is going on for others as well as the self" (Sinclair, 2007, p. 68).

Altering the way we use our body changes *who we are* and *how we are perceived*: "the notion of flesh tells us that the dynamic between us and those who perceive us will also shift" (Ladkin, 2010, pp. 69-71). Ladkin shows the direct way in which a manager held himself physically impacted on his ability to interact effectively. Body language and voice represent the essential component of our communications in the way a woman enters a room, takes up space, uses her voice and lowers her tone, and put herself forward (Leimon *et al.*, 2011).

Peeters' study of leadership notes that followership begins with the body: the will to change begins with the body and not in the mind (Bekkenkamp *et al.*, 1998). Binney *et al.* (2013, p. 333) state that good leadership needs to recognize interdependence in order to bring any effective transformation: "leading is a social in between activity".

Ladkin takes the idea of physical leadership one step further by arguing that the physical and vocal presence changes how female leaders are experienced not only outwardly but also inwardly. Ladkin names the conscious and unconscious relationship between any leader and follower as an "intersubjective experience". This relationship moves beyond a traditional Cartesian understanding of a mind/body split into an acknowledgement that embodiment is central to perception (Ladkin, 2010, pp. 70, 71). The relationship between the leader and the follower shifts in the subconscious mind as a result of physical perceptions. Her premise is based on the work of Merleau-Ponty's theory of intersubjectivity, in which "the world is not what I think but what I live through" (Ladkin, 2010, p. 59). "We do not just interrogate the world around us through questioning it intellectually, but that our bodies prompt questions as well as responses to the world around us" (Ladkin, 2012, p. 59).

Ladkin continues to argue that any perception of a leader goes beyond their flesh—it is the way in which my entire sense of being is created—a person's interaction with the world (Ladkin, 2010).

There are benefits of physical difference. Leaders can use their leadership differently precisely because they do not match the prototype. Power and communication can be used differently through stature, gestures, physical attributes and the movements that they make. The difference for leader, Chris Sarra, of Aboriginal descent and male, and Christine Nixon, a white middle aged female, allowed a space for a different kind of bodily practice of leadership (Sinclair, 2007). They both used their body to communicate and bring about significant changes in their organizations.

Chris Sarra used *physical power* and presence as principal of an Aboriginal primary school: physical contact, acknowledgement of his pupils' physical needs, a vision for "Strong and Smart", and a focus on physical wellbeing. He enacted physical authority by lifting children up to congratulate them in assembly, physically sitting with them and playing football at break time and used an indigenous approach to discipline called "growling". After six years at the school, vandalism became rare, absenteeism fell to below average and academic performance increased (Sinclair, 2007).

As state commissioner, Christine Nixon broke down boundaries between community and the police and between uniformed and non-uniformed police in Melbourne. She was physically out and about, consulted on and changed police uniforms, and deliberately seen in the toughest areas of policing in the state. Her openness to listening and receiving feedback, in contrast to the remoteness prior to her appointment, produced significant change in trust in the police force and better working relations within communities. She used her body to form relationships; a common touch, maintaining living contacts and having consistent concern (Sinclair, 2007).

The body *can* function to free the leader and followers to achieve by intentional interaction styles. Both leaders listened to their communities and were open to learning from the communities they served, which some might suggest is the feminization of leadership, emphasising *interpersonal* relations more than men (Jackson *et al.*, 2011). Astin and Leland (1992) highlight the gender differences in leadership behaviours. Women believe more strongly than men in listening to and empowering followers and are more likely to use conferences and networks to achieve results. Interpersonal leadership "improves long-term organizational effectiveness and well-being, success and profit" (Leimon *et al.*, 2011, pp. 19, 20).

Eagly's social role theory concludes that women will strive to be nurturing and caring, while men will be more task-focused, ambitious and competitive (Jackson *et al.*, 2011). A woman is better suited to the subordination of her own power: "women teachers become trapped in their own concept of nurturance ... women will favour devolution and self-direction over coercion" (Sinclair, 2007, p. 51). However, "subordination" of a kind is positive in models of collaborative leadership practice. Wesley Carr (2004, p. 84) states that to collaborate[7] is "to devolve

---

7 Collaborative leadership is working together in a manner which recognizes others' gifts, acknowledges interdependency and the importance of relationship, and enables active

responsibility, to put the resource for the task where it is appropriate". This does not mean abdicating responsibility but enabling others. Gillian Stamp (2004, p. 119) also recognizes the importance of nurture in creative leadership: "rather than imposing a vision, the leader must seek to establish what is really going on by listening to deeper patterns in the community; helping the community discover its core values and then find a way of nurturing them". Leaders who conform to a feminized stereotype of relationship orientation as well as task orientation will be the better leaders (Jackson *et al.*, 2011).

However, as strength and heroism are portrayed as a leadership social norm, often when women function in a relational manner they communicate powerlessness (Steyeart and Van Loiy, 2010). Neuger (cited in Miller McLelmoe *et al.*, 1999) writes that "relationality" is taken as the cultural responsibility of women who are driven towards a life of relatedness and caring by a culture that demands them to be unconscious of the masculine context. Neuger therefore suggests that women must question the relational foci of their work and their emphasis on *interpersonal* relations "which is more than is usual for men" (Jackson *et al.*, 2011, p. 28).

Embodied leadership in the Church of England

While looking at the leadership research on bodies, I cannot escape the imagery of male leadership in the stories of the Bible and the liturgy: the "hard upright male" (Isherwood, 2007, pp. 20, 21), or assumption of a "masculine bodiless God" (Biezeveld, 1998, p. 185). Masculine concepts of leadership and the male body are made divine in the person of Christ (Isherwood, 2007), while "the female body is portrayed in many biblical stories, traditions and theology as chaotic, and female sexuality as distasteful" (Isherwood, 2007, pp. 116, 117). This distaste is upheld by the institutional church, which supports the concept of tainting[8] by providing

---

decision making that contributes to a common purpose, vision and mission within the church (Nash *et al.*, 2008). Leadership is seen as a collective responsibility which is not reliant on heroes but on the unique skills that have been developed in ordinary people. Grint explores the concept of collaboration through "Collective responsibility" and "Distributed leadership" (Grint, 2005, p. 143). Gronn names similar concepts and values in distributed leadership, leadership activity that moves from person to person in their dedication to achieve shared purposes (Ladkin, 2010, p. 35). Gill defines collaboration as leadership that values dialogue, is based on an individual or an organization's gifts and avoids duplication of programmes and roles (Sofield and Juliano, 1987).

8 With the appointment of women bishops, the Act of Synod has been rescinded but parishes are still allowed to request the priestly and episcopal ministry of a man on the grounds of "theological" conviction; of "headship" and "Apostolic succession", which argues that the succession of Peter is now tainted: "Since those within the Church of England who, on grounds of theological conviction, are unable to receive the ministry of women bishops or priests continue to be within the spectrum of teaching and tradition

external supervision by bishops who have not ordained women, for parishes who object theologically to female priests and bishops.[9]

It is within this theological and ideological context that women in the Church of England have officially been leading as priests.

One of the arguments in favour of women's leadership has been the "complementary" view of women's leadership, in which gendered characteristics, such as relationality, which have been highlighted above, are given as reasons in favour of accepting women priests and bishops.

However, Williams (2011, p.11) argues that this idea is

> simplistic in that it implicitly regards women as all and exclusively possessing certain attributes (for example, of compassion or empathy) with which they complement the existing ordained male ministry, whereas the truth is much more complex ... There may be aspects of women's experience which incline them to approach issues in certain ways rather more than men might do. What is important is for the Church to recognize the implications of issues such as pregnancy, maternity and child care responsibilities and to create models of ordained ministry which not only accommodate those factors but also ensure that opportunities for deployment are not artificially and unnecessarily curtailed... (Williams, 2011, p. 11).

Williams' point is valid as Leimon *et al.* (2011) also highlight that job prospects and opportunities available are another aspect of gendered embodiment which need to be acknowledged. She states that mentoring and coaching needs to be available to women in their early 20s and 30s, with the average age of childbearing at 29, to enable women to rejoin the workplace with confidence and to negotiate a career path.

When women were first ordained to the priesthood in the early 1990s, Lynda Katsumo Ishii (1992) argued that women were accustomed to thinking of themselves as powerless especially with a model of "servanthood" in the Church. This servant leadership concept is still promoted and exemplified in the phrase used by Bishop

---

of the Anglican Communion, the Church of England remains committed to enabling them to flourish within its life and structures; and Pastoral and sacramental provision for the minority within the Church of England will be made without specifying a limit of time and in a way that maintains the highest possible degree of communion and contributes to mutual flourishing across the whole Church of England". House of Bishop's Declaration on the Ministry of Bishops and Priests (General Synod, 2014).

As illustrated in Forward in Faith's leaflet entitled "Women as Priests and Bishops: What's the Problem?" states: "A bishop is a 'Father in God'. This role relates to the fatherhood of God. (Christ and the Scriptures teach us to call God our Father—never our Mother)" (p. 2). "To be present when a woman presides at the Eucharist can be painful, because this visible mark of the Church's disunity conflicts with the nature of the Sacrament of unity" (p. 1).

9 In 2011 6% of parishes were allowed under Church of England laws of Synod to state that they would not appoint a woman priest to celebrate Holy Communion, 9% would not accept a woman as incumbent or priest in charge, 3% asked for alternative episcopal oversight.

Libby Lane, the first female bishop in the Church of England. "I am very conscious of all those who have gone before me, women and men, who for decades have looked forward to this moment…" She added:

> I stand in a long line of women and men *whose self-giving service* has changed the world for good. So today, I pray, will not be simply about one woman called up a new ministry in the Church but much more than that, an opportunity to acknowledge all that has gone before and to look ahead to what is still to be done (Bingham, 2014).

The Church of England's historical and social context means that when women reach powerful positions they can still be afraid to share power (Ishii, 1992).

> When I'm asked …"what difference you do you think you make as a woman?" I'm often stuck for an answer: bearing in mind I've worked with immensely empathetic collaborative and sensitive men and some authoritarian, task focussed women, it's not right to make any generalisations; but some of the difficulty for women is that if the institution itself seems to have been vaguely or at times strongly reluctant to embrace this change, the temptation for women is to try too hard to fit in; to do it like the men have done it. It is at times very hard to remain alive in here as we navigate between the twin dangers of seeking too much approval from the ones who reject us or becoming the kind of jaw jutting "this is me take it or leave it" (Winkett, 2011, p. 8).

Charlene Li states that the most important consideration in any leading, whether individual or group, is trust: "the most important currency of the Twenty First century" (Li, 2010, p.1). New technologies have reinforced the need to respond in an open and fast manner which has highlighted the cultural shift necessary in all leadership. "At a time when customers are redefining how they make and maintain relationships … let go of the need to be in control to develop the confidence that the people to whom you will pass the power will act responsibly" (Li, 2010, p. 9). Caulat (2013) states that leaders feel they need to pretend and present the best image of themselves in virtual space but that if authenticity is a value they hold, and is worked through into virtual space, then it can bring higher levels of performance. It can also promote task *and* relationship through the willingness of leaders to be personal and express how they really feel about a task.

So leadership becomes more than the body; a set of values that enable people to participate in leadership roles themselves. Embodied leadership is risky but can liberate. How has it liberated me?

A case study of my own embodiment

I am a full-time female incumbent, in charge of two churches in Wiltshire, with a population of 14,000. I arrived, in January 2013, at the age of 41, as the first female in charge of the parish. The vote for women bishops had been defeated but leading women priests were invited onto a panel to explore a way forward with other lead bishops. I was the first female incumbent in the deanery in which one parish had passed resolutions not to accept women priests and in which there are seven other male incumbents. The average age of my congregation members is 70 years old. In many areas of the parish 74% of the population is over 55 years old.[10]

My experience as leader within this context illustrates the fact that leadership and followership are unquestionably interconnected and that as a younger female leader questions have been raised about my experience and leadership style purely through bodily communication. I have led strategically through choices of how I use my body.

Bodily comments

I have been surprised and challenged by comments that I have received and actions that have affected me since my change in roles. To know that my experiences are named in academic literature validates my experience and I feel less isolated in my role. It has reinforced my desire to be authentic and at the same time take account of the fears that are being articulated in comments about my gender and age: How can I build trust? I have built trust through the use of my body.

Gender- and age-related comments were never made when I was on the management team at a school. However, in my encounters in the parish such comments abound. A few examples are: "Can you look older by the funeral next week?" "I didn't think people like you could be a vicar", and in the middle of a PCC meeting, "How are you looking after your husband?" I believe these comments would not have been made if I were a man. It has drawn my attention to the undercurrents of gender that are often hidden and the expectations of a "dominant male" style of leadership as used by the 65-year-old male incumbent who was my predecessor and who had worked here for 20 years. He could symbolize power, father, chief, strength whereas I am very different physically in height, gender, voice and age. A majority of the congregation members are aged 70 or above. It has confirmed my notion that the male body is hidden, and exposed to scrutiny that people associate it with the ability to lead. One older woman in the congregation commented "Her skirts are getting shorter and shorter" in a time of silence so all could hear. People have commented on the heels or the flatness of my shoes. So I have changed my style and wear jackets and trousers. It feels cumbersome but gives a professional look that counterbalances "youth". I feel more androgynous and that I am letting my femininity down. My dress, out of role, has become more colourful and "individual" since I have altered my role dress code.

10 Census data 2011 E00163249 Salisbury Harnham. Retrieved from http://www.ukcensus data.com/salisbury-harnham-e00163249#sthash.qDhogdgV.dpbs

I am very aware of the way I use vestments (clergy uniform) in church. The chasuble[11] set in one of the churches is far too large for me, too long and too wide. I had opted for putting it on as I step up to the altar. However, I noted my reaction to the different servers helping me to robe in the chasuble. One server is my husband and I did not mind him helping me robe. The other server is a retired gentleman and I found it uncomfortable with him robing me. Sinclair (2007, p.78) notes the gendered reactions to dressing and undressing: "I realized the act of removing a jacket … seemed to detract and dramatically reduce my credibility". It brought to my attention the difference between women and men's actions of robing and de-robing. I now dress myself and have asked for the robes to be altered in order to fit. I had been robing in my alb[12] with the vestry door open, as there are males and females in the vestry but have now revised my thinking. It highlighted for me the "hidden socialized sexuality" in that act (Jackson *et al.*, 2011, p. 54).

My body also represents societal expectations of female roles. When I was asked at PCC whether I was looking after my husband properly I laughed it off with a joke, which can dissolve a difficult question and leave space to return to the main issue at hand. However, I am aware of the feelings at least one person held towards my role as leader—the implication was: how could I both "look after my husband" and ensure my role as vicar was being done competently?

The local and wider Church of England must acknowledge and value women's experience *and* that their experiences are often different from those of men. The church must work on training and coaching programmes that enable female clergy to learn endurance and resilience in such a culture and to provide role models of young female leaders.

Mentoring women and providing role models for women is key to continued embodied practice. Leimon *et al.* (2011) shows the effectiveness of women in leadership: the cash benefits of gender diversity, the positive association between company performance and female participation, and the increase in profits as women lead for the shareholders, for equity and assets. Not a single study shows women-rich management teams have poorer performance than male-rich management teams and yet it is perceived as such. She argues that by 2030 most European countries will experience a significant gap between leadership age and population supply and the leadership demand driven by economic growth. Non-participants in this leadership pool are women. Coaching women at crucial stages of their careers could ensure a higher quality of leadership than current practice and fulfil the need (Leimon *et al.*, 2011).

My female body has liberated me to lead an embodied compassionate care by sitting on the steps at the same level with children in church, by touching those who are ill, by kissing the elderly, by holding someone's hand when he or she is dying or upset. I have deliberately chosen to lead with embodied touch in close bodily proximity to build trust.

11 A chasuble is an ornate outer garment worn when a priest celebrates Holy Communion.
12 An alb is a simple white garment which comes down to the ankles and has sleeves and is worn under other vestments.

I have also deliberately chosen not to use the pulpit[13] as a way of being closer to the congregation when preaching. It symbolizes the openness I would like to foster in preaching and the initial steps to make it more interactive. I have narrowed the physical distance between the congregation and myself and encouraged a model of engagement in which I am not elevated. This bodily stance has been combined with interaction with the congregations as encouragement for them to own their own thoughts and learning. Two years on, both congregations interact more concerning what they are learning about Christianity both with each other and with me.

Leading from an individual relational perspective again builds trust and confidence and allows space for deeper conversations about strategy. I am very aware that I do not have time to speak to people and shake their hands after the services on a Sunday, as I have to move from one church to the next. I deliberately shake hands with everyone during the service as a way of compensating. The question remains: When else can I be physically present to listen? Visiting? Can I build time in my diary to visit a few people each week who do not necessarily respond well to electronic communication? Balkundi and Kilduff (2006) speak of the quality of individual relationships affecting perceptions of leadership. Leadership is not experienced as the leader and followers as a homogeneous group but through the experiences of individual followers. When individuals are included or excluded an individual can influence the perception of who belongs or is excluded as "in and out" groups (Ladkin, 2010, p. 56). In an age when popular culture and public leadership often sideline those who are elderly, my physical presence counteracts this value.

A number of younger families have started coming to church since I have been vicar. I wonder whether this is because "like attracts like" and the social theory of prototype is at work (Jackson *et al.*, 2011, p. 57). Yet when I read the words; "leadership effectiveness depends more on the match of the leader to the group prototype", I wrote "Help!" in my diary. I fear the desires for younger people attending church are being fulfilled in me as a "younger" leader.[14] A change of culture in the church congregation is needed, change will not happen from just me being at the front. I need to manage people's hopes and expectations and communicate clearly, so that I am not setting myself apart in what I say. I need to listen to their values and to "get on board" respected members of the congregation who are older than me so that others can link their trust to the group and not just myself. I must be careful how I present myself when dealing with issues that are contentious, as I do not conform to the prototype of a majority of the congregation. I need to continue to be aware of this dynamic. Change may take longer than I hope for.

When I arrived, one of the first changes I made to the church magazine was to put in my photograph by the side of my monthly "letter"; we now include different

---

13 A pulpit is a raised platform from which the vicar teaches through sermons.
14 The average age of a full-time female Church of England clergy person is 52 (most recent Archbishops' Council statistics).

photographs of the congregation at events on the front cover. I have removed the logo of the church buildings, and replaced it with a visible representation of the people. When I meet people on the street, most of an older generation have seen my photo, as they are the magazine readership. Our new website will include visual images of the congregation and leadership team in informal settings to promote accessibility and presence in everyday situations.

I find it even more necessary to focus on the importance of inclusive language and female imagery for God in my own spiritual growth. I hope to gradually challenge the concepts of God that are oppressive and heroic without alienating the congregation through choice of words and images that are used to explain faith.

I struggle to understand how leadership in the organization of the Church of England can progress without a change in culture, which includes language and imagery of feminine aspects of God and therefore female ways of relating (Reuther and Maitland in Loades, 1990). "Sacred power is not power *over* derived from the one divinity that has power over all else but rather power from within or power *for*" (Raphael, 1999, p. 60).

The naming and valuing of women's experience is crucial in the culture change.

Being a female cleric has enabled me to meet the community in a different way from that of my predecessor and to see this positively. The most surprising result of my study of the body is that it has made me more aware of the need to develop knowledge and strategy *beyond* my body, in particular my verbal communication skills and written strategic planning. However, the Church both locally and nationally must acknowledge new ways for leadership, without falling into the heroic leadership style as Church membership declines. As an overall organization it must remodel the key imagery used to proclaim its message that Christ was an embodiment of God on Earth and as such *all* bodies are valued. This must be reflected in policy and practice.

Credible communication is a vital element (Gibbs, 2005). My strategy for communicating vision and goals needs careful planning. If change is to be encouraged through trust as a two-way process, I need to adopt some traditional heroic ways of leading until I can *explain* positively the benefits of leading differently, or have a smaller task in which a collaborative style of leadership can succeed. In PCC meetings, I have been handing over leadership of each committee to the people who attended that meeting in order to create ownership and develop leadership and less dependency at meetings. For me, this was encouraging leadership, but when discussing this with the standing committee it was seen as an abdication of my role as chair*man* and negative. I had either not communicated the reasons for this strategy clearly enough for them to see it as me leading and developing the PCC or they did not want the responsibility I was handing them.

My body has definitely affected the way I am perceived as a leader. I hope that it can also change the way in which my core values can be transmitted. I firmly believe in the practice of "wearing skin" (Brown Taylor, 2009, pp. 35-51). "Christianity is to have one's body shaped, one's habits determined, in such a way that the worship of God is unavoidable" (Brown Taylor, 2009, p. 45).

Bibliography

Archbishops' Council (2008). *Canons of the Church of England.* London: Church House Publishing. Retrieved from https://www.churchofengland.org/media/35588/complete.pdf

Archbishops' Council (2014). *Statistics for Mission 2012.* London: Archbishops' Council.

Astin, Helen & Leland, Carole (1991). *Women of Influence, Women of Vision: A Cross Generational Study of Leaders and Social Change.* San Francisco: Jossey Bass.

Balkundi, Prasad & Martin Kilduff (2006). The ties that lead: A social network approach to leadership. *The Leadership Quarterly,* 17, 419-423.

Bekkenkamp, Jonneke, & De Haardt, Maaike (eds.) (1998). *Begin With the Body: Corporeality, Religion and Gender.* Leuven: Uitgeverij Peeters.

Biezeveld Kune, E. (1998). The body of God: A key for unlocking male monotheism? In J. Bekkenkamp & M. De Haardt (Eds.), *Begin With the Body: Corporeality, Religion and Gender* (pp. 157-183). Leuven: Uitgeverij Peeters.

Bingham, John (2014, December 17).   First woman bishop: parish priest Libby Lane is surprise choice. *The Telegraph.* Retrieved from http://www.telegraph.co.uk/news/religion/11298342/Woman-bishop-announced-as-Libby-Lane.html

Binney, George, Wilke, Gerhard & Williams, Colin (2013). *Living Leadership: A practical Guide for Ordinary Heroes* (3rd ed.). London: Pearson.

Brown Taylor, Barbara (2009). *An Altar in the World.* Norwich: Canterbury Press.

Carr, Wesley, (2004). Leading without leadership: Managing without management. In Adair, John & Neilson, John, (Eds.), *Creative Church Leadership.* Norwich: Canterbury Press.

Caulat Ghislaine (2013). Viewpoint: Why authenticity is most crucial in the virtual space. In Donna Ladkin and Chellie Spiller (Eds.), *Authentic Leadership: Clashes, Convergences and Coalescences.* Cheltenham, UK: Edward Elgar Publishing.

Coakley, Sarah Revd (2011). Panel presentation. *Transformations: Theology and Experience of Women's Ministry, 19 September 2011.* Retrieved from https://womenandthechurch.org/wp-content/uploads/2015/07/Transformations-Report-9-Nov-11.pdf

Forward in Faith (n.d.). *Women as Bishops and Priests: What's the Problem?* London: Forward in Faith. Retrieved from http://forwardinfaith.com/jscripts/tiny_mce/plugins/image manager/files/4_Women_Priests_for_print.pdf

General Synod (2014, May 19). *House of Bishops' Declaration on the Ministry of Bishops and Priests.* Retrieved from https://www.churchofengland.org/media/2011184/gs%20 misc%201076%20-%20women%20in%20the%20episcopate%20house%20of%20bishops% 20declaration.pdf

Gibbs, Eddie, (2005). *Leadership Next: Changing Leaders in a Changing Culture.* Leicester, UK: IVP.

Grint, Keith, (2005). *Leadership: Limits and Possibilities.* Basingstoke and New York: Palgrave McMillan.

Heiftetz, Ronald A. & Linsky, Marty (2002). *Leadership on the Line: Staying Alive through the Dangers of Leading.* Boston, MA: Harvard Business Review Press.

Hirschhorn Larry, (1997). *Reworking Authority: Leading and Following in a Postmodern Organisation.* Cambridge, MA: MIT Press.

Hughes, Ian & Ferguson, Kate (2014, December 17). Libby Lane: Manchester United-supporting, saxophone-playing mum-of-two is Church of England's first female bishop. *The Mirror.* Retrieved from http://www.mirror.co.uk/news/uk-news/libby-lane-manchester-united-supporting-saxophone-playing-4827716

Ishii, L.K. (1992). To be a servant leader. In: Kanyoro, M.R.A. & Robins, W.S. (Eds.), *The Power We Celebrate: Women's Stories of Faith and Power.* Geneva: World Council of Churches

Isherwood, Lisa, (2007). *The Fat Jesus.* London: DLT.

Jackson, Brad and Parry, Ken (2011). *A Very Short, Fairly Interesting and Reasonably Cheap Book about Studying Leadership.* London: Sage.

Ladkin, Donna, (2010). *Rethinking Leadership.* Cheltenham, UK: Edward Elgar Publishing.

Ladkin, Donna, (2012). Perception, reversibility, "flesh": Merleau-Ponty's phenomenology and leadership as embodied practice. *Integral Leadership Review,* January 2012. Retrieved from http://integralleadershipreview.com/6280-perception-reversibility-flesh-merleau-pontys-phenomenology-and-leadership-as-embodied-practice/

Ladkin, Donna, & Spiller, Chellie (Eds.) (2013). *Authentic Leadership: Clashes, Convergences and Coalescences.* Cheltenham, UK: Edward Elgar Publishing.

Lamdin, Keith, (2012). *Finding Your Leadership Style.* London: SPCK.

Leimon, Averil, Moscovici, Francois & Goddier, Helen (2011). *Coaching Women to Lead.* London: Routledge.

Li, Charlene, (2010). *Open Leadership: How Social Technologies Transform the Way you Lead.* San Francisco: Jossey Bass.

Loades, Ann Ed, (1990). *Feminist Theology: A Reader.* London: SPCK.

Miller McLelmoe, Bonny, & Giill-Austen, Brita (eds.) (1999). *Feminist and Womanist Pastoral Theology.* Nashville, TN: Abingdon Press.

Nash, Paul, Nash, Sally & Pilmott, Jo (2008). *Skills for Collaborative Ministry.* London: SPCK.

Palaver, Wolfgang, (2013). *Rene Girard's Mimetic Theory.* East Lancing, MI: Michigan State University Press.

Raphael, Melissa, (1999). *Introducing Theology.* Sheffield, UK: Sheffield Academic Press.

Schaller, Mark, Simson, Jeffry A. & Kenrick, Douglas (2014). *Evolution and Social Psychology: Frontiers of Social Psychology.* New York and Hove: Psychology Press, Taylor & Francis.

Sinclair, Amanda, (2005). *Doing Leadership Differently: Gender, Power and Sexuality in a Changing World.* Melbourne: Melbourne University Press.

Sinclair, Amanda, (2007). *Leadership for the Disillusioned: Moving Beyond Myths and Heroes to Leadership that Liberates,* New South Wales: Allen & Unwin.

Sinclair, Amanda, (2013). Can I really be me? The challenges for women leaders constructing authenticity. In Donna Ladkin and Chellie Spear (Eds.), *Authentic Leadership: Clashes, Convergences and Coalescences.* Cheltenham, UK: Edward Elgar Publishing.

Sofields, Loughlan, & Juliano, Carroll, (1987). *Collaborative Ministry.* Notre Dame, IN: Ave Maria Press.

Stamp, Gillian, (2004). But me no buts. In Adair, John & Neilson, John, (Eds.), *Creative Church Leadership.* Norwich: Canterbury Press.

Steyeart, Chris & Van Looy, Bart (eds.) (2010). *Relational Practices, Participative Organising.* Bingley, UK: Emerald Group Publishing.

Strauss, William & Howe, Neil (1998). *Generations: The History of America's Future, 1584 to 2069.* New York: Perennial

Van Knippenburg and Hogg (2011). Social identity theory. in: Jackson, Brad & Parry, Ken (Eds.), *A Very Short, Fairly Interesting and Reasonably Cheap Book about Studying Leadership* (pp. 57-59). London: Sage.

Western, Simon (2008). *Leadership: A Critical Text.* London: Sage Publications.

Williams, Rowan The Most Rev'd (2011). *Transformations: Theology and Experience of Women's Ministry, 19 September 2011.* Retrieved from https://womenandthechurch.org/wp-content/uploads/2015/07/Transformations-Report-9-Nov-11.pdf

Winkett, Lucy Revd Canon (2011). Panel presentation. *Transformations: Theology and Experience of Women's Ministry, 19 September 2011.* Retrieved from https://womenandthechurch.org/wp-content/uploads/2015/07/Transformations-Report-9-Nov-11.pdf

Reverend **Rebecca Roberts** is a full-time female priest-in-charge of a large Parish in Wiltshire that includes two churches. She arrived, in January 2013, at the age of 42, after leaving a management position as a full-time teacher in a local school. She has been an ordained priest for 12 years and is currently studying for an MA in Leadership at Sarum College, Salisbury.

Part III

**Factors beyond
the workplace that
can foster greater
gender equality at
work**

7

To impact the workplace, think beyond the workplace

Lessons about gender equality in industry from the International Women's Coffee Alliance (IWCA)

Mary Johnstone-Louis

Saïd Business School, University of Oxford, UK

As executives pursue gender equality in their workplaces, which steps might they take towards this goal, and which barriers might they encounter along the way? This case details the experience of the International Women's Coffee Alliance (IWCA), a non-profit organization founded by executives working in the coffee industry. IWCA's aim is to advance gender equality throughout the coffee supply chain. IWCA's experience highlights at least six contributors to gender inequality in the coffee industry: challenges related to women's time; physical mobility; skills and knowledge; industry visibility; control over resources; and personal safety. The lesson of this case is that at least four of these exist outside the "workplace". Therefore, executives who seek to promote gender equality in their industries must become attentive to and conversant with these—and similar—contextual contributors to gender inequality.

Introduction

> When I started going to coffee growing countries... I'm going to the fields. I'm going into the processing mills. I'm going into the trading offices. I'm going into little cafes. And I'm seeing women everywhere. But when I'm going to the [industry] leadership conferences, I'm not seeing them on the stage. I'm not seeing them on the boards of directors of their local organizations. And I asked myself, "What's wrong with this picture"?... So there was a group of us who started to talk to each other and ask, "What if we looked at the global supply chain? What if we could connect women from seed to cup"? ... If you look at the resources that some of the women who work in the global industry have ... there really should be tremendous support available (Margaret Swallow, Executive Director of the Coffee Quality Institute (2002–2006), IWCA Co-founder).[1]

As executives pursue gender equality in their workplaces, which steps might they take towards this goal, and which barriers might they encounter along the way? This chapter presents the findings from a case study of the International Women's Coffee Alliance (IWCA), which is a non-profit organization founded and directed by women holding positions of corporate leadership in the global coffee industry. This case is the result of original qualitative research conducted by the author. Data collection was conducted across 2013 via desk research, participant-observation, field visits, and more than 40 individual interviews with IWCA leaders and partners based in 12 countries. Interviewees included the organization's co-founders, board of directors, presidents of ten IWCA country chapters, IWCA's global president, industry leaders, the organization's partners and funders, as well as women IWCA sought to support. In-person interviews were conducted around the IWCA 10th Anniversary Conference held in Guatemala in February 2013, and follow-up interviews were conducted by phone. Names have been used with permission.

Participants in this international cadre of coffee buyers, importers, roasters, and retailers tend to share lengthy industry experience and an interest in overcoming barriers to gender equality throughout the coffee value chain. The organization represents an example of how executives and managers, while maintaining their positions within the private sector, can organize to advance gender equality in the industries in which they work.

Gender forms a fundamental aspect of social systems and contributes to the entrenchment of manifold forms of hierarchy in societies across the globe (Sisson Runyan and Peterson, 2013). IWCA's experience illustrates that overcoming gender inequality in workplaces and industries requires strategic and sustained engagement with political, legal, cultural and economic aspects of contexts in which workplaces and industries are embedded.

---

1 This and subsequent quotes are drawn from original interviews conducted by the author.

IWCA was born out of a visit to coffee farms in Central America for US-based roasters and buyers, organized by several women with significant corporate experience in the coffee trade. Such trips are commonplace in the industry; however, unlike standard buyer visits, these tours in particular sought to establish dialogue with women involved in coffee production. IWCA's founders-to-be had the impression that while women formed a fundamental aspect of coffee production, gender inequality within the coffee supply chain was rife. IWCA co-founder Karen Cebreros explained, of their flagship trip to Nicaragua in 2003:

> Traders, importers, exporters, roasters, buyers; [representatives of] all segments of the [coffee] industry [came on the trip]... We learned a lot as we went on our way... about domestic violence, about poverty ... and [female coffee producers] telling us ... "We just want do business with dignity, and put our children to school, we are no different than you." [and we decided]... "We can't go home and do business as usual."

IWCA's founders emphasize that industry leaders were often surprised to discover that women made a crucial contribution to coffee production. They recount that, despite years of commercial experience, many buyers and roasters had never undertaken sustained consideration of their industry using a gender lens. By the early 2000s, the future founders of IWCA were persuaded that women were too often invisible to local and global coffee industry leadership, perpetuating gender inequality in workplaces throughout the coffee value chain (Jacobs and Cote, 2015; Stanculescu *et al.*, 2011).

Convinced of the need to address contributors to gender inequality in their industry, but unsure of the steps to take towards this goal, IWCA's co-founders hosted a follow-up meeting at the next annual coffee trade meeting, the Specialty Coffee Association of America (SCAA), held in Boston, Massachusetts in 2003. IWCA's founders recount that each coffee executive who had travelled to Central America with them also attended this follow-up meeting, along with more than 70 other managers and executives who had heard about the experience. The growing group continued to consult an expanding set of actors across the globe regarding the needs and interest of women working in the coffee industry. By 2005, the International Women's Coffee Alliance was founded as a non-profit organization in the United States (with the legal status of a 501(c)3), with a mission to work from within industry to pursue gender equality across all aspects of the coffee trade.

The world of coffee

IWCA's task is a daunting one. Coffee represents a complex, truly global business made up of producers, exporters, importers, roasters, brand managers, and numerous other agents (Jan van Hilten, 2012). Because coffee grows best at high altitudes in tropical climates, it is primarily cultivated in the globe's equatorial belt;

an expansive geography encompassing a variegated set of cultural, political and economic contexts (Euromonitor, 2012). Coffee can be cultivated on mechanized plantations, on large farms where it is picked, sorted and dried by hand, or on small household plots (Jan van Hilten, 2012). Each setting provides unique challenges and opportunities to those who gain their livelihood from the industry.

Women's contributions to coffee production are significant and growing (Jacobs and Cote, 2015; Oliveira Silva, 2015; International Trade Center, 2008). Nevertheless, IWCA's founders noticed that women tend to be "clustered at the bottom" of the industry, rarely occupying positions of commercial influence and disproportionately undertaking poorly remunerated, precarious labour on land they do not own (Elder *et al.*, 2012; Pehu *et al.*, 2009). Research suggests that women and children perform work required for coffee production, until the crop is taken to market; from there, men tend to take over (Jacobs and Cote, 2015; Oliveira Silva, 2015; Lyon *et al.*, 2010; International Trade Center, 2008). This dynamic is not unique to coffee, but characteristic of the gendered nature of much agricultural production (Manchón and MacLeod, 2010; Pehu *et al.*, 2009). Women, therefore, are central to agricultural outputs (Tandon, 2010). However, because they often possess relatively little training or market experience, they may be even more vulnerable than male farmers to the vicissitudes of agricultural livelihoods (Jacobs and Cote, 2015; DeSchutter, 2012; Pehu *et al.*, 2009).

IWCA's founders perceived that gender inequality also persists in the coffee industry at the corporate level, with women remaining under-represented relative to men in many corporate and industry leadership settings. IWCA's mission, therefore, became tackling gender inequality across the coffee value chain, seeking to "Empower women in the international coffee community to achieve meaningful and sustainable lives; and to encourage and recognize the participation of women in all aspects of the coffee industry" (International Women's Coffee Alliance, 2014).

IWCA's approach

Aware that mainstream efforts towards corporate social responsibility and ethical trade may not manage to engage effectively with marginalized individuals and groups (Barrientos and Evers, 2013; Barrientos, 2010; Lyon *et al.*, 2010; Thompson, 2008), and with gender in particular (Barrientos *et al.*, 2003; Grosser and van der Gaag, 2013; Kilgour, 2007, 2013; Grosser and Moon, 2005), IWCA developed three strategies to help ensure their activities contributed to gender equality in the coffee industry.

First, the organization works through chapters in coffee-producing nations, rather than primarily from its US base. IWCA encourages country chapters to register as legal, independent entities, which permits women working in coffee to interact with national governments and local markets as a group. A chapter typically comprises a leadership team of four to eight women from a wide range of coffee-related roles including smallholder farmers, larger exporters or quality experts. Most chapters have several hundred members, again characterized by representation from across the coffee value chain. IWCA has chapters in 19 countries across the globe, and regularly adds to this number.[2] IWCA provides country chapters with training on organizational design, strategic planning and fundraising. In addition, IWCA supports community-based programmes emphasizing women's health and youth education in coffee-producing communities. IWCA also provides extensive training to female coffee producers and exporters on tactics to enhance coffee quality and improve outcomes of negotiations with buyers.

Second, IWCA partners with policy and research organizations outside the private sector in order to further its mission. The International Trade Center (ITC), a subsidiary of the World Trade Organization and the United Nations, has provided funding and technical assistance on ensuring gains from export trade reach women throughout the coffee value chain. IWCA also works with industry bodies such as the African Fine Coffees Association (AFCA) to, for example, encourage the adoption of a gender policy to guide such organizations' work, and to develop gender-related programming.

Third, IWCA has continued to ensure their presence is felt at gatherings of industry leaders. Their inaugural meeting at SCAA quickly became an annual event at the trade body conference, drawing a growing range of industry professionals into regular conversation about gender equality. In addition, IWCA members with access to industry bodies such as the Coffee Quality Institute (an influential trade organization) work to raise issues of gender equality in the industry with these institutions on an ongoing basis.

IWCA focuses on challenges to gender equality in workplace settings ranging from corporate offices to coffee farms. IWCA has managed to develop programming and interventions to address challenges related to women's skills and knowledge access, as well as visibility and advancement in the industry. However, issues outside the workplace setting also significantly impact gender equality in the coffee trade and have proved to be more difficult to address. These include: women's available work time, physical mobility, access to and control over assets (including income and land), and personal safety. The lesson of IWCA's experience is that these and similar issues, which are present outside the "workplace" setting, hold enormous sway over gender equality outcomes.

---

2 At the time of writing, IWCA has chapters in: Brazil, Burundi, Colombia, Costa Rica, Democratic Republic of Congo, Dominican Republic, El Salvador, Guatemala, Honduras, India, Japan, Kenya, Mexico, Nicaragua, Peru, Philippines, Rwanda, Tanzania and Uganda.

Time and mobility

The role of a woman in her family and her society means that coffee is only a small part of what faces a woman in her daily life ... How much time does a woman possibly have on her hands to attend training and still do everything else that her domestic situation demands without some level of flexibility? (Mbula Musau, African Fine Coffees Association, 2007–12 and IWCA Kenya Member).

Fathers don't like it if their daughters travel [to training sessions] alone, because who knows what they might learn there? Who knows what people will say to them? And it's not good that other men see your daughter going places alone. Who knows what they will think of her? (coffee worker and father, Quetzaltenango, Guatemala).

In many countries, ensuring that government services and technical assistance programmes reach women is notoriously difficult (International Trade Center, 2008; Holmes and Jones, 2013). This is particularly true when women are concentrated at the beginning of a long agricultural value chain (Pehu *et al.*, 2009; Barrientos *et al.*, 2003). Access to training on coffee quality, export protocols and managing negotiations with buyers can be crucial for success in the coffee industry. However, via their country chapters, IWCA learned that participation in such events remains out of reach for many women. Care responsibilities in their communities may mean that women rarely venture far from home. If taken, IWCA learned, such a trip could entail an arduous or dangerous journey, often prohibitively expensive in the scope of household affairs. IWCA came to understand that, in many contexts, the prospect of women travelling to a market or training session can be unsettling to relatives, who may fear women could bring dishonour while away, come to harm, or even choose not to return. Further, chapter leaders reported that women frequently have little or no access to cash, relying on male relatives for travel money.

IWCA chapters intentionally comprise women working in every aspect of the coffee value chain, but women's lack of time and freedom of mobility often presents a barrier to chapter organization. In Burundi, for instance, it took coffee quality expert Isabelle Sinamenye three years to found an IWCA chapter, and doing so found her initially obligated to work through "gatekeeper" male presidents of regional coffee federations across the country to identify women who were "free to come to meetings without facing pressure from her husband". Because of this, many of her first chapter members were "widows, or women without a husband". Of the experience, she recounted, "[Women I was trying to recruit] all asked me 'How can we meet together?' This is a problem because they all need to take busses for many hours, and they cannot leave the family behind..." Since the chapter has been established, Sinamenye and her team have worked tirelessly to ensure that women from a wide range of personal circumstances can participate in IWCA Burundi.

Lorena Calvo, a leader in IWCA Guatemala, tried to overcome the challenge of women's lack of time and mobility by holding training programmes at her own farm. She recounted that, in her context, relatives and partners frequently hesitate to "allow" women to travel. This is ostensibly for safety reasons, but Calvo suspects that it is also due to a concern about female propriety, and who women will meet along their journeys. "Husbands don't like the women to travel in the bus and they don't like the women to be classmates with other people", she detailed. Calvo used her position as the first women on Guatemala's national coffee board to pressure the board to partner with IWCA's fledgling local chapter and provide training for women on farms, rather than in capital cities.

IWCA's experience suggests that such decentralized training appears to be important for gender equality in the coffee industry. Indeed, a review conducted for the African Fine Coffees Association's work with the ITC and IWCA suggested that of more than 40 major coffee-related training events financed by bilateral aid and held in more than ten African countries between 2004 and 2009, women comprised on average only 15% of participants (Musau, 2009). In response to this report, AFCA began to work with their own partners to draft their first official policy on gender in the coffee trade in East Africa. Of this process, one IWCA leader observed: "Men in these societies are also realizing the importance of these activities; it's no longer a confrontation in every country". A coffee grower from Burundi echoed the sentiment, explaining, "Even though I am a man, I've understood the importance of the IWCA Burundi project. My wife is a member … when a wife is promoted [advances economically] … the promotion is for the whole family."

Control over assets

In my country, women in coffee do not have land. The fact is, in Burundi, the owner of the land is the man. Your husband. The fruit of the agriculture belongs to the man. When you get married, you go to another family. You live on the land, but it belongs to your husband. You are not honoured. It is not yours. You can work on it, but you can't decide what to do with it. For example, if you have coffee, you grow and pick the coffee. But the sale of the coffee and the money, the man needs to manage. He says, "This for my own spending, this for my cousin." Women, they need to wait. Wait and see what is left over for them, and for the children (Isabelle Sinamenye, Founder and President, IWCA Burundi).

For many years, I picked coffee from trees that belonged to my husband's family. I had the coffee cherries I picked with my hands, but I did not know their proper price. And it was not me, but my husband, who went to sell them. The coffee belonged to him. If he left me, I would no longer be allowed to pick coffee from his land. I had nothing to pass on to my daughters. I knew I needed to become part of IWCA so I could learn about coffee and how the business is done (IWCA member, IWCA Burundi).

In many nations with IWCA chapters, women are unable to own or inherit land (World Bank, 2013). In addition, IWCA has learned that, because the person who owns the land is often seen as the owner of its agricultural output—and wives may not be perceived to share in that ownership—women in coffee could work at a never-ending job from which they benefit very little (Peterman *et al.*, 2014; Verhart and Pyburn, 2012). Gender-disaggregated data on asset ownership within the coffee industry is at an early stage, but research conducted by the International Trade Center across 15 countries suggests women own an average of 15% of the land, traded produce and companies related to coffee (International Trade Center, 2008). Women's property rights, as well as other rights germane to the conduct of business (such as the right to sign contracts or take out a loan), thus represent an important systemic barrier to gender equality in the coffee industry. Additionally, because the sale of cash crops is typically a male pursuit (Jacobs and Cote, 2015; Pehu *et al.*, 2009), women are often unable to gain and maintain control over income from coffee production (Stanculescu *et al.*, 2011). Lack of formal savings institutions, especially in rural areas, and difficulty in accessing such accounts without formal documents or financial literacy, leaves women's earnings vulnerable (Stanculescu *et al.*, 2011, Lyon *et al.*, 2010). These challenges to gender equality, which may appear distant from the context of a corporate workplace, in fact have immense impact on gender equality in the coffee industry as a whole.

Personal safety

> In Congo, we find that women who grow coffee with their husbands do not have access to income generated after harvest. The coffee harvest is an occasion for men to drink alcohol and to marry several women, as they have money. And during this time, women are beaten and driven from their homes with their children without anything. Apart from that, while working in the field, women are often victims of rape by armed militia[3]... To fight against these practices, we educate women and girls about their human rights and sexual violence that they face daily in their coffee cultivation and in their households... That is why we have found useful to join the IWCA and seek the involvement of other women around the world so that together we can find solutions to various problems faced by women in the cultivation of coffee in our country (Chantal Binwa, Founder, IWCA Democratic Republic of the Congo).

Gender-based violence is notoriously difficult to measure accurately. Yet, IWCA chapters frequently report that violence impacts women working in the coffee industry in their countries. On one of their early trips to Central America, IWCA's founders-to-be were shaken to hear a local NGO estimate that domestic violence may affect more than 80% of the women in the region hosting their visit. In Uganda, where IWCA has a chapter, some legal scholars have argued that a key reason for

---

3 Note that men were also victims of such militia. However, women were especially likely to be left to cultivate coffee, and yet were often particularly vulnerable when working outside unaccompanied.

establishing inheritance rights for women is to curtail the violence that often occurs upon the death of a husband, including ritual rape, as male kin attempted to reclaim ownership of land and transfer "ownership" of the widow with the other property (Loftspring, 2007). Similarly, IWCA chapters report that women may be liable to be attacked while working outside unaccompanied; indeed fear of violence was a key reason for hesitation to travel on the part of women and their families. Some IWCA leaders were initially shocked to learn that women in some coffee growing communities may become mothers through sexual assault, and that forcible early marriage was commonplace in some settings. However, as their work has progressed, IWCA has become increasingly convinced that gender-based violence represents yet another concern apparently situated outside the workplace, but impacting gender equality in the coffee industry in fundamental ways.

IWCA: lessons learned

> A lot of people [in our industry] talk about how important women are— they talk about the need for diversity, empowerment, and equality. They talk about it. They don't necessarily do something about it. When you go to farm level in any agricultural commodity, you find women don't even get paid. Or the money disappears. Or they are abused. These issues are out in the open. We're attempting to [do something]... By giving a voice to women, they improve the living conditions for families, which in turn improves their community as a whole. They deserve to be heard about what their needs are in order to benefit the world around them. And we should be able to do that, especially if as consumers, we're willing to pay seven dollars for a couple of lattes, right? (Jennifer Gallegos, Director of Business Development for Coffee, Fair Trade USA and IWCA Board Member).

IWCA represents an effort on the part of executives and senior managers to engage their own industry towards gender equality. IWCA's experience highlights at least six contributors to gender inequality in the coffee industry: challenges related to women's time; physical mobility; skills and knowledge; industry visibility; control over resources; and personal safety. The lesson of this case is that at least four of these exist outside the "workplace". Therefore, executives who seek to promote gender equality in their industries must become attentive to and conversant with these—and similar—contextual contributors to gender inequality.

Several organizational lessons are evident from the IWCA experience. First, the organization is notably volunteer-led; strategically parlaying existing influence and resources of industry leaders for its own ends. Second, IWCA has learned that working through the establishment of independent national chapters is a crucial aspect of the group's success. Third, IWCA works primarily through the provision of skills training, networks and market opportunities; a role they can fulfil efficaciously due to their industry experience. IWCA has learned that partnering with industry associations such as the African Fine Coffees Association and policy bodies such as the International Trade Center is crucial to their work.

IWCA leaders also believe that many of the barriers to gender equality in their industry possess a seemingly intractable quality, existing at the level of law or custom. While the organization was founded with the desire to pursue gender equality within coffee workplaces, it is clear that challenges to gender equality often originate from outside the commercial sphere. In addition, IWCA has learned that challenges regarding women's time and mobility, access to and control over assets, and personal safety are not unique to the coffee industry. Rather, they represent truly global challenges to gender equality. The lesson of IWCA's experience is thus twofold: industry leaders can organize to enact change from within their industries in powerful ways; however, in order to effectively pursue gender equality in the workplace, it is crucial to engage the gendered nature of the contexts in which workplaces are situated.

Bibliography

Barrientos, S. (2010). Gender and ethical trade: Can vulnerable women workers benefit? In S. Chant (ed.), *The International Handbook of Gender and Poverty* (pp. 440-445). London: Edward Elgar.

Barrientos, S. & B. Evers (2013). Gender production networks: Push and pulls on corporate responsibility? In S. Rai & G. Waylen (eds.), *New Frontiers in Feminist Political Economy* (pp. 43-71). London: Routledge.

Barrientos, S., C. Dolan, & A. Tallontire (2003). A gendered value chain approach to codes of conduct in African horticulture. *World Development* 31(9), 1511-1526.

DeSchutter, O. (2012). *Women's Rights and the Right to Food: Report to the Human Rights Council.* New York: United Nations.

Elder, S.D., H. Zerriffi, & P. LeBillion (2012). Effects of Fair Trade certification on social capital: The case of Rwandan coffee producers. *World Development*, 40(11), 2355-2367.

Euromonitor (2012). *Hot Drinks 2012 Overview: Trends and Opportunities.* London: Euromonitor International.

Grosser, K. & N. Van der Gaag (2013). Girls can save the world? In T. Wallace, F. Porter & M. Ralph-Bowman (eds.), *Aid, NGOs, and the Realities of Women's Lives: A Perfect Storm* (pp. 73-87). Rugby, UK: Practical Action Publishing.

Grosser, K. & J. Moon (2005). Gender mainstreaming and corporate social responsibility: Reporting workplace issues. *Journal of Business Ethics*, 62(4), 327-340.

Holmes, R. & N. Jones (2013). *Gender and Social Protection in the Developing World: Beyond Mothers and Safety Nets.* London: Zed Books.

International Trade Center (2008). Women in coffee. *International Trade Forum*, 3/4, 24-6.

International Women's Coffee Alliance (2014). About IWCA. Retrieved from http://www.womenincoffee.org/about-iwca/

Jacobs, I. & S. Cote (2015). *The Way Forward: Accelerating Gender Equity in Coffee Value Chains.* Aliso Viejo: Coffee Quality Institute.

Jan van Hilten, H. (2012). *The Coffee Exporter's Guide: Third Edition.* Geneva: International Trade Center.

Kilgour, M.A. (2007). The UN Global Compact and substantive equality for women: Revealing a "well hidden" mandate. *Third World Quarterly*, 28(4), 751-773.

Kilgour, M.A. (2013). The Global Compact and gender inequality: a work in progress. *Business & Society*, 52(1), 105-134.

Loftspring, R.C. (2007). Inheritance rights in Uganda. *University of Pennsylvania Journal of International Law*, 29(1), 243-281.

Lyon, S., J.A. Bezaury, & T. Mutersbaugh (2010). Gender equity in fairtrade–organic coffee producer organizations: Cases from Mesoamerica. *Geoforum*, 41(1), 93-103.

Manchón, B.G. & M. MacLeod (2010). Challenging gender inequality in farmers' organisations in Nicaragua. *Gender and Development*, 18(3), 373-386.

Musau, M. (2009). *Women in the Coffee Sector.* International Trade Centre and African Fine Coffees Association, Internal Report.

Oliveira Silva, R. (2015). The role of women in the coffee industry: Remarks by the Executive Director of the International Coffee Organization. Presented at *Trade Beyond Barriers: International Women's Coffee Alliance Convention, Bogotá, Colombia, 15 October 2015.*

Pehu, E., Y. Lambrou, & M. Hartl (2009). *Gender in Agriculture Sourcebook.* Washington, DC: World Bank.

Peterman, A., J. Behrman, & A. Quisumbing (2014). A review of empirical evidence on gender differences in nonland agricultural inputs, technology, and services in developing countries. In A. Quisumbing, R. Meinzen-Dick, T. Raney, A. Croppenstedt, J. Behrman & A. Peterman (eds.), *Gender in Agriculture: Closing the Knowledge Gap* (pp. 145-186). Rotterdam: Springer.

Sisson Runyan, A. & V.S. Peterson (2013). *Global Gender Issues in the New Millennium, Fourth Edition.* Boulder, CO: Westview.

Stanculescu, D., L. Gibson, & M. Schole (2011). *Microfinance in East Africa: Schemes for Women in the Coffee Sector.* Geneva: International Trade Center.

Tandon, N. (2010). New agribusiness investments mean wholesale sell-out for women farmers. *Gender and Development*, 18(3), 503-514.

Thompson, L.J. (2008). Gender equity and corporate social responsibility in a post-feminist era. *Business Ethics: A European Review*, 17(1), 87-106.

Verhart, N. & R. Pyburn (2012). Gender equality in certified agricultural value chains. In Harcourt, W. (ed.), *Women Reclaiming Sustainable Livelihoods: Spaces Lost, Spaces Gained* (pp. 62-82). London: Palgrave MacMillan.

World Bank (2013). *Women, Business and the Law 2014: Removing Restrictions to Enhance Gender Equality.* Washington, DC: World Bank.

Mary Johnstone-Louis is an Economic and Social Research Council Scholar at the University of Oxford's Said Business School. Her research interests include women's entrepreneurship (particularly in emerging economies), corporate social responsibility, and collaborations between corporations and development agencies. She has contributed to academic articles and business cases and has recently been awarded a grant from the Skoll Centre for Social Entrepreneurship for her research.

Transport and workplace accessibility
Routes to improved equity

Deanna Grant-Smith
Queensland University of Technology, Australia

Natalie Osborne
Griffith University, Australia

Paolo Marinelli
go2team, Australia

While there has been progress on a range of issues influencing gender equity in the workforce, getting to and from work can be a fundamental barrier to participation and equity. Issues such as: access to transportation, the routes taken, modes used, distance travelled, and time and money spent in transit are often shaped by gender. In this chapter we adopt an intersectional feminist lens to explore the structural inequities in transport accessibility and workplace mobilities and consider ways to begin to redress or mitigate their impact. We describe a cross-section of organizational and public policy responses to the broader societal challenge of gendered transport disadvantage primarily from an Australian perspective. We consider its impacts on equal workforce participation within the formal economy, including the mainstreaming and normalization of flexible working and transport policies. We identify a mix of transport and non-transport initiatives from selected OECD nations aimed at reducing barriers to workforce participation and contributing to improved workplace equity through improved accessibility and mobility, particularly for women.

While there has been progress on a range of issues influencing gender equality in the workforce, getting to and from work can be a fundamental barrier. An equity-focused approach to transport dilemmas takes individual circumstances and needs into account when seeking to improve workplace accessibility and equality (Espinoza, 2007). Issues such as: access to transportation, the routes taken, modes used, distance travelled, and time and money spent in transit are often shaped by gender. As such, the constraints on women's access to transport represent a signifi-cant obstacle for achieving workplace equality. In this chapter we adopt an inter-sectional feminist lens (Crenshaw, 1989, 1991) to explore strategies for promoting equity in transport accessibility and mobility to achieve equality in workforce par-ticipation. This requires exploring the structural inequities in transport accessibility and workplace mobilities, focusing primarily on gender but also considering how gender intersects with class, race, ethnicity, dis/ability and caring responsibilities in shaping transport options and the accessibility of workplaces. This is not a stock-take of all extant measures; rather, we describe a cross-section of organizational and public policy responses to the challenge of gendered transport disadvantage primarily from an Australian perspective. We consider the impacts on equal work-force participation within the formal economy, including the mainstreaming and normalization of flexible working and transport policies. We identify a mix of trans-port and non-transport initiatives from selected OECD nations aimed at reducing barriers to workforce participation and contributing to improved workplace equal-ity through improved accessibility and mobility, particularly for women.

Women and transport

Transport is often discussed as if it were a gender-neutral concern (Scholten *et al.*, 2012). However, women's transportation options tend to be more constrained than men's and these constraints have been demonstrated to impact upon women's ability to take up available job opportunities (Braff and Barrett Meyering, 2011). Since the late 1980s researchers have been calling for the need to better understand the relationships between gender, transport and employment to address what they consider to be the "consequences of lessor mobility" on employment outcomes (Whipp and Grieco, 1989, p. 2). This lessor mobility can be understood as the result of the coalescence of a number of factors.

First, despite some increases in fathers' childcare responsibilities and increasing female employment participation rates, travel patterns remain gendered, particu-larly trips centred on commuting (McQuaid and Chen, 2012). Because women con-tinue to bear the primary responsibility for caring for children and other domestic responsibilities, their travel behaviour reflects this more complex and dispersed programme of activity and involves more "household and family support trips" (Hjorthol, 2008, p. 196). As a result, women's commuting trips often incorporate trip chaining, that is, completing multiple tasks and making multiple stops within a single journey to meet the complex demands of their roles (Greed, 2008). For example, their trips to and from work may involve completing a range of household chores (Dobbs, 2005) alongside picking up/dropping off children, who are more than five times as likely to travel with their mothers than their fathers (McDonald, 2006). These complex linked trips have also been observed to be subject to considerable daily variation (Rosenbloom, 1989). As such, many women require more travel flexibility because they carry a greater transport burden than men (Mashiri *et al.*, 2005) and are less likely than men to undertake single purpose trips within any one journey (Hodgson, 2012). Furthermore, there is a persistent tendency for women in heterosexual relationships to find that their employment is considered subordinate to their male partner's, with the location of residences relative to workplaces tending to suit his, rather than her, career advancement and employment prospects (Fine, 2002).

Second, women are more likely than men to feel insecure and vulnerable to attack, which can restrict their travel at particular times, for example at night (Hodgson, 2012). This fear of being subjected to violence can impact on patterns of both travel and work, prompting some women to avoid night work or to change their commuting habits when working nightshifts to avoid perceived or real threats to their personal safety (Scholten *et al.*, 2012). These "self-imposed precautionary measures" significantly limit women's mobility and contribute to the underrepresentation of women in certain workplaces and settings (Law, 1999, p. 570). Although transport research in the past has been "gender-blind" (Law, 1999, p. 567) and transport systems constructed as universal and neutral, they are designed around patterns of mobility that are inherently gendered, classed and racialized. As a result, transport may not only be inaccessible and impractical but also unsafe for women, children, people of colour and members of other marginalized groups. Indeed, women are more likely to perceive public transport and the spaces around it (e.g. bus stops, walking between stops and destinations) as dangerous (particularly at night), which may affect their usage (Loukaitou-Sideris and Fink, 2009; Rosenbloom, 2005; Wekerle, 2005), while ethnicity, age, and dis/ability also shape women's sense of safety and how accessible public transport may be (Hine and Mitchell, 2001; Sweet and Escalante, 2010). These intersectional factors may be both independent of and/or complexify gendered experiences.

Finally, women tend to have less access to private transport than men (Hjorthol, 2008). The ability to service the costs associated with purchasing, running, servicing, insuring, registering and parking a car may be more difficult for women given the continuing wage disparity between men and women, and between white people and people of colour. Furthermore, the travel burden on poorer women tends to be higher as they are more likely to live further away from employment centres, less likely to have access to frequent, reliable and safe public transport, and less able to afford to run and park a private vehicle. The complexity of women's travel movements and the fact that their trips are more likely to involve others (such as children) also limit women's ability to adopt alternative and often cheaper forms of commuter transport such as cycling, which continues to be dominated by men (Mackett, 2014).

Despite acknowledgement of these gendered differences in transport accessibility and mobility, the needs of women are often overlooked in the planning and delivery of transport services, and transport considerations at both the organizational and public policy level rarely reflect gendered differences (Buiten, 2007; Greed, 2008; Hanlon, 1996). However, research suggests that there are sufficiently significant differences in women's transport demands and experience in terms of access, patterns of commuting and in childcare responsibilities to justify specific attention paid to their needs (Hamilton and Jenkins, 2000). Calls for gender equality in the workplace must also consider how gender, class, race, dis/ability and other identity factors shape transport needs and access to different modes of transportation and consequently employment opportunities. It also requires consideration of how diverse and intersectional identities shape transport needs and equity responses required by organizations and governments to improve workplace equality outcomes.

Women's access to transport "encompasses economic concerns related to affordability, sociocultural aspects related to safety and security in public space, and the physical issues of comfort and ease of design in the use of transport and its related infrastructure" (Levy, 2013, pp. 53-54). Transport-related inhibitors affect women's participation and their choices in the workplace (Hjorthol, 2008) and thus should be a matter of concern for both policy makers and employers. In the remainder of this chapter we explore a range of policy and organizational responses to improve women's mobility. These transport and non-transport initiatives are organized around three key themes: 1) providing more flexibility; 2) ensuring safety; and 3) addressing affordability.

Providing more work and transport flexibility

Transport needs are shaped by both origin and destination. Women's trips, modal choice and routes are influenced by not only the location of their destination relative to their home, but also their household dynamic, role in household labour and caring responsibilities. In single vehicle, heterosexual households, men tend to have primary use of the car (Hjorthol, 2008; Næss, 2008), despite women having greater responsibility for household and care-related labour, and that they often combine these with paid employment. This has a significant influence on women's mobilities, their ability to access the workforce and their choice of workplace. Mobility is concerned with the movement of people through space as a social or cultural artefact. Mobility as a construct understands the ways in which being mobile impacts many aspects of social life, civil society and political participation and how "uneven and unequal" the practice and outcomes of mobility can be (Adey et al., 2014, p. 3).

Women tend to have more constrained mobilities than men in that they may have fewer transport options and resources available to them which impacts their travel choices and outcomes. Their mobilities also are often shaped by caring responsibilities and household sustaining labour (Skinner, 2003). As such improving workplace accessibility for women requires attention to these differences including mobilities of care (Sánchez de Madariaga, 2013) and socio-economic positionality (Murray, 2008). Women's travel needs, particularly the need to engage in multiple trips within a single journey (trip chaining), can be addressed through non-transport interventions. An example is the practice in some east Asian cities to co-locate shopping and childcare facilities with metro stations (Pojani, 2014, p. 1731). A common non-transport solution used by workplaces includes providing on-site childcare, thus simplifying women's trips to and from the workplace. It should be noted, however, that commuting with children can present its own problems which are often underestimated by transport planners (see Hamilton and Jenkins, 1989; Hine and Mitchell, 2001).

Some employers also institute organizational policies which limit the impact of transport constraints on workforce participation. These include promoting greater flexibility in working hours such as compressed working weeks and flexible start and finish times, and flexibility in workplace attendance such as working from home and telecommuting (Breaugh and Farabee, 2012; Glauber, 2011; Walls *et al.*, 2010). Flexible work policies such as these encourage employees to integrate a range of work and non-work commitments; while care responsibilities tend to dominate discussions of the benefits of such schemes, some employees also require flexibility in order to manage non-family obligations (Cathcart *et al.*, 2014). However, such practices can have unforeseen negative impacts on the transport choices available to workers (McMahon and Pocock, 2011).

Governments have also been keen to capitalize on the perceived benefits of more flexible work practices to reduce reliance on private vehicles (Wheatley, 2012), congestion management and workforce participation. However, a major hurdle in the effective implementation of such schemes is persistent "values of presenteeism and infinite availability" (Watts, 2009, p. 37) which construct the ideal worker as one who is unencumbered by family or other external obligations (McDonald *et al.*, 2013).

More flex in the city: a case study of flexible work and transport

During 2009 almost 900 employees across ten government agencies and ten private sector organizations in Brisbane (Australia) participated in a four week programme designed to evaluate the uptake of a range of flexibility measures. Participants were mainly managers, professional, clerical, sales and service workers who typically fit the commuter profile of a standard Monday to Friday 9 a.m.–5 p.m. work pattern (Marinelli *et al.*, 2010). Policies were not changed as part of the pilot; rather a proactive implementation and promotion of existing policies was employed to encourage employees to use them. This subtle change in the workplace culture saw shifts of more than 30% out of the morning and afternoon peak travel; employees staggering their travel arrangements reduced overcrowding on public transport and allowed them to avoid peak hour traffic if using a private vehicle. The majority of participants (80%) reported enhanced work–life balance, and depending on the choice of flexible work arrangement adopted, up to 70% of participants reported productivity increases (Cleary *et al.*, 2010). However, these shifts and benefits were not evenly shared across the workforce. Professionals (45%), managers (21%) and advanced and intermediate clerical and service workers (21%) were disproportionately over-represented as participants in the pilot compared with the general Brisbane workforce (Marinelli *et al.*, 2010). Participants in the pilot also tended to hold organizational roles with greater than average independence and the ability to manage their own workload (Nielsen, 2009). This suggests that flexible work schemes may be limited to certain employees, including those in more powerful positions and those who are not required to be physically present within specific hours to do their job. This is likely to constrain the participation of lower level and administrative staff in flexible work initiatives. Further, the study found that those workers who adopted flexible working hours were more likely to be male (65%) than female (57%) (Nielsen, 2009) and that male participants had a higher tendency to start work before 7 a.m. (Marinelli *et al.*, 2010). This might suggest that many women are more constrained in the extent to which they can push the boundaries of flexible work practices as their degree of flexibility tends to be mediated by mobilities of care (Sánchez de Madariaga, 2013) and the fact that schools, childcare facilities and other services have fixed operating times (Whipp and Grieco, 1989).

Although this pilot was primarily concerned with achieving congestion management outcomes through the application of workplace flexibility measures, it demonstrates that such practices can have benefits in terms of work–life balance for those who have the capacity to participate. They may also work towards normalizing care work because it allows employees to structure their work life and hours such that they can autonomously manage their multiple responsibilities without having to seek managerial approval. However, broader managerial support remains critical for the success of flexible work initiatives (Hornung *et al.*, 2008; Cathcart *et al.*, 2014; McDonald *et al.*, 2008). Participants reported that full participation in the scheme was limited by individual workplace cultures and the actions of line managers. An example of this was the perception that choosing to work from home carried a stigma, which had to be addressed by ensuring a workplace presence through email traffic to demonstrate that they were working productively (Nielsen, 2009).

Addressing actual and perceived community safety risks

It is often considered that women's mobility constraints are "their own fault and not an urban structural issue" (Greed, 1994, p. 43). However, there are a number of socio-spatial and cultural factors which can inhibit or constrain women's mobility. Safety is primary among these. Indeed, safety concerns are likely to be a greater consideration in modal choice and transport routes for women, as they are more likely to be victims of violence and sexual harassment while in public space and while taking public transport (Levy, 2013). This risk may be heightened for women (and men) who belong to other visible minorities such as if they are read as gay or transgender or if they belong to a marginalized race, ethnicity and/or religion (Pain, 2010; Sandercock, 2003; Stotzer, 2009).

These risks are sometimes broadly recognized, as evidenced by the #IllRide-WithYou campaign following the 2014 Martin Place shooting in Sydney (Australia). In a movement that began with Rachael Jacobs, in Brisbane (Australia), and Sydney-based Twitter user Sir Tessa (@sirtessa) (Jacobs, 2014), many individuals recognized that Muslim people—particularly Muslim women who wear religious attire—would face increased danger on public transport as a result of heightened bigotry and hatred following the shooting perpetrated by a self-identified Muslim man. Using the twitter hashtag, "#IllRideWithYou", people offered themselves as escorts on specific public transport routes for Muslim commuters and travellers who were concerned about the increased risk to their safety as a result of this incident and were worried about using public transport alone. This campaign was a moving display of support for the Australian Muslim community; however it highlighted the increased danger that women and minority travellers face while using public transport, and the fact that public spaces are more or less safe (or perceived to be so) depending on one's positionality and identity.

Strategies to improve workplace accessibility for women must consider how accessibility is influenced by safety, and by perceptions of safety. It is important to acknowledge that perceived risks are just as influential on behaviour as actual risks, and the likelihood of a person perceiving a situation, modal choice or transport route to be risky depends a great deal on identity factors like gender (Loukaitou-Sideris and Fink, 2009; Pain, 2010). Organizations cannot unilaterally make a city or society safer, nor can they (or should they) seek to change perceptions of danger. There is a considerable body of work on crime prevention through environmental design (CPTED) and helping people feel safer in public spaces, including transit spaces but much of this work is focused on the cityscape and urban design scale, and is thus more the purview of local and state governments, rather than workplaces. However, organizations can seek to ensure that their individual premises are well-lit and employ safety features such as security guards after dark. Closed-circuit televisions, although often used to improve security, may have little effect on women's perceptions of danger (Loukaitou-Sideris and Fink, 2009).

Organizations can seek to institute measures that are sensitive to these risks and perceptions, and attuned to particular risk factors in their local area and for their workforce. For example, Griffith University (Brisbane, Australia) has a security shuttle bus that operates on the half hour from 6 p.m., with a final run after the library closes for the night (times vary throughout the semester). The sprawling campus is situated within remnant bushland, and getting to one's car in the late afternoon or evening can require a long walk to remote, dimly lit areas of the campus, often using poorly lit bush paths with limited passive surveillance. Within the CPTED literature, passive surveillance is focused on limiting opportunities for crime and violence by taking steps to increase the perception that people can be seen through the design and placement of physical features, activities and people in such a way as to maximize visibility. Measures to improve passive surveillance can include street lighting, landscaping that promotes visibility, the use of glass and clear plastic in bus shelters, and the design of public spaces which result in greater pedestrian traffic throughout both the day and night (Clancey *et al.*, 2012). Due to the size of the campus, the university provides a free shuttle service to car parking areas and escorts to accompany staff and students to their cars. Because the on-campus bus stops are located in close proximity to the main security office and have better lighting and more opportunities for passive surveillance this safety-focused service is targeted at car users, who are perceived to be more at risk on campus.

Queensland University of Technology works with its Student Guild to offer LGBTIQ (Lesbian, Gay, Bisexual, Transgender, Intersex and Questioning) safety escorts at night to promote safety on campus. It has also developed a free smartphone app, SafeZone, for use by students and staff. Once the user has registered, the app is available to be used at any time by opening it and tapping on the required icon. When used on campus the user's location is highlighted on a map in the Central Monitoring Station and security staff are able to talk directly to the student or worker in distress and coordinate the immediate attendance of the campus security team to their location to assist them.[1] It should be recognized, however, that workers may still be at risk once off campus either during travel or at the other end of their journey.

Photo 8.1 **Initiatives such as security shuttle buses can impact employees' actual and perceived safety**

1 https://www.qut.edu.au

Guaranteed ride home from work schemes: a case study in ensuring worker transit safety

An increasingly common measure for addressing actual and perceived risks to worker transit safety for the entire journey, particularly for workers required to work late or at night, is guaranteed ride home schemes. Guaranteed ride home from work schemes can be a voluntary initiative on the part of an organization but also have been incorporated as part of organizational compliance with congestion management programmes in North America (Brownstone and Golob, 1992; Victoria Transport Policy Institute, 2013). Congestion management programmes see the employer provide or subsidize car-sharing (using private employee vehicles) or van-pooling (using employer supplied vehicles or a third party provider) schemes often through connecting employees through a central carpool database, providing information about carpooling, and offering preferential parking for carpooling employees. However, the rigidity of such schemes and their reliance on compatible travel arrangements with other employees can cause issues for workers when faced with unforeseen circumstances which affect their ability to return home the same way they arrived. The guaranteed ride home supports carpooling schemes by improving their accessibility, viability, flexibility, safety and cost because the eligible employee is guaranteed some form of free or subsidized ride home from work if they cannot use the mode they normally use as a result of work or personal circumstances such as being required to work late or needing to go home early in an emergency (Vanoutrive *et al.*, 2012).

The benefits of such schemes include the ability for employees to manage the transport implications of emergent or unplanned situations in a way which limits potential costs to the employee and does not compromise their safety. Who pays (employer or partially the employee) can vary depending on the company, the local jurisdiction and whether it is a legally required or voluntary action by the company (Menczer, 2007; Transit Cooperative Research Program, 2010). In the United States some local transit authorities provide guaranteed ride home schemes outside the normal operating hours of the transit system as part of ticket sales programmes for their staff and specific institutions such as universities (Boslaugh, 2014, p. 1448).

Guaranteed ride home schemes address important concerns employees may have when considering participating in carpooling programmes; especially women, who may have particular concerns about safety (e.g. should they miss their ride) and lack of flexibility (e.g. should they need to collect children unexpectedly). Studies have shown that the availability of these guaranteed ride home schemes thus constitutes a psychological safety net but that employees tend not to overuse or abuse them (Victoria Transport Policy Institute, 2014).

Addressing transport affordability and accessibility

The intersectional feminist lens (Crenshaw, 1989) adopted in this chapter requires that factors in addition to, or in concert with, gender, and their influence on transport accessibility are considered. Gender is not the sole determinant of a person's experiences of inequality (hooks, 2000; Schüssler, 1992). The constraints on women's mobilities and concomitant impact on workplace accessibility may be complicated by factors including (but not limited to) race, ethnicity, class and occupational status. Race and ethnicity have been discussed earlier; in this section, we particularly consider class and occupational status and the impact of these on transport affordability and accessibility. It is also important to understand that these factors—class and occupational status—can intersect with race; in many places, women of colour are more likely to be in lower paid, lower status employment than white women (Berry and Bell, 2012)—in some cases, even when their qualifications and level of experience are comparable (Creese and Wiebe, 2012).

Many organizations have made efforts to compensate workers for costs incurred travelling to work. Measures may include salary sacrificing for vehicles or public transport tickets, providing company cars, subsidizing the costs of on-site parking and organizing company carpools. However, these measures privilege—or indeed are only offered to or effective for—certain kinds of workers. Carpools tend to be unworkable for employees who trip chain (that is, those whose journey to and from work comprises multiple stops—they may have to drop off and collect children at school or childcare, they may stop to buy groceries or conduct other household errands) or who work variable hours. Similarly, subsidizing on-site parking is only a benefit for those who can afford or have access to a car. Salary sacrificing is not available to all workers; for example, pink collar workers (service workers in fields traditionally associated with women) and casual and contract workers generally do not have this option. Relative to male employees, women have traditionally had comparatively low access to company cars (Law, 1999) and the company funded parking spaces attached to them. This is not to say that these measures are without value; rather, that organizations seeking to offset travel costs for their workers to improve workplace accessibility may need to offer a suite of measures, some of which may be more suitable for some employees than others. Organizational strategies designed to improve workplace accessibility must consider their workforce profile and their patterns of work. For example, shift workers have different transport needs and experiences from those employees working conventional diurnal shifts and standard hours.

Governments can also assist business to address the unequal distributional impacts of policy initiatives and may implement modifications to mitigate negatives for specific groups. For example, in the central business district of Melbourne (Australia) a parking congestion levy of AU$1,300 per annum applies to most public and private car parking spaces (Victoria State Revenue Office, 2014). This has the potential to increase costs for commuters who must pay for their own parking. However, the scheme also allows a levy exemption for parking spaces guaranteed exclusively for the use of shift workers, which may benefit low-income workers such as cleaners and other ancillary staff in which women constitute the majority.

Cycling and other forms of active transport have gained prominence in recent years, and as a result many workplaces (or in some cases, municipal governments) are providing end-of-trip facilities for their workers. This often involves providing secure storage for bicycles, as well as showers and changing rooms. While active transport is an important and valuable goal, it is important to acknowledge that uptake is affected by gender. Employees may find cycling to work difficult if they also need to pick up children from school and buy groceries on their way home; and as previously discussed, such trips remain largely the responsibility of women. Indeed, Scheiner (2014) found that cycling to work was significantly lower among women with children. This encounter by Clara Greed (2008, p. 246) summarizes the tension between active transport, gender, commuting, care and household labour:

> As I struggle along through a pedestrianized part of my local city centre carrying tons of bags to a meeting far from the car park, I often encounter a young man, dressed up in the latest fashionable "Lycra cycling gear" coming up silently behind me and then whooshing past aggressively, cursing at me under his breath for daring to be on a footpath (presumably because he is purer than I because he is a cyclist) without so much as a warning on his bell. I wonder about him. Who does your shopping? Who does your washing? Who is looking after your children?

Even where a cycling commute may be viable for a woman, she is likely to encounter additional difficulties preparing for work. In many professional workplaces it is expected that women wear a full face of makeup and have styled hair (expectations generally not applied to men), and conforming to these expectations may be essential for job security and for promotion (Bartlett, 1994; Steinle, 2006). For end-of-trip facilities to accommodate those needs, they would need to provide sufficient counter space and electrical outlets and secure storage for hairdryers, makeup and toiletries. These considerations rarely form part of end-of-trip design decisions.

Sharing responsibility for transport: case studies of employer-provided transport

It can be beneficial for employees when employers provide specific transport services or lobby for their provision by government or private providers. An example of this is the Australian telecommunications company Optus. When Optus moved its facilities from the Sydney central business district to a business park in the suburb of Macquarie Park, approximately 17 km from the central business district, commuter transport was a concern to its employees. Optus facilitated a range of employee transport options including preferential access to on-site secure parking for those choosing to ride share. Discounted fares for "exclusive access" to public transport services between the campus, the central business district and local public transport interchanges are also available (Singtel Optus, 2015).

Another example of employer supported and funded travel is the free inter-campus shuttle service provided by the Queensland University of Technology (Brisbane, Australia) for travel by staff and students between its city and Kelvin Grove campus. Staff and students who show their staff/student card are able to access this shuttle service for free while other users are charged. The shuttle timetable varies in frequency during the year, with a service provided every 10 minutes on weekdays during the main teaching semesters and every 15 minutes at other times, excluding public holidays, weekends and the days between Christmas Day and New Year's Day when the university is closed. The university also operates a night shuttle bus service (between 5:45 p.m. and 10:00 p.m., Monday to Friday) between the two campuses during the key teaching and examination periods. The bus operates on a "hail and ride" basis and travels a route that covers the Kelvin Grove campus including the major on-site car parks, while at the city-based Gardens Point campus the service includes drop points at the nearby major commercial car parks and railway stations.[2]

Photo 8.2 **Employer-provided or subsidized transport, such as free shuttle buses, can help to relieve employees' transport burdens**

2 https://www.qut.edu.au

Routes to improved equity

In the past "women's needs have too often been assumed to be identical with men's, or simply to be unworthy of note" (Hamilton and Jenkins, 1989, p. 17). However, while it is important to ensure that women's specific needs are considered, the cases described show how mainstreaming transport concerns can have the potential to benefit all employees. Although the cases discussed in this chapter represent moves towards improving women's mobility and accessibility, transport solutions implemented without broader social and culture change "merely scratch the surface" (Pickup, 1989, p. 220). Similarly, approaches which assume that all women experience the same levels of transport disadvantage are problematic. They must be complemented by approaches which disaggregate fundamental factors such as caring responsibilities, hours and times of work, and work performed; how these affect differences within each gender and between genders (McQuaid, 2009; McQuaid and Chen, 2012); and which consider how women's experiences are also shaped by other identities and by other social, political and economic factors. As discussed, some of the strategies mentioned in this chapter may particularly benefit certain (privileged) groups of women and ignore the needs of others, and employers must then consider any strategies aimed at improving women's mobilities through an intersectional lens; that is, gender should not be the only identity factor considered when devising strategies to improve women's mobilities for improved workplace equality. The examples drawn upon in this chapter have highlighted the importance of also considering the race and/or ethnicity of workers and their class and occupational status.

Employers seeking to support more flexible work practices must ensure that workplace cultures and line managers support their uptake and do not impose negative consequences for those who take them up (Wheatley, 2012, p. 813). Negative stereotypes relating to women's mobilities—as potentially unreliable, contingent and detrimentally affected by care and domestic labour—must be challenged. Indeed, rather than perceiving women's constrained transport mobility as a deficit, managing multiple roles, responsibilities and complex transport arrangements involves considerable creativity in managing time, task and travel (Whipp and Grieco, 1989, p. 4); traits that should be valued by employers. Further, working and transport arrangements sensitive to care and domestic labour need to be normalized, not only to improve women's equality in the workplace, but also their equality at home. As workplaces become more flexible and responsive to these needs for the whole workforce, we may see the priority given to men's paid work, and the imbalanced burden of care and domestic work on women, begin to shift.

Certainly, women's reduced transport mobility can impact on their social mobility and prevent progress towards gender equality in the labour market (Schmucki, 2012, p. 75). However, it should also be recognized that "travel to work is not only a reflection of the need and desire of women to work but also of the spatial use of the city and its intersection with the gendered spatial labour markets in cities", and transport is one of the key ways through which women claim their right to the city (Levy, 2013, p. 58). Thus, facilitating women's transport mobility is important not only for individual employees, but also for organizations, and for a more just society.

References

Adey, P., D. Bissell, K. Hannam, P. Merriman, & M. Sheller (2014). Introduction. In P. Adey, D. Bissell, K. Hannam, P. Merriman, & M. Sheller (eds.), *The Routledge Handbook of Mobilities* (pp. 1-20). Abingdon: Routledge.

Bartlett, K.T. (1994). Only girls wear barrettes: Dress and appearance standards, community norms, and workplace equality. *Michigan Law Review*, 92(8), 2541-2582.

Berry, D. & M.P. Bell (2012). Inequality in organizations: Stereotyping, discrimination, and labor law exclusions. *Equality, Diversity and Inclusion: An International Journal*, 31(3), 236-248.

Boslaugh, S.E. (2014). Transit finance. In M. Garrett (ed.), *Encyclopedia of Transportation: Social Science and Policy*. Thousand Oaks, CA: Sage.

Braff, R. & I. Barrett Meyering (2011). *Seeking Security: Promoting Women's Economic Well-being Following Domestic Violence*. Sydney: Australian Domestic & Family Violence Clearinghouse.

Breaugh, J.A. & A.M. Farabee (2012). Telecommuting and flexible work hours: Alternative work arrangements that can improve the quality of work life. In N.P. Reilly, J. Sirgy and C.A. Gorman (eds.), *Work and Quality of Life: Ethical Practices in Organisations* (pp. 251-274). Netherlands: Springer.

Brownstone, D. & T.F. Golob (1992). The effectiveness of ridesharing: Discrete-choice models of commuting in California. *Regional Science and Urban Economics*, 22(1), 5-24.

Buiten, D. (2007). 'Gender, transport and the feminist agenda: Feminist insights towards engendering transport research. *Transport and Communications Bulletin for Asia and the Pacific*, 76, 21-33.

Cathcart, A., P. McDonald & D. Grant-Smith (2014). Challenging the myths about flexible work in the ADF. *Australian Defence Force Journal*, 195, 55-68.

Clancey, G., M. Lee & D. Fisher (2012). Crime prevention through environmental design (CPTED) and the New South Wales Crime Risk Assessment Guidelines: A critical review. *Crime Prevention and Community Safety*, 14, 1-15.

Cleary, N., H. Worthington-Eyre & P.A. Marinelli (2010). More flex in the city: A case study from Brisbane of spreading the load in the office and on the road. *Australasian Transport Research Forum 2010 Proceedings 29 September – 1 October*. Canberra: Australasian Transport Research Forum. Retrieved from http://www.atrf.info/papers/2010/2010_Cleary_Worthington-Eyre_Marinelli.pdf

Creese, G. & B. Wiebe (2012). Survival employment: Gender and deskilling among African migrants in Canada. *International Migration*, 50(5), 56-76.

Crenshaw, K. (1989). Demarginalizing the intersection of race and sex: A black feminist critique of antidiscrimination doctrine, feminist theory and antiracist politics. *The University of Chicago Legal Forum*, 1989, 139-167.

Crenshaw, K. (1991). Mapping the margins: Intersectionality, identity politics, and violence against women of color. *Stanford Law Review*, 43(6), 1241-1299.

Dobbs, L. (2005). Wedded to the car: Women, employment and the importance of private transport. *Transport Policy*, 12(3), 266-278.

Espinoza, O. (2007). Solving the equity-equality conceptual dilemma: A new model for analysis of the educational process. *Educational Research*, 49(4), 343-363.

Fine, B. (2002). *Women's Employment and the Capitalist Family: Towards a Political Economy of Gender and Labour Markets*. London: Routledge.

Glauber, R. (2011). Limited access: Gender, occupational composition, and flexible work scheduling. *The Sociological Quarterly*, 52(3), 472-494.

Greed, C. (1994). *Women and Planning: Creating Gendered Realities*. London: Routledge.

Greed, C. (2008). Are we there yet: Women and transport revisited. In T. Uteng & T. Cresswell (eds.), *Gendered Mobilities* (pp. 243-253). Surrey: Ashgate.

Hamilton, K. & L. Jenkins (1989). Why women and travel? In M. Grieco, L. Pickup & R. Whipp (eds.), *Gender, Transport and Employment: The Impact of Travel Constraints* (pp. 17-45). Aldershot: Avebury.

Hamilton, K. & L. Jenkins (2000). A gender audit for public transport: A new policy tool in the tackling of social exclusion. *Urban Studies*, 37(10), 1793-1800.

Hanlon, S. (1996). Where do women feature in public transport? In *Women's Travel Issues: Proceedings from the Second National Conference*. Retrieved from http://www.fhwa.dot.gov/ohim/womens/chap34.pdf

Hine, J. & F. Mitchell (2001). 'Better for everyone? Travel experiences and transport exclusion. *Urban Studies*, 38(2), 319-332.

Hjorthol, R. (2008). Daily mobility of men and women: A barometer of gender equality? In T. Uteng & T. Cresswell (eds.), *Gendered Mobilities* (pp. 193-210). Surrey: Ashgate.

Hodgson, F. (2012). Escorting economies: Networked journeys, household strategies and resistance. *Research in Transportation Economics*, 34(1), 3-10.

hooks, b. (2000). *Feminist Theory: From Margin to Center*, 2nd edition. London: Pluto Press.

Hornung, S., D. Rousseau & J. Glaser (2008). Creating flexible work arrangements through idiosyncratic deals. *Journal of Applied Psychology*, 93(3), 655-664.

Jacobs, R. (2014, December 16). How #illridewithyou began with Rachael Jacobs' experience on a Brisbane train. *Brisbanetimes.com.au*. Retrieved from http://www.brisbanetimes.com.au/queensland/how-illridewithyou-began-with-rachael-jacobs-experience-on-a-brisbane-train-20141216-128205.html

Law, R. (1999). Beyond "Women and Transport": Towards new geographies of gender and daily mobility. *Progress in Human Geography*, 23(4), 567-588.

Levy, C. (2013). Travel choice reframed: "Deep Distribution" and gender in urban transport. *Environment & Urbanization*, 25(1), 47-63.

Loukaitou-Sideris, A. & C. Fink (2009). Addressing women's fear of victimization in transportation settings: A survey of U.S. transit agencies. *Urban Affairs Review*, 44(4), 554-587.

Mackett, R.L. (2014). The health implications of inequalities in travel. *Journal of Transport and Health*, 1(3), 202-209.

Marinelli, P.A., N. Cleary, H. Worthington-Eyre & K. Doonan (2010). Flexible workplaces: Achieving the worker's paradise and transport planner's dream in Brisbane. *Australasian Transport Research Forum 2010 Proceedings 29 September–1 October*. Canberra: Australasian Transport Research Forum. Retrieved from http://www.atrf.info/papers/2010/2010_Marinelli_Cleary_Worthington-Eyre_Doonan.pdf

Mashiri, M., D. Buiten, S. Mahapa & R. Zukulu (2005). Towards setting a research agenda around mainstreaming gender in the transport sector. *Proceedings of the 24th Southern African Transport Conference, 11–13 July 2005, Pretoria*.

McDonald, N. (2006). Exploratory analysis of children's travel patterns. *Transportation Research Record*, 1977, 1-7.

McDonald, P., L. Bradley & K. Brown (2008). Visibility in the workplace: Still an ingredient for career success. *International Journal of Human Resource Management* 19(12), 2198-2215.

McDonald, P., K. Townsend & A. Wharton (2013). The legitimation and reproduction of discourse–practice gaps in work–life balance. *Personnel Review*, 42(2), 205-222.

McMahon, C. & B. Pocock (2011). *Doing Things Differently: Case Studies of Work-life Innovation in Six Australian Workplaces*. Adelaide: Centre for Work + Life, University of South Australia and Equal Opportunity for Women in the Workplace Agency.

McQuaid, R.W. (2009). A model of the travel to work limits of parents. *Research in Transportation Economics*, 25(1), 19-28.

McQuaid, R.W. & T. Chen (2012). Commuting times: The role of gender, children and part-time work. *Research in Transportation Economics*, 34(1), 66-73.

Menczer, W.B. (2007). Guaranteed ride home programs: A study of program characteristics, utilization, and cost. *Journal of Public Transportation*, 10(4), 131-150.

Murray, L. (2008). Motherhood, risk and everyday mobilities. In T. Uteng & T. Cresswell (eds.), *Gendered Mobilities* (pp. 47-64). Surrey: Ashgate.

Næss, P. (2008). Gender differences in the influences of urban structure on daily travel. In T. Uteng & T. Cresswell (eds.), *Gendered Mobilities* (pp. 173-192). Surrey: Ashgate.

Nielsen (2009). *Flexible Workplace Program Brisbane Central Pilot Report*. Unpublished technical report prepared for Queensland Department of Transport and Main Roads, Brisbane.

Pain, R. (2010). The new geopolitics of fear. *Geography Compass*, 4(3), 226-240.

Pickup, L. (1989). Women's travel requirements: Employment, with domestic constraints. In M. Grieco, L. Pickup & R. Whipp (eds.), *Gender, Transport and Employment: The Impact of Travel Constraints* (pp. 199-222). Aldershot: Avebury.

Pojani, D. (2014). Women's issues/gender issues. In M. Garrett (ed.), *Encyclopedia of Transportation: Social Science and Policy*. Thousand Oaks, CA: Sage.

Rosenbloom, S. (1989). Trip chaining behaviour: A comparative analysis and cross cultural analysis of the travel patterns of working mothers. In M. Grieco, L. Pickup & R. Whipp (eds.), *Gender, Transport and Employment: The Impact of Travel Constraints* (pp. 75-82). Aldershot: Avebury.

Rosenbloom, S. (2005). Women's travel issues. In S.F. Fainstein & J.L. Servon (eds.), *Gender and Planning: A Reader* (pp. 235-255). New Brunswick: Rutgers University Press.

Sánchez de Madariaga, I. (2013). Mobility of care: Introducing new concepts in urban transport. In I. Sánchez de Madariaga & M. Roberts (eds.), *Fair Shared Cities: The Impact of Gender Planning in Europe*. Surrey: Ashgate.

Sandercock, L. (2003). *Cosmopolis II: Mongrel Cities in the 21st Century*. London: Continuum.

Scheiner, J. (2014). Gendered key events in the life course: Effects on changes in travel mode choice over time. *Journal of Transport Geography*, 37, 47-60.

Schmucki, B. (2012). "If I walked on my own at night I stuck to well lit areas": Gendered spaces and urban transport in 20th Century Britain. *Research in Transportation Economics*, 34(1), 74-85.

Scholten, C., T. Friberg, & A. Sandén (2012). Re-reading time-geography from a gender perspective: Examples from gendered mobility. *Tijdschrift voor Economische en Sociale Geografie*, 103(5), 584-600.

Schüssler, F. (1992). *But She Said: Feminist Practices of Biblical Interpretation*. Boston, MA: Beacon Press.

Singtel Optus (2015). Working at Optus. Retrieved from http://www.optus.com.au/about/careers/working-at-optus

Skinner, C. (2003). *Running Around in Circles: Coordinating Childcare, Education and Work*. Bristol: Policy Press.

Steinle, A.T. (2006). Appearance and grooming standards as sex discrimination in the workplace. *Catholic University Law Review*, 56(1), 261-298.

Stotzer, R.L. (2009). Violence against transgender people: A review of United States data. *Aggression and Violent Behavior*, 14(3), 170-179.

Sweet, E.L. & S.O. Escalante (2010). Planning responds to gender violence: Evidence from Spain, Mexico and the United States. *Urban Studies*, 47(10), 2129-2147.

Transit Cooperative Research Program (2010). *TCRP Report 95 Traveler Response to Transportation System Changes: Chapter 19—Employer and Institutional TDM Strategies*. Washington, DC: Transportation Research Board.

Vanoutrive, T., E. Van De Vijver, L. Van Malderen, B. Jourquin, I. Thomas, A. Verhetsel & F. Witlox (2012). What determines carpooling to workplaces in Belgium: Location, organisation, or promotion? *Journal of Transport Geography*, 22, 77-86.

Victoria State Revenue Office (2014). *2013-14 Budget Update Amendments*. Retrieved from http://www.sro.vic.gov.au/cgl2014

Victoria Transport Policy Institute (2013). *Commute Trip Reduction*. Retrieved from http://www.vtpi.org/tdm/tdm9.htm

Victoria Transport Policy Institute (2014). *Guaranteed Ride Home*. Retrieved from http://www.vtpi.org/tdm/tdm18.htm

Walls, M., E. Safirova & Y. Jiang (2010). 'What drives telecommuting? Relative impact of worker demographics, employer characteristics, and job types. *Transportation Research Record*, 2010, 111-120.

Watts, J.H. (2009). "Allowed into a Man's World": Meanings of work–life balance. *Gender, Work and Organization*, 16(1), 37-57.

Wekerle, G.R. (2005). Gender planning in public transit. In S.F. Fainstein & L.J. Servon (eds), *Gender and Planning: A Reader* (pp. 275-295). New Brunswick: Rutgers University Press.

Wheatley, D. (2012). Work-life balance, travel-to-work, and the dual career household. *Personnel Review*, 41(6), 813-831.

Whipp, R. & M. Grieco (1989). Time, task and travel: Budgeting for interdependencies. In M. Grieco, L. Pickup & R. Whipp (eds.), *Gender, Transport and Employment: The Impact of Travel Constraints* (pp. 1-16). Aldershot: Avebury.

Deanna Grant-Smith is a Senior Lecturer in the QUT Business School, Queensland University of Technology, Australia. Deanna maintains an active research interest in gender issues associated with employment, transport, and urban planning and policy. Prior to an academic career, she worked in the government sector in transport policy and planning, and in organizational development.

Natalie Osborne is a lecturer in human geography and planning at Griffith University, Australia. Natalie's research on transition planning processes and social justice draws from radical and insurgent planning practices, emotional and feminist geographies, and critical and participatory epistemologies.

Paolo Marinelli is director of the transport policy consulting firm *go2team*. Paolo has over 25 years' experience developing, implementing and evaluating transport policies. Paolo has worked for the Australian and Queensland Governments and established the TravelSmart programme in Queensland. He is a PhD candidate at QUT Business School, Queensland University of Technology.

Domestic violence as a management challenge
How trade unions can help

Gemma Wibberley, Carol Jones, Anthony Bennett and Alison Hollinrake
University of Central Lancashire, UK

Domestic violence is a key workplace gender equality issue. Although domestic violence affects everyone, it is predominantly women who are the victims and who suffer from the most severe abuse. This chapter focuses on female employees in the United Kingdom. While rarely acknowledged in UK literature or practice, domestic violence can also affect women at work. It can hamper their performance, attendance and career development. Furthermore, perpetrators can continue the abuse at the workplace. Conversely the workplace can be a haven from domestic violence, offering support and resources. Yet far too often employers lack the capacity and capability to handle domestic violence, resulting in many victims losing their job. Our research explored the role played by trade unions in domestic violence cases, and found that representatives were a source of support for both victims and organizations in helping them better handle domestic violence in the workplace.

Domestic violence is a key workplace gender equality issue. Although domestic violence affects everyone, it is predominantly women who are the victims and who suffer from the most severe abuse. While rarely acknowledged in UK literature or practice, domestic violence can also affect women at work. It can hamper their performance, attendance and career development. Furthermore, perpetrators can continue the abuse at the workplace. While this chapter focuses on UK female employees, it is important to note that domestic violence and its horrific impact on women and their employment are global problems (Chappell and Di Martino, 2006).

Managing domestic violence is challenging for employers. Employers can support their staff to escape the violence, providing victims with financial independence and safe access to services and information (Faichnie, 2010). Best practice organizations also offer practical help, such as relocation and paid time off (Swanberg *et al.*, 2006, TUC, 2014). These employers are likely to have policies that acknowledge the impact of domestic violence, and recognize their role in addressing it. Others may want to help but lack the resources to handle cases. Also employees may not disclose to managers (Swanberg and Logan, 2005). In addition, many employers see domestic violence as a private issue, and do not recognize the legal, moral and business cases for more effectively supporting victims. Unfortunately, many victims are unsupported by their employers. In some cases, employees may face disciplinary sanctions as a result of the impact of the abuse upon their work (Atterbury, 1998).

Trade unions already play an important role in the area of domestic violence and can assist managers in handling domestic violence cases. They can provide resources for employers and representatives to support victims, raise awareness and influence policies. Trade union representatives can also assist employees directly in cases of domestic abuse impacting on their work (Parker and Elger, 2004).

However, there is limited specific knowledge of the role of trade unions in handling domestic abuse in the workplace (Atterbury, 1998; Parker and Elger, 2004; Foreman, 2006; Beecham, 2009; EHRC, 2009), which provided the impetus for the small-scale qualitative research project reported upon in this chapter. The research was based on in-depth interviews with 18 union representatives from a range of organizations. A key objective was to establish the support that they and their unions gave to their members who are experiencing domestic violence.

The findings demonstrate that representatives can be a source of support for both victims and organizations in helping them handle domestic violence in the workplace. In particular, they are able to support individual workers: as an avenue for disclosure; signposting members to other services; or representing them in disciplinary cases. They also have a strong role to play in working in partnership with management to help victims continue safely in work, and to make changes that benefit the wider workforce. The research also highlights the challenges for managers in dealing with domestic abuse cases, and argues that employers need to develop policies and practices to support managers.

The chapter begins with a discussion on domestic violence and the workplace, drawing on international and policy sources, due to the lack of UK academic studies in this field. The chapter goes on to describe the research study and present the findings, highlighting best practice. The conclusion discusses the implications for practice.

Domestic violence in the workplace

In the UK, domestic violence is defined as:

> Any incident or pattern of incidents of controlling, coercive, threatening behaviour, violence or abuse between those aged 16 or over who are or have been intimate partners or family members regardless of gender or sexuality. The abuse can encompass but is not limited to: psychological, physical, sexual, financial, emotional (Strickland 2013, p. 2).

It is a serious and widespread problem, with 30% of women and 16% of men in the UK suffering from domestic abuse during their lifetime (Bardens and Gay 2014, p. 2). Although it affects both genders, women are at a higher risk of experiencing domestic abuse and are more likely to suffer more severe abuse or die as a result (Hester, 2009). Refuge/Respect (2010, p. 19) state that approximately two women are killed every week as a result of domestic violence. Data from the Office of National Statistics (ONS, 2013) reveals that, contrary to popular belief, abuse affects women of all races, ages, sexualities, incomes, occupations and other personal characteristics.

There is a lack of UK academic literature on domestic violence in the workplace; however, policy and practitioner papers and literature from other regions reveal important issues. Evidence suggests that domestic violence can intrude into the workplace in a number of ways. The UK Equality and Human Rights Commission (EHRC) suggested that on average 10% of staff in every organization could be suffering from abuse (EHRC, 2010a, p. 5). A survey by the Trades Union Congress (TUC)[1] found that 13% of the respondents who were experiencing domestic violence said it continued while they were at work (TUC, 2014, p. 4).

This abuse can take many forms: for example, harassing the victim via phone or email; entering the workplace or stalking the surrounding premises such as staff car parks; and physically assaulting the employee (EHRC, 2010a; Refuge/Respect, 2010). This increases victims' fears for their safety (Faichnie, 2010). It is common for victims to report being prevented from going to work or having to take time off, due to threats, being locked in the house, sleep deprivation, destruction of work clothing, verbal abuse and/or being unable to use transportation (Swanberg and Logan, 2005; McFerran, 2011). Wettersten *et al.* (2004) report that children are often utilized to reduce victims' attendance at work, through threats or perpetrators' refusal to provide childcare.

Physical violence, and its resulting injury, have a major impact on victims' ability to work (Moe and Bell, 2004). At its most extreme there is a risk of staff being murdered during their commute or at the workplace, particularly at work sites that

---

1 The TUC is the umbrella organization for trade unions in the UK. They describe themselves as "the national trade union centre in the UK, representing the vast majority of organized workers" (TUC, https://www.tuc.org.uk/).

are accessible to the general public (Tiesman *et al.*, 2012). In the UK it has been suggested that one-third of deaths resulting from domestic violence take place on work premises.[2]

When at work, the majority of victims felt their abuse had a negative effect on their performance (Swanberg *et al.*, 2006). This is because of the physical and mental after-effects of the abuse, inability to concentrate, exhaustion and their ongoing fear (Wettersten *et al.*, 2004). This typically negatively affects an employee's performance, attendance and behaviour (Bell and Kober, 2008). Walby and Allen (2004, p. 38) highlight the severity of this impact in the UK, with more than 20% of women having to take time off work because of domestic abuse. The TUC survey found that 86% of those who had experienced domestic violence said it had affected their performance at work by making them feel distracted, tired or unwell (TUC, 2014, p. 5, Fig. 5). Unfortunately, domestic violence, and its serious impact on women and their employment, is an international issue (ILO, 2013a, b).

However, the workplace can support employees to escape the violence, providing victims with financial independence (TUC, 2014). Faichnie (2010) shows how work may also be a safe place to access services and information, such as refuges and shelters and the legal system. Furthermore, Beecham (2014) suggests some employees may perceive work as a "safe haven" away from the violence. Best practice organizations also offer practical help, such as relocation, paid time off, people to talk to (formally or informally), safety plans, flexibility around their work and working arrangements, and making it harder for perpetrators to contact victims (Swanberg *et al.*, 2006; TUC, 2014).

Unfortunately, many victims are unsupported by their employer. Staff may face disciplinary sanctions or dismissal because of the impact of the abuse upon their work, particularly if their attendance or performance declines (Walby and Allen, 2004; Faichnie, 2010). Swanberg and Logan (2005) report that some feel pressurized to resign. The EHRC (2009, p. 13) argues "[at] the time when a person is experiencing domestic violence their employment is most under jeopardy". The increased risk of female employees losing their job, just because they are suffering from domestic violence, thus reinforces and increases gender inequalities (Brown, 2008/09).

Managing domestic violence is challenging for employers. They may want to help but lack the specific knowledge, training or policies to handle cases (Parker and Elger, 2004; TUC, 2014). Managers may be fearful of potential negative outcomes if the organization tries to address a case and mishandles it (Brown, 2008/09). Alternatively, Chappell and Di Martino (2006) argue many employers see domestic violence as a private issue. This is reinforced by stereotypes and myths that blame the victim and suggest that domestic violence only happens to "other" people (Brown, 2008/09).

Organizations may also perceive costs or workplace pressures as disincentives to addressing abuse for individuals or more generally across the company (Samuel

2 Corporate Alliance Against Domestic Violence website (http://www.caadv.org.uk/why.php)

et al., 2011). Many employers do not recognize the legal, moral and business cases (Swanberg *et al.*, 2012) for more effectively supporting victims. Yet Walby (2009, p. 8) demonstrates domestic violence causes British businesses to lose at least £1.9 billion annually. This figure does not take into account the costs of replacing all the former employees who have left employment as a consequence of domestic violence.

Crucially, staff may not disclose that they are experiencing domestic violence to managers (Samuel *et al.*, 2011). Victims are typically reluctant to discuss the abuse in any setting because of fears that their disclosure will not remain confidential; have a negative impact upon their safety; or lead to an unsupportive response (Berry *et al.*, 2014). In the workplace, there is the added worry that disclosure will have a negative effect on one's career or job security, or will not make any difference (Swanberg and Logan, 2005; Faichnie, 2010). Parker and Elger (2004) suggest it is more likely that the manager will become aware of the situation through associated issues such as absence monitoring or poor work performance.

Overall, in addition to the moral case, there are substantial positive outcomes if organizations are able to handle domestic violence more appropriately including: lower costs; increased performance, productivity, morale and reputation; and the ability to retain staff (Swanberg *et al.*, 2006). The EHRC (2010b) calculated that employers could save over £15,000 per case if they managed it supportively. Furthermore, this support may save lives, give victims an opportunity to escape abuse and continue to maintain their employment (EHRC, 2009).

The role of trade unions in handling domestic violence cases

Trade unions have had a long-standing interest in providing services and support for victims of domestic violence, and representatives are well-placed to be able to discuss the scale and scope of support that is needed and to illuminate what remains a hidden problem for many victims. The limited evidence available suggests trade unions are supporting members in a variety of ways. These include:

- Negotiating for domestic violence policies
- Raising awareness and providing training
- Working collaboratively with stakeholders, especially domestic violence specialists
- Working to improve legislation and services
- Providing information about resources available to victims
- Supporting individual victims, practically and emotionally

- Encouraging employers to offer flexible working arrangements to those experiencing domestic violence (Atterbury, 1998; Parker and Elger, 2004; Foreman, 2006; Beecham, 2009; EHRC, 2009)

In the UK, UNISON[3] is frequently cited as demonstrating best practice in supporting members who are experiencing domestic violence, in particular through their work in developing workplace policies with employers (Elger and Parker, 2006; Foreman, 2006; Faichnie, 2010), and its campaign work (Beecham, 2009). UNISON provides a model workplace agreement on domestic violence and abuse, along with negotiating packs to assist representatives in their discussions with management (UNISON, 2014). Internationally, union action in Australia is seen as providing a useful model to adopt (TUC, 2014; ILO, 2013a and b). For example, Australian unions have negotiated for domestic violence clauses that entitle employees to paid leave and other rights, including that they will not face disciplinary action if their performance or attendance declines because of the abuse, and the right to request an array of flexible working conditions (Baird *et al.*, 2014).

It is, however, recognized that union representatives need more training and support for these practices to become more widespread (ILO, 2013b). Furthermore, it is vital that there are good relations between unions and members so that staff feel comfortable to disclose (Parker and Elger, 2004). It is argued that all unions should be helping victims avoid disciplinary action, through effective individual representation and collective negotiations for better workplace support (Atterbury, 1998), and awareness raising (ILO, 2013b).

Unfortunately, there has been little research that looks specifically at the role and experiences of UK trade unions in the area of domestic violence (Parker and Elger, 2004; Elger and Parker, 2006). This research therefore adds to our understanding of this issue and will provide insights into the support that union representatives offer members experiencing domestic violence. To put this in the context of the UK labour force, approximately 26% of the total workforce were union members in 2013. Furthermore, the proportion of women workers who were in a trade union was 28%, exceeding the 23% of all male workers who were union members (DfBIS, 2014, p. 5).

The research involved in-depth, semi-structured interviews with a sample of trade union representatives to explore their experiences of and views about the support given to victims of domestic violence in the workplace. The main objective was to develop our understanding of what is effective in handling domestic violence cases and the complexity of responding to victims.

In order to access trade union representatives, the researchers approached a TUC regional women's committee, and it very kindly offered access. Based on this initial contact a cross-section of unions in the region was contacted to participate in the research. Eighteen interviews were completed with union representatives and officers. They were drawn from a range of unions, and represent members across

---

3 A large trade union that represents workers in both the private and the public sector.

an array of industries, but to ensure confidentiality these will not be disclosed. All but one of the respondents was female. Most of the domestic abuse referred to by union representatives was experienced by female employees, but there were also a few cases experienced by male employees. All interviews lasted an hour on average and the interview transcripts were thematically analysed by the research team to explore key concepts and dominant issues.

The limitations of this research must be acknowledged. It was a small study, and only focused on the views of trade union representatives. Furthermore, the participants were self-selecting, and therefore were likely to have volunteered due to their experiences of supporting members experiencing domestic violence. We would not argue that these results are generalizable. However, due to the lack of specific literature in this area we believe it is valuable to share our findings to enable more light to be shed on this important subject. We recommend that future research be conducted with other organizational stakeholders such as line managers, HR practitioners and, where ethically appropriate, those who have experienced domestic violence.

Findings

The research suggests that domestic violence remains a "hidden issue" in the workplace (Chappell and Di Martino, 2006). Several interviewees noted that within their workplaces there continued to be a perception that domestic violence was a "private" matter:

> You will always get employers out there that say, "Well, that's your home life, this is your work life and that's got nothing to do with me." [Employers have] ... a duty of care to an individual while they're in their workplace and if they're saying that their partner's going to come in and it's going to have an impact ... [employers] need to help and support (Representative 17).

Respondents argued that domestic violence can affect both an individual employee and the wider workplace (see also EHRC, 2010a):

> It is going to have a major impact if say a member was in a situation where they are experiencing domestic violence at home because it is going to affect their demeanour, it's going to affect their confidence, it's going to affect maybe the level of time they take off work, it may have to be hidden with sick [leave], it could affect their performance because of the worries, the way they are at work (Representative 6).

The representatives' experiences highlighted that abuse can prevent an employee from getting to work (for example, through injury suffered or by tactics such as hiding keys or money needed to access transport) or it can make an employee late for work (for example, where childcare arrangements are disrupted).

The illusion that there is a clear boundary between home and work can be shattered very dramatically if the abuse continues when the employee is at work (Swanberg and Logan, 2005). Many of the interviewees had experiences of working with victims whose partners continued to abuse them even when they were at work and on work premises: "I've had people turning up and phoning, we've had to move [the member] to different workplaces. It's really a problem when they get stalked by a previous partner" (Representative 1).

These actions cause both stress and fear and can impact negatively on performance (Bell and Kober, 2008). This is not always understood by managers who may simply see an "underperforming" employee, as encapsulated in the following comment: "They're serving customers, they might say 'Gosh, that girl never smiles', but ... you don't know what's going through their minds or what they worry [about] ... or if they're ... going home to everything being sold" (Representative 2).

At other times the actions of perpetrators could be more overt and raise more obvious concerns about security and health and safety. Interviewees reinforced findings from previous studies by noting that workplaces, especially those with open access, such as retail environments and "public" spaces such as car parks, are areas where partners can easily access victims (Tiesman *et al.*, 2012).

In 2013 the EHRC and the Chartered Institute for Personnel and Development (CIPD) produced a guide for employers to advise them how to support employees who were experiencing domestic violence (EHRC/CIPD, 2013). This laid out clearly the steps organizations should take when developing and implementing a policy. These include: information for employees to enable them to identify domestic violence; outlining the specific roles and responsibilities of managers and HR; details of external sources of support and advice; and a commitment to provide training for all employees and to engage in awareness raising measures within the workplace. However, within our sample, although all of the organizations had a range of equality policies, in only a few cases were the interviewees aware that there was a specific policy on domestic violence. Interviewees felt that the "business case" needed to be presented to employers, and particularly that domestic violence policies could be a low cost but high impact initiative:

> We want you to have a clear written policy on this, we're not expecting you to put loads of money into it, we're not asking you to employ a whole load of staff to deliver it, we're just saying that we want you to be visibly supportive of people who've suffered domestic violence and we want that message to be filtered through your documents. If somebody raised it in that way, I think a lot of employers, given that there isn't ... a huge cost ... would be persuaded to do it (Representative 7).

A significant stumbling block in the effectiveness of many organizational responses to domestic violence is that access to support is predicated on an employee coming forward to discuss his or her personal circumstances. Unfortunately, victims are often very reluctant to disclose what they are experiencing to anyone (Samuel *et al.*, 2011). Several representatives described having been aware of people they worked with who they suspected were experiencing domestic violence but who would not speak about it.

The concerns that inhibit victims from disclosing the abuse at work are the same barriers that generally affect disclosure (Berry *et al.*, 2014); namely, shame, embarrassment, fears about confidentiality and the belief that being a victim of violence would in some way reflect badly on them. In workplaces these barriers are reinforced through the tendency for domestic violence to be seen as a "private" matter that should be kept at home, and worries that disclosure will alter how co-workers and managers see victims:

> [Disclosure] is a really difficult question because there is a lot of things that can go on in the workplace that prevent people from bringing it to our attention … management who might not feel comfortable talking to people… might be, once they've opened up and said, "Look I'm suffering from domestic violence", is it going to be the talk for everybody now? … it is embarrassing. … Management disclosing that they are suffering from domestic violence. So are they going to be undermined as a manager in that position? Is it going to be taken away? (Representative 10).

As this comment illustrates, managers themselves can also experience domestic violence and their organizational position could make them more reluctant to disclose. The positive self-image associated with managerial or professional work, combined with the enhanced workplace autonomy and access to greater financial resources, can also underpin personal coping strategies (Beecham, 2014). However, this can be a fragile and easily undermined position.

Without disclosure, representatives explained that not only are victims unable to access support, but they also risk coming into conflict with organizational rules around attendance and performance. There are a number of reasons why an employee who is experiencing domestic violence might have a pattern of increased absenteeism or low productivity. Interview findings reinforced international evidence (Wettersten *et al.*, 2004; Swanberg and Logan, 2005; McFerran, 2011), with examples of: employees who had been beaten and were physically unable to attend work; destruction of property, including work uniforms; taking away a phone so the employee cannot call in to work or conversely being called by the abuser demanding that the employee leaves work to meet them.

However, managers are rarely trained in responding to domestic violence; therefore they are unlikely to recognize that it could be a factor in erratic attendance. Managers' first response is more likely to implement absence procedures:

> Weekends are sort of like when they get the battering and then on Monday they're not able to come in to work…initially [management] were looking to put my member on the procedure with a view to dismissal for attendance management because they recognized there was a pattern emerging in terms of her attendance… she didn't share that [abuse] with them; she was just saying that she felt unwell (Representative 16).

Unfortunately respondents stated that because of the effects of the violence and employees' fears of disclosing the real reasons behind their absenteeism, managers often prescriptively follow attendance management policies, which can result in victims facing disciplinary action or even dismissal (Walby and Allen, 2004). Further challenges for organizations in handling domestic violence appropriately included: little understanding about domestic violence; limited aptitude in handling sensitive issues; unawareness that this is a "duty of care" issue.

The research suggested that trade union representatives were able to help organizations overcome some of these challenges (Parker and Elger, 2004). They could often access resources from their union that increased their understanding of the signs, risks and impacts of domestic abuse upon the workplace. Unions may also offer training for representatives to better support members who are victims. Representatives were also able to work with employers to introduce policies and procedures to address the impact of domestic violence in the workplace. Furthermore, most unions undertook awareness raising campaigns among members and representatives (TUC, 2014).

Through working together, managers and representatives appeared to increase their potential to handle cases more appropriately. Sometimes, victims first disclosed to the representative:

> [A] member … was just chatting when suddenly she was hysterical and said "I've got to tell you this" … And she just pulled up her jumper … oh my god she was bruised … in between the tears that she was able to start to tell me that she'd been experiencing domestic violence (Representative 16).

Representatives discussed that in some situations, with the agreement of the employee, the union had helped staff to raise their situation with management. In many cases, once they were made aware that domestic violence was affecting an employee, managers were understanding. Representatives then worked in partnership with the manager on changes in the workplace to help victims continue in work. This normally involved changes to work patterns, blocking access to a victim's work phones, and ensuring security was in place for when the victim came to and left work. Examples were also given where employees were allowed special time off, support from in-house occupational health teams, or, redeployment and financial assistance. The following quotes demonstrate the array of support good practice organizations do offer:

> So we negotiated a flexible start, a safe parking area to get from her car to work and a choice of entrance to the workplace just to try and make that a little bit safer for her (Representative 9).

> They supplied her … with a mobile phone that her husband knew nothing about … a second uniform to keep in a friend's house confidentially, so if she was thrown out of her home then … she could go to, to collect her uniform so she could still get to work, … as well as being obviously signposted for help (Representative 17).

> Give him extra support so there [were] people he could go and talk to, so he could go for counselling, so his manager knew, so his targets were reduced (Representative 4).

In cases where the employee's situation had resulted in them facing managerial action, representatives often talked about their ability to intervene to try to find a more appropriate course of action:

> I had a ... conversation with the senior manager, without breaking any confidentiality, and said this guy needs our help. He said, "Yeah, I can see that ... I'm going to do 'no further action' and leave it with you and we'll work to try and give him as much support and help as we can", which is what we did (Representative 4).

Representatives also discussed times when they had provided additional support to individual workers, signposting them to other services and support such as refuges and domestic violence services. They have also accessed additional assistance from the union, in one case enabling the employee to be re-housed.

It is important to acknowledge that a representative's ability to respond was generally reliant on that particular individual having a specific interest in domestic violence and being willing and able to take the case on. Additionally the representatives in the sample tended not to have specialized training and relied more on experiential knowledge. Furthermore, the ability of representatives to support staff is limited to those that are members of unions, and to organizations that recognize unions. However, our findings suggest that where present representatives did offer assistance to both employees and employers in handling domestic violence cases.

Conclusions

The chapter focuses on gender inequality in the workplace and offers real examples of good practice in terms of managing domestic violence at work, a still too often ignored but devastating situation confronting many millions of women workers every year, globally. A limitation is that not all organizations have unions. However, the strategies of supporting victims will still be of value to all organizations.

This is a small-scale study but there are, however, a number of points that emerge from this research that highlight the challenges for organizations in responding effectively to domestic violence. At the most basic level, this involves raising awareness within the workplace; respondents were concerned that this was a hidden issue for too many organizations and felt that this must change. Many of the representatives stated that their unions have been actively involved in such initiatives, such as developing communication and campaign materials, but should continue and increase their efforts to do so. Raising awareness also needs to include providing information on the support, both internally and externally to the organization, that employees can access should the need arise.

Within workplaces participants highlighted that there continues to be a lack of understanding concerning domestic violence. Few organizations have a specific domestic violence policy, as recommended above by EHRC/CIPD or UNISON, and most managers are unlikely to have had any specific training in relation to domestic violence. Even where there is a policy, interviewees felt there needs to be more practical advice about what both employees and managers can do in response to domestic violence. A "toolkit" approach guiding the individuals through the actions, support and processes, made freely available and well publicized (beyond an intranet) would be helpful in this respect. Unions often have materials that could support organizations in designing these toolkits, as outlined above.

Organizational responses tend at present to be reactive and ad hoc and although often positive, it requires a huge leap of faith for a victim of violence to disclose to anyone when it is unclear from the outset how this information will be received. Handling domestic violence cases, particularly their implications for absence management, should be included in managerial training.

Representatives can and do work in partnership with management to enable them to handle domestic violence in the workplace. They can access training and resources that increase their knowledge of abuse and how to respond to cases. Their role within the workplace enables representatives to offer an alternative route to disclosure; to help organizations implement workplace changes that will enable staff to remain safely at work; and to offer personalized support to victims.

This study has contributed to our understanding of the challenges of dealing with domestic abuse in British workplaces. It highlights that the problems experienced by women workers internationally (Swanberg and Logan, 2005; Chappell and Di Martino, 2006; ILO, 2013a, Baird *et al.*, 2014) are unfortunately repeated in the UK. They suffer from abuse at home and often perpetrators also access them at work to continue the abuse, having a detrimental impact upon their wellbeing and employment. Furthermore, organizations can struggle to handle these cases. Managers are often unaware of the realities of domestic violence and ill-equipped to address it. This puts victims at risk of losing their jobs and even their lives. It thus reinforces and increases gender inequalities. However, organizations can support their employees in dealing with domestic abuse, as illustrated above. The findings suggest that support appears more likely when managers and representatives work together to handle cases.

The research offers more detail on the experiences of trade union representatives in these cases, and demonstrates that they can have a substantial role to play in supporting both victims and managers. That is not to argue that all representatives offer the same level of support, as they too require a greater level of training and resources to consistently enable them to provide the most effective service.

The challenge remains for all employers to see that there is a business case for dealing with domestic violence that does not come at a huge cost but has huge benefits, as demonstrated above by EHRC (2010b) and Swanberg *et al.* (2012). Managers need the training and experience to deal with such cases. Employers need to develop fully functioning policies and practices to support managers. Trade union representatives should draw upon the resources of their unions to enable organizations to develop these policies, implement them effectively and offer the support that victims deserve.

References

Atterbury, J. (1998). Employment protection and domestic violence: Addressing abuse in the labor grievance process. *Journal of Dispute Resolution*, 2(3), 165-182.

Baird, M., McFerran, L. & I. Wright (2014). An equality bargaining breakthrough: Paid domestic violence leave. *Journal of Industrial Relations*, 56(2), 190-207.

Bardens, J. & O. Gay (2014). *Domestic Violence: Standard Note: SN/HA/6337*. London: House of Commons Library, Home Affairs Section.

Beecham, D. (2009). *The Impact of Intimate Partner Abuse on Women's Experiences of the Workplace: A Qualitative Study.* unpublished thesis, Warwick, UK: Warwick University.

Beecham, D. (2014). An exploration of the role of employment as a coping resource for women experiencing intimate partner abuse. *Violence and Victims*, 29(4), 594-606.

Bell, K. & C. Kober (2008). *The Financial Impact of Domestic Violence*. London: Family Welfare Association/ Gingerbread.

Berry, V., Stanley, N., Radford, L., McCarry, M. & C. Larkins (2014). *Building Effective Responses: An Independent Review of Violence against Women, Domestic Abuse and Sexual Violence Services in Wales.* Cardiff: Welsh Government Social Research.

Brown, J. (2008–2009). The costs of domestic violence in the employment arena: A call for legal reform and community-based education initiatives. *Virginia Journal of Social Policy & the Law*, 16(1), 1-45.

Chappell, D., & V. Di Martino (2006). *Violence at Work*, 3rd Edition. Washington, DC: International Labour Office.

DfBIS (2014). *Trade Union Membership 2013 Statistical Bulletin, May 2014.* Retrieved from www.gov.uk/government/uploads/system/uploads/attachment_data/file/313768/bis-14-p77-trade-union-membership-statistical-bulletin-2013.pdf

EHRC (2009). *Better Public Services: Breaking the Silence on Violence against Women.* Retrieved from https://www.ipcc.gov.uk/sites/default/files/Documents/smallbreaking-silenceonviolence.pdf

EHRC (2010a). *Domestic Abuse is Your Business: Employers Campaign Pack.* Retrieved from http://www.equalityhumanrights.com/publication/domestic-abuse-your-business-employers-campaign-pack

EHRC (2010b). *Domestic Abuse is Your Business: Bridget's Story—the Business Case for Having a Policy.* Retrieved from http://www.equalityhumanrights.com/en/publication-download/domestic-abuse-your-business-bridget%E2%80%99s-story-%E2%80%93-business-case-having-policy

EHRC/ CIPD (2013). *Managing and Supporting Employees Experiencing Domestic Abuse.* London: EHRC.

Elger, T. & A. Parker (2006). *Union Policies to Combat Domestic Violence: An Analysis of the Widening and Reframing of Union Agendas.* CCLS Working Paper 23, Warwick, UK: Warwick University.

Faichnie, C. (2010). *"Work was an Escape for Me": The Impact of Domestic Abuse on Employment.* Manchester, UK: Greater Manchester Employment Rights Advice Service.

Foreman, A. (2006). *Domestic Abuse and the Workplace: A Report Looking at the Impact of Domestic Abuse on Women's Employment.* Manchester, UK: Greater Manchester Employment Rights Advice Service.

Hester, M. (2009). *Who Does What to Whom? Gender and Domestic Violence Perpetrators.* Bristol, UK: University of Bristol in association with the Northern Rock Foundation.

ILO (2013a). *Impact of Domestic Violence in the Workplace: Joint Government of Australia/ ILO Side Event at the 57th Session of the CSW.* Retrieved from http://www.ilo.org/gender/ Events/WCMS_208336/lang–en/index.htm

ILO (2013b). *Commission on the Status of Women 57th Session, Australia/ILO Side Event on the Impact of Domestic Violence in the Workplace.* Retrieved from http://www. ilo.org/wcmsp5/groups/public/—dgreports/—gender/documents/briefingnote/ wcms_212746.pdf

McFerran, L. (2011). *Safe at Home, Safe at Work? National Domestic Violence and the Workplace Survey.* Australia: Centre for Gender Related Violence Studies UNSW.

Moe, A. & M. Bell (2004). Abject economics: The effects of battering and violence on women's work and employability. *Violence Against Women,* 10(1), 29-55.

ONS (2013). *ONS Focus on: Violent Crime and Sexual Offences, 2011/12 Coverage: England and Wales.* Retrieved from http://www.ons.gov.uk/ons/dcp171778_298904.pdf

Parker, A. & Elger, T. (2004). *Combating Domestic Violence: A Role for Workplace Union Organisation?* CCLS Working Paper 22, Warwick, UK: Warwick University.

Refuge/ Respect (2010). *Domestic Violence Resource Manual for Employers,* second edition. Retrieved from http://respect.uk.net/wp-content/uploads/2014/06/Respect.Refuge_ DV_Manual_A4_76pp.pdf

Samuel, L., Tudor, C., Weinstein, M., Moss, H. & N. Glass (2011). Employers' perceptions of intimate partner violence among a diverse workforce. *Safety and Health at Work,* 2(3), 250-259.

Strickland, P. (2013). *Domestic Violence: Standard Note: SN/HA/6337.* London: House of Commons Library, Home Affairs Section.

Swanberg, J., & T. Logan (2005). Domestic violence and employment: A qualitative study. *Journal of Occupational Health Psychology,* 10(1), 3-17.

Swanberg, J., Macke, C., & Logan, T. (2006). Intimate partner violence, women and work: Coping on the job. *Violence and Victims,* 21(5), 561-578.

Swanberg, J., Ojha, M. & C. Macke (2012). State employment protection statutes for victims of domestic violence: Public policy's response to domestic violence as an employment matter. *Journal of Interpersonal Violence,* 27(3), 587-619.

Tiesman, H., Gurka, K., Konda, S., Coben, J., and H. Amandus (2012). Workplace homicides among U.S. women: The role of intimate partner violence. *Annals of Epidemiology,* 22(4), 277-284.

TUC (2014). *Domestic Violence and the Workplace.* London: TUC.

UNISON (2014). *Domestic Violence and Abuse: A Trade Union Issue, A UNISON Guide, October 2014.* Retrieved from www.unison.org.uk/content/uploads/2014/10/On-line-Cata logue226662.pdf

Walby, S. (2009). *The Cost of Domestic Violence: Update 2009.* Lancaster, UK: Lancaster University.

Walby, S. & J. Allen (2004). *Domestic Violence, Sexual Assault and Stalking: Findings from the British Crime Survey.* London: Home Office.

Wettersten, K., Rudolph, S., Gallagher, K., Transgrud, H., Adams, K., & S. Graham (2004). Freedom through self-sufficiency: A qualitative examination of the impact of domestic violence on the working lives of women in shelter. *Journal of Counselling Psychology,* 51(4), 447-462.

Gemma Wibberley is a Research Associate at iROWE (Institute for Research into Organizations, Work and Employment), at the University of Central Lancashire. Her research interests include employees' experiences in the contemporary workplace, workplace conflict and relationships with unions.

Carol Jones is Division Leader for the Human Resource Management and Leadership Division and a member of iROWE, at the University of Central Lancashire. She has research interests in workplace conflict and in workplace violence, with specific reference to domestic violence.

After careers in data technology management, the union movement and then higher education, **Anthony Bennett** is now a freelance researcher and consultant with interests in conflict management, equality and diversity, employee engagement and employee representation. He is a trained and practising workplace mediator and writer on employee relations.

Alison Hollinrake is a Senior Lecturer in the HRM and Leadership Division and a member of iROWE at the University of Central Lancashire. Her research interests are human resource development, workplace learning, trade unions and learning. Alison is an active trade unionist, a trained and practising workplace mediator and business and executive coach.

10

Thinking outside the classroom to promote gender equality
A rationale and roadmap for translating service-learning to organizations

Meghan E. Norris
Saint Mary's University, Canada

Katelynn Carter-Rogers
Maastricht University, Netherlands

Organizations are unique in their cultures, and paths to gender equality may vary depending on context. The necessary solution for gender equality, therefore, may rely on the opportunities to provide organizations with contextualized insights into the dynamic barriers specific to that workplace, and the ability of that organization to identify creative and evidence-based solutions so that everyone can thrive in a dynamic context. This chapter presents the SOLL Model (The Service-, Operational, and Lecture Learning Model) as a guide for how to facilitate contextualized insights into barriers towards equality in the workplace. SOLL stresses the importance of content learning, skills practice and skill application through service-learning to facilitate thoughtful awareness of problems and credible mastery of relevant skills. Service-learning benefits include reduced stereotypes, increased

capacity for diversity and increased sense of social responsibility. Although designed for academic contexts, the current work is
the first initiative to translate SOLL into an applied organizational
learning method.

Mounting evidence demonstrates that there is gender inequality in the workplace (e.g. Catalyst, 2013; Lauzen, 2014; Sandberg, 2013; Statistics Canada, 2012;
Stone, 2007, 2013). Gender inequality is a complex issue and, as such, one size will
likely not fit all in terms of developing solutions within every organization. Context matters. This chapter identifies useful points of translation from the literature
on service-learning within education to organizations to provide a roadmap for
organizations looking to implement service-learning principles.

Introduction to service-learning

What is service-learning?

Service-learning is a pedagogy that attempts to combine meaningful community
service with experiential learning. Although scholars often debate the nuanced
definition of service-learning, it is typically accepted that service-learning is an
experiential learning paradigm that is intended to equally benefit the provider and
recipient (Furco, 1996). In service-learning engagements, providers (typically students) will work with a recipient (typically community organizations) to promote
mutual benefits: providers learn about real-world skill application challenges and
recipients benefit from knowledgeable providers assisting with a challenge the
organization is facing. Because providers and recipients can vary greatly in terms
of areas of expertise and need, service-learning is necessarily flexible.

A cornerstone of service-learning is active reflection where participants (ideally both providers and recipients) intentionally reflect critically on their experiences throughout the service-learning process (Eyler, 2002). Indeed, the hyphen in
the term service-learning is intentional among scholars; it serves as a reminder of
the necessary equality between provider and recipient (Migliore, 1995 as cited in
Jacoby, 2003), and a reminder about the importance of active reflection throughout
the service-learning process (Eyler, 2001). [1]

Benefits of service-learning

Service-learning is typically conducted in educational settings including high
schools, universities and business schools (Astin *et al.*, 2006; Cadwallader *et al.*,

---

1　For resources on service-learning, the National Service-Learning Clearinghouse is a good
resource (https://gsn.nylc.org/clearinghouse)

2013; Godfrey, 2000; Govekar and Rishi, 2007; Norris, 2014; Norris, in press). Through these initiatives, students engage in hands-on work within a community to facilitate student skill development in such a way that builds and strengthens the community. Service-learning initiatives have demonstrated a number of concrete positive outcomes. For example, participating in service-learning has been shown to increase awareness of social inequality (e.g. Everett, 1998) and increase civic participation on behalf of providers (e.g. Morgan and Streb, 2001). Notably, Everett (1998) has demonstrated that when 30 hours of service was mandatory for a course on social inequality and social stratification, 87% of students reported that the experience enhanced their understanding of social inequality. Research has also demonstrated a number of positive humanistic outcomes associated with service-learning: it helps providers to develop a new perspective of the world, new personal views related to stereotypes and ethnocentrism, and a better understanding of social and culture diversity (Astin *et al.*, 2000).

Reinforcing the benefits from service-learning engagements, in a thorough review of the research, Eyler *et al.* (2001) provide a comprehensive overview of positive outcomes associated with such service-learning initiatives. Specifically, as highlighted by Eyler *et al.* (2001), service-learning providers have been shown to demonstrate positive changes to personal outcomes including: increased senses of personal efficacy, moral development and leadership; positive changes to social outcomes including reduced stereotypes, increased racial understanding, increased commitment to service and increased social responsibility; important learning outcomes such as improved ability to apply course content to "real-world" situations, increased complexity of understanding and increased cognitive development; and an increased capacity for diversity.

Service-learning and gender inequality

In addition to many well-documented humanistic outcomes, some scholarly work has directly commented on the benefits of service-learning with respect to gender equality outcomes. Indeed, faculty involved in a service-learning initiative within an economics class directly reported students gaining insights into gender inequities: "Students, I believe … had eye opening experiences [with respect] to gender, racial, etc. inequities" (McGoldrick, 1998). Consistent with this insight, Schutz and Gere (1998) report on a service-learning project where a team of students directly tackled gender equality in the context of university athletics. Through this project, the students who initially intended to focus on the "fairness" of gender equality ended up developing a published paper in the student newspaper that instead highlighted their community's complicity in attitudes towards women's athletics. Thus, the project not only served to teach the students involved in the project about the complexity of gender equality issues, but it also prompted students to engage in their own dissemination of their findings. This is indeed a most impressive tangible outcome. Gender equality outcomes have been additionally noted in other work.

For example, in a Spanish language programme in the USA where students were placed with immigrant Mexican families, the host female heads of households were reported to learn and incorporate issues related to gender equality (Jorge, 2003).

When considering both global humanistic and specific gender equality outcomes associated with service-learning engagements, there appear to be powerful indicators that service-learning may be one path to make meaningful differences in both understandings of social barriers to gender equality and in the likelihood of change behaviours to promote gender equality.

Making a case for service-learning in industry

Service-learning in industry, although gaining in popularity, is largely a new frontier. The emerging data available to support this movement is promising, and is evident through corporate social responsibility initiatives including pro bono work and skills-based volunteering. PepsiCo's PepsiCorps is one notable example in this field. PepsiCo estimates that in 2012 over 33,000 volunteer hours were completed by PepsiCo employees globally (PepsiCo, 2015). These volunteer initiatives include a one-month volunteer-based effort when PepsiCo employees spent one month in Ghana working to improve access to safe water (PepsiCo, 2015). Another example is Project Ulysses, administered by PricewaterhouseCoopers (PwC). Through this initiative, nominated PwC members work with NGOs, social entrepreneurs or international organizations in developing countries to address significant problems including poverty and health. A number of positive outcomes have emerged from Project Ulysses including participant learning of responsible mind-set, ethical literacy, cultural intelligence, global mind-set, self-development and community building (Pless *et al.*, 2011).

In addition to community benefits from industry social responsibility initiatives, evidence of personal employee impact is apparent from interviews with professionals who have participated in skills-based volunteering through their employers. For example, Susan Wedge, a partner in IBM's Global Business Services Public Sector, was quoted by IBM after a group of IBM consultants travelled pro bono to Romania to assist with a project:

> When you are working with people who speak a different language and live in a different culture than you do, your sensitivity to communication is heightened in new ways... That is a learning experience that you bring back to your own more familiar work environment. It changes you (IBM, 2009, 2011).

Wedge is not alone in her feelings of personal change resulting from a work-related volunteer experience. After working in Kenya to promote malaria treatment, Katherine Scott, a Clinical Research Associate with GlaxoSmithKline, reported: "My volunteer experience provided lessons in working with people from different cultures and backgrounds that has deeply affected my sensitivity to more subtle differences among people with whom I work back home" (GlaxoSmithKline, 2013; Korngold, 2012).

   Although some may be sceptical of the authenticity of reports of change due to self-promotion biases within industry, the academic literature suggests that service-based initiatives can indeed lead to significant personal change. Industry examples of skills-based volunteering, such as those outlined above, thus appear to be emerging examples of how facilitating social responsibility within the workplace may result in positive moral and ethical outcomes.

Translating academic service-learning principles to the workplace

When considering the empirical evidence for positive service-learning out-comes in education in tandem with the industry-provided insights on employee responses to skills-based volunteering, a path emerges through which to formally apply service-learning principles in industry to facilitate community benefits and employee personal and professional growth. Within the field of higher education, the **Service, Operative, and Lecture Learning (SOLL) Model** (Norris, 2014) has been suggested as a template for developing successful service-learning initiatives (see Fig. 10.1). SOLL is a multi-level method of learning that focuses on outcomes across three learning domains: developing knowledge that can be transferred among con-texts; developing creative and critical thinking skills; and building bridges between evidence-based research and application. Learning across these three domains should occur at three levels: the content level, the skills level and the applied level. Within the higher education system, these levels of learning are discussed in terms of learning in lectures (the content level), operative laboratory sessions (the skills level) and through service-learning (the application level). When translating this model to industry, it is important to be aware that the mode of education is less important than the nature of education. That is, learning should occur at a content level, a skills level and an application level in whatever way is most effective given the context. Concrete examples are provided below.

Figure 10.1 **The SOLL framework for developing multidisciplinary curricula in higher education**

Source: Norris (2014).

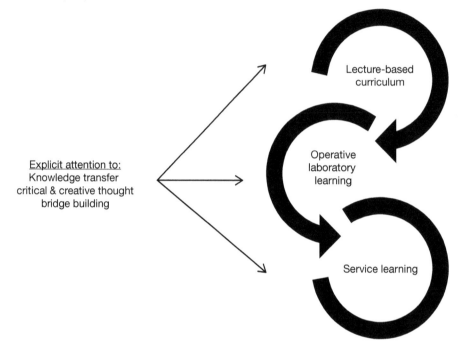

Understanding SOLL

Domain 1: Developing knowledge that can be transferred among contexts

Being educated in a certain field does not mean that one has the ability to take the knowledge learned and apply it effectively. Indeed, there is some speculation that learning content in discrete classroom-style experiences leads to something called fragmented learning. Fragmented learning is when pieces of information are learned, but there is a lack of ability to build connections among those pieces of information, and a lack of ability to facilitate application (e.g. Berryman, 1991). This challenge is elegantly demonstrated by the following quote:

> From a very early age, we are taught to break apart problems, to fragment the world. This apparently makes complex tasks and subjects more manageable, but we pay a hidden, enormous price. We can no longer see the consequences of our actions; we lose our intrinsic sense of connection to a larger whole. When we try to "see the big picture," we try to reassemble the fragments in our minds, to list and organize all the pieces. But, as physicist David Bohm says, the task is futile—similar to trying to reassemble the fragments of a broken mirror to see a true reflection. Thus, after a while we give up trying to see the whole altogether (Senge, 1990, p. 3).

To prevent this, a goal of the SOLL model is to foster the learning of content in such a way that points of application can be identified so that the content knowledge can be remembered and effectively translated.

Domain 2: Developing creative and critical thinking skills

Critical thinking is an often used concept. Although the academic definition of critical thinking varies (Kennedy *et al.*, 1991), it is commonly accepted that critical thinking encompasses the ability to both identify and analyse a problem to identify a solution (Pithers and Soden, 2000). Traditionally left out of the definition of critical thinking is *creative* thinking. Creativity is the ability to construct something, and this need not be artistic. Indeed, we argue that generating innovative solutions requires creativity, in addition to critical evaluation of that solution based on available evidence. The bridge between creative and critical thinking for skill application is only beginning to gain attention within the literature (e.g. Gruenfield, 2010), yet industry has already highlighted the importance of creative thinking time for solution generation. For example, Google allows employees a day per week (20% of their time) to pursue their work-related interests, 3M allows 15% of time to be spent on innovation (Baldwin, 2012). Further, companies like Facebook, Apple and LinkedIn also reportedly allow for innovation time (Tate, 2013). The University of Pennsylvania has "Exploration Days" once per year to allow IT employees time for creative solution generation (Baldwin, 2012). As yet, there remains a lack of publicly available empirical evidence for outcomes associated with these creativity days, and this is an important opportunity for future research. Perhaps more importantly, there is a dearth of acknowledgement on how to facilitate and evaluate connections between creative solution generation and critical thinking. Table 10.1 provides suggestions for how to accomplish this in the field of gender inequality.

Domain 3: Building bridges between evidence-based research and application

Unfortunately, academics have often been accused of residing in an "ivory tower" (e.g. Schön, 1983). For example, academics may not have the experience to have insight into real-world problems at the same level of abstraction as a front-line worker. For this reason, we take the stance that effective practices are built not only on evidence-based research, but also on experiential learning that allows for an understanding of context effects including, but not limited to, cultural context, political climate within and outside of the organization, and available resources. It very well may be that despite evidence-based knowledge of best practice, front-line workers do not have access to assumed resources. Thus, creative solution generation is needed that can be critically evaluated for efficacy, built upon a thorough and comprehensive basic understanding of the problem.

To most successfully fulfil the three domain outcomes of developing knowledge that can be transferred among contexts, developing creative and critical thinking skills, and building bridges between evidence-based research and application, learning experiences should occur at each of three learning levels: 1) the content level (where information is gathered and retained); 2) the skill creation and development level (achieved in practice sessions where mistakes can be treated as opportunities for future growth); and 3) the skill application level (achieved through skill application in a service-learning context). The following overview of learning levels includes a comprehensive table that describes how each level of learning can be achieved across the three domains.

Learning level 1: Content—lecture learning in the workplace

In higher education, set times occur at which students are provided with large amounts of engagement-relevant information via a lecture. Within the workplace, although employers may host workshops, there is likely a higher expectation on employees to gather information on issues of interest. This is perhaps especially true when considering issues that may not be directly relevant to the product or service being provided by the organization, as would be the case with respect to gender inequality and barriers to gender equality. This pursuit of knowledge may be achieved through various avenues including, but not limited to, ongoing continuing education, self-directed knowledge pursuit, and personal experience. It is important to clearly define the problem to be addressed at this phase so that information gathering can be targeted to the issue of interest.

Although not necessary, it is recommended that attitudes toward the problem statement are measured prior to engaging in Level 1 content learning. This is so that attitudes can be re-measured at the end of the engagement process to determine whether attitude change has taken place. Within the field of social psychology, attitudes are considered overall evaluations of some object (Petty and Cacioppo, 1996). Attitudes are often discussed as having primarily **affective** (emotion) or **cognitive** (thought/belief) bases. Attitudes may also be more global in nature (e.g. Fabrigar and Petty, 1999). It is recommended that when measuring attitudes, these affective and cognitive bases of attitudes be specifically measured, as suggested by Crites *et al.* (1994). When these attitude bases are known, it is possible to develop more successful messaging campaigns related to any identified contextual issues and to potentially develop more targeted and effective engagement opportunities for overcoming identified barriers (see Fabrigar and Petty, 1999).

Learning level 2: Skill development—operative learning in the workplace

Once content knowledge has been attained across all three domains, providers are in a strong position from which to begin developing applied skills. Borrowing from the mathematical literature, having a chance to make mistakes relatively free from consequences when practising new skills provides a "springboard" for future inquiries (Borasi, 1994; Brown and Callahan, 1985). In the education system, with careful application, laboratory-style learning can be effective at teaching skills at least in science-based disciplines (Hofstein and Lunetta, 2004). Within an organization, laboratories for skill development are likely to be scarce. As one alternative, research has demonstrated the ability for comprehensive case study evaluation to increase ethical considerations within management (Laditka and Houck, 2006). To make this learning level relevant, organizations would perhaps benefit most from identifying competitors and then comparing and contrasting on identified points of most interest. This method is an extension of the retailing model of "Look, Compare, Innovate" when doing self-business assessments (Bell and Ternus, 2006). Table 10.1 provides concrete examples of skill development across all three domains.

Learning level 3: Application—service-learning in the workplace

Once providers have both content and skill expertise, they are better equipped to engage in skill application through service-learning. Recall that service-learning is one way of allowing providers to *experientially* understand a problem, and to apply relevant skills. With respect to the engagement, providers must be thoughtful about the best recipient with whom to work. In Level 1, a critical first step is identifying the problem/content area to be addressed. This is so that the foundational work being done in Levels 1 and 2 can comprehensively support this final level of skill application. With respect to gender inequality in the workplace, this may mean that the engagement focuses on only one aspect of the complex problem. Table 10.1 provides a concrete example of such an engagement initiative.

A challenge with service-learning is that the identified problem to be solved will vary greatly depending on the organization, the current cultural climate and available resources. Thus, this guide is intentionally flexible, recognizing that each organization has its own context to work within. Using gender inequality as a focus, Table 10.1 provides a guide for how to adapt and apply SOLL principles within an organization. The predominant skill being developed in this example is the skill of empathy. Empathy is the ability to relate to and understand experiences that others have. Empathy is not sympathy. Sympathy involves an "I've been there" perspective. Empathy does not require one to have similar experiences, but rather to view a situation through the lens of another. When considering social injustice issues such as gender inequality, empathy is thus a helpful skill for development. For detailed instructions of how to facilitate development of empathy skills in the workplace, see Gentry *et al.* (2007).

Just as attitudes toward the problem were measured in Level 1, attitudes should be re-measured following Level 3. This will allow formal testing to see whether attitude changes have occurred at the affective, cognitive and/or general level.

Table 10.1 **A general guide for applying service-learning principles to industry**

	Domain 1: Translational Knowledge	Domain 2: Creative and critical thinking	Domain 3: Building bridges between research and application
Level 1: Content *Knowledge gathering in place of lecture learning* This phase should be done well in advance of the beginning of the hands-on initiative. It is recommended that this phase is completed 2–4 months prior to the hands-on initiative to allow those involved time to become comfortable with the idea of looking within.	Clearly define the problem to be addressed by the initiative Provide concrete evidence when defining the problem to highlight the impact of the problem. For example, "75% of women are leaving the organization within 5 years of joining" Disseminate this defined problem and related evidence to all involved well ahead of the initiative Gather knowledge regarding perceived barriers that are tied to the problem from multiple sources most directly impacted by the barrier. For example, one might inquire about barriers to long-term employment from both junior and senior female employees, and those who work with them *All responses should be anonymous at this stage to promote honest responding	Encourage employees to privately reflect on their knee-jerk reactions to the identified barriers Foster a non-judgemental environment. This phase is not intended to be judgmental; rather it is intended to cultivate mindfulness of current reactions to the barriers prior to any engagement initiation Encourage employees to write down their thoughts through private journalling so that they can be revisited at the end of the process	Encourage participants to independently consult past research regarding perceived barriers to determine any evidence-supported insights Allow a venue for employees to forward these findings to the group, along with any comments they would like to share at this point Create a private web forum with anonymous accounts to facilitate open and honest sharing Anonymously measure provider attitudes toward the problem to measure for initiative success

Level 2: Skill development *Operative learning* At this point, there is a transition from knowledge gathering to skill development. Knowledge gathering is encouraged to continue as appropriate, but the main focus of the engagement shifts. It is recommended that this phase take place 0–2 months before the hands-on initiative.	Highlight instances of successful skill application in other domains, and within other organizations/competitors Compare and contrast between the current engagement opportunity and other identified successful organizations. For example, if other organizations have lower female attrition rates, what are they doing differently from you? What are they doing that is the same? At what levels are the similarities and differences? Identify gaps in needed skills and identify evidence-based ways to fill that gap (e.g. workshops, consultants, self-study, etc.)	Engage those involved in anonymous brainstorming of creative and out-of-the-box ways to overcome anticipated barriers Encourage those brainstorming to critically evaluate their own ideas through the lens of their colleagues. *Why and why not* might this idea be a good one? Encourage reflection on both thoughts and feelings related to generated solutions Remind those involved that this phase is a development phase intended to teach empathy and perspective taking. Participants should be made to feel comfortable generating ideas and then critically evaluating their own solutions through the lens of their colleagues. Depending on the workplace culture, this phase may need to be done anonymously for honest responding. An anonymous, but locked, web forum may be an appropriate place for such a discussion if face-to-face discussions would be hostile	Link successful skill application identified in Domain 1, and compare against published data. Reflect on any discrepancies between academic and applied examples, and note where creatively brainstormed ideas do and do not fit with research Identify areas where your organization is able to improve or capitalize on an identified gap based on your comparison

	Domain 1: Translational Knowledge	Domain 2: Creative and critical thinking	Domain 3: Building bridges between research and application
Level 3: Skill application *Applied service-learning* It is recommended that this phase only occur after the appropriate groundwork has been conducted. Especially with respect to gender inequality, concerns of stigma are associated with various interventions. Engaging in hands-on initiatives without the proper preparation can result in a negative outcome. If you've done the background but the initiative feels forced, invite the group to return to Level 1. It may be that underlying concerns were not brought up as a result of mistrust, misunderstanding or inability to elucidate the concern. Taking the time to return to earlier phases where appropriate should facilitate trust and participation	Revisit the goals of the initiative Ensure engagement opportunity matches the problem defined in Level 1. For example, if the problem is that "75% of women are leaving the organization within 5 years of joining", be specific and intentional in the ways that the proposed engagement initiative is expected to shed light on this issue. Job shadowing one employee for one day is not likely to shed light on a potential 5-year problem that may vary depending on career timeline. Facilitate knowledge transfer by exploring the applied problem from multiple perspectives. As the provider, you might say, "I want to do X so that you can see what I see" Remind participants to practice empathy skills learned in Level 2 Reinforce the goal of understanding resolving the problem	Brainstorm creative solutions to identified barriers after those barriers have been experienced first-hand. Explicitly discuss how *anticipated* barriers are (in)consistent with *experienced* barriers Facilitate a cooperative environment where solutions are generated that address the barrier, and where constructive critical evaluation of solutions is welcomed Encourage participants to privately reflect back on their journals from Level 1 and 2 What has changed about their evaluation of the barrier? Has there been a shift in the nature of solutions generated?	Evaluate generated solutions against published data and competitors Will this solution be a trail blazing solution? If so, what are potential risks? Is there any reason to believe that the generated solutions will create increased or new barriers? Generate a list of concrete steps to implement chosen strategies Present strategies for change as a united front to the larger organization Re-measure attitudes and compare against the Level 1 attitude measurement to assess for provider attitude changes

Implementation challenges and solutions

Despite many positive outcomes associated with service-learning, there are road-blocks to implementation that warrant consideration. For example, at least among business students, there is a perception that service-learning is "less attractive" in comparison to other methods of learning (i.e. internships, case analysis, discussions) (Karns, 2005). Some service-learning providers report that volunteered hours are being wasted because they personally feel that the volunteer work is not related to business or marketing (Kohls, 1996; Kolenko *et al.*, 1996). In the case of gender inequality, a risk is that employees may not be aware of more subtle forms of gender inequality (e.g. Lundeberg, 1997), and thus might initially feel that the process is a waste of time. Although this position is likely to change by the end of the process, it certainly makes beginning the process challenging. Additionally, there may be discomfort in confronting personal beliefs or in openly accepting that one (un)intentionally played a role in the defined problem. Thus, it is crucial to create dedicated time to thoroughly prepare for the determined initiative in Level 1. For example, developing a thorough content knowledge base surrounding the problem, whether participants agree with the content or not, gives participants shared background knowledge from which to begin discussions.

In addition to overcoming potential discomfort of those participating in the service-learning process, providers need the support of upper level management for these initiatives to be successful. These initiatives are resource intensive, and thus must be supported by those who control the resources. Based on experience, a clearly defined and data supported problem statement from Level 1 is a necessary (albeit insufficient) condition for gaining this support. Admittedly, for these initiatives to be successful, those controlling the resources have to be committed to change and open to learning.

A strength and weakness in service-learning implementation and research is that each service-learning engagement inherently looks very different, as matches between providers and recipients can vary depending on contextual needs. A clearly defined problem statement is required. If the chosen application engagement does not match with the identified problem, learning that addresses that problem is unlikely to occur.

Throughout the chapter, we have highlighted the importance of reflection. What we have not detailed is the many methods for reflection including journalling, intentional considering of (non)ethical case studies and discussions. There are many options, and readers are encouraged to see Bringle and Hatcher (1999) for examples of possible reflection methods. Regardless of the nature of reflection, providers must be aware of potential risks associated with reflection (see Rodgers, 2002 and Boud and Walker, 1998). For example, if an employee discloses too much through reflection and that reflection is not private, there could be implications for job security, discomfort within the workplace and potentially negative relationships ensuing. For that reason, within the workplace it is recommended that reflections are private, or that it is very clearly understood that reflections will be read by others. If choosing to de-identify reflections for sharing, ensure that hand-writing cannot be identified, and ensure that disclosure through the reflection does not inadvertently identify the participant.

Reflection admittedly may sound "hokey", and the first author was reluctant to buy in to the value of reflections. First-hand experience with reflections done in a safe space revolutionized how the first author has come to think about the value of reflection. When undertaken with care, reflection has been demonstrated to facilitate meaning-making resulting from experiences, to update beliefs to fit with new experiences, and to facilitate insights into problem solving; thus we see it as an integral piece of the process (see Mezirow, 1990, for a review). Indeed, specific to service-learning initiatives, reflection has been shown to promote deeper learning among academic, social, moral, personal and civic dimensions (Hatcher *et al.*, 2004, p. 39). Furthermore, service-learning participants who engaged in reflection reported greater learning as a result of the project (Eyler *et al.*, 1996). These reflections can be private, but are encouraged for all who are involved in the initiative, even those leading. Organizations might consider providing participants with journals specifically devoted to reflection to demonstrate commitment to this part of the process.

Future directions

There is a clear need and growing call for organizations to engage in initiatives that promote community benefits, and that allow for experiential learning on behalf of those within the organizations. Large organizations are beginning to answer this call through skills-based volunteering, but there is no formal process in place to ensure that these initiatives are grounded by comprehensive understanding of the domain, that the initiatives foster creative and critical problem solving, or that they are connected with the larger academic empirical literature. Furthermore, although service-learning efficacy has been demonstrated in academia, there has been scant data published on the ability of these engagements to facilitate goals within organizations. Rather than viewing this lack of data as a drawback, we see this as an open opportunity for delineating and justifying a new path to facilitate gender equality in an evidence-based way. This chapter takes a first step in laying out a clear format for how to approach change from an organizational perspective, in such a way that identifies and attenuates barriers to gender inequality within the workplace, and that intentionally measures for efficacy during the process. This format is adapted from the SOLL model of service-learning suggested for implementation in business schools (Norris, 2014).

Business schools and business are two very different venues. Indeed, students necessarily graduate or leave their programme. Students have many classes and may be able to avoid colleagues who create barriers. The workplace provides no such easy escape, which creates a new tension when seeking change. Looking within at clearly identified problems can be very uncomfortable, especially as employees may learn they were unintentionally complicit in the problem. As with any new framework, this model is still developing. Service-learning outcomes are currently being explored in both graduate and undergraduate higher education within the United States and Canada. For example, research is currently being conducted to determine the effects of service-learning on ethical beliefs, perceived responsibility for outcomes, the degree of knowledge complexity and understanding surrounding ethical issues, and attitudes towards specific issues among graduate students. Similar research can be conducted in organizations which embrace a service-learning model.

In conclusion, service-learning engagements have resulted in a number of positive outcomes for students, communities and within organizations. These include an increased sense of self-efficacy, increased political engagement, reduced stereotypes and increased capacity for diversity (e.g. Eyler *et al.*, 2001). There is an opportunity to extend this pedagogy in a very meaningful way to address gender equality within the workplace. Service-learning, when conducted within a SOLL-model framework, provides an opportunity for skill development and application that is based on a comprehensive foundation of evidence-based, problem-related knowledge that can be applied creatively in ways supported by critical thinking. Through intentional application of service-learning engagements, data can be collected throughout the process to concretely identify effective methods within and across organizations.

References

Astin, A. W., Vogelgesang, L., Ikeda, E., & Yee, J. (2000). *How Service Learning Affects Students*. Los Angeles, CA: Higher Education Research Institute, UCLA.

Astin, A. W., Vogelgesang, L. V., Misa, K., Anderson, J., Denson, N., Jayakumar, U., Saenz, V., & Yamamura, E. (2006). *Understanding the Effects of Service-Learning: A Student of Students and Faculty*. Report to the Atlantic Philanthropies, Los Angeles, CA: Higher Education Research Institute, Graduate School of Education and Information Studies, University of California.

Baldwin, H. (2012). Time off to innovate: Good idea or a waste of tech talent? Computer World. Retrieved from http://www.computerworld.com/article/2506129/it-management/time-off-to-innovate–good-idea-or-a-waste-of-tech-talent-.html?page=2

Bell, J. A., & Ternus, K. (2006). *Silent Selling: Best Practices and Effective Strategies in Visual Merchandising*. Fairchild Publications, Incorporated.

Berryman, S. E. (1991). *Designing Effective Learning Environments: Cognitive Apprenticeship Models*. ERIC Clearinghouse

Borasi, R. (1994). Capitalizing on errors as "springboards for inquiry": A teaching experiment. *Journal for Research in Mathematics Education*, 166-208.

Boud, D., & Walker, D. (1998). Promoting reflection in professional courses: The challenge of context. *Studies in Higher Education*, 23(2), 191.

Bringle, R. G., & Hatcher, J. A. (1999). Reflection in service learning: Making meaning or experience. *Educational Horizons*, 179.

Brown, S. & Callahan, L. (1985). Using errors as springboards for the learning of mathematics [Special issue]. *Focus on Learning Problems in Mathematics*, 7.

Cadwallader, S., Atwong, C., & Lebard, A. (2013). Proposing community-based learning in the marketing curriculum. *Marketing Education Review*, 23(2), 137-149.

Catalyst (2013). *Fortune 500: Women Board Directors*. Retrieved from: http://www.catalyst.org/system/files/2013_catalyst_census_fortune_500_women_board_director.pdf

Crites, S., Fabrigar, L., & Petty, R. E. (1994). Measuring the affective and cognitive properties of attitudes: Conceptual and methodological issues. *Personality and Social Psychology Bulletin*, 20, 619-634.

Everett, K. D. (1998). Understanding social inequality through Service Learning. *Teaching Sociology*, 26(4), 299-309.

Eyler, J. (2001). Creating your reflection map. *New Directions for Higher Education*, 114, 35-43.

Eyler, J. (2002). Reflection: Linking service and learning—Linking students and communities. *Journal of Social Issues*, 58(3), 517-534.

Eyler, J., Giles, D. E., Jr., & Schmiede, A. (1996). *A Practitioner's Guide to Reflection in Service-Learning: Student Voices and Reflections*. Nashville, TN: Vanderbilt.

Eyler, J., Giles, D. E., Jr, Stenson, C. M. & Gray, C. J. (2001). *At a Glance: What We Know about the Effects of Service-Learning on College Students, Faculty, Institutions and Communities, 1993–2000* (3rd ed.). Retrieved from https://www.mnsu.edu/cetl/academicservicelearning/Service-Learning.pdf

Fabrigar, L.R., & Petty, R.E. (1999). The role of the affective and cognitive bases of attitudes in susceptibility to affectively and cognitively based persuasion. *Personality and Social Psychology Bulletin*, 25, 363-381.

Furco, A. (1996). Service-learning: a balanced approach to experiential education. In Taylor, B. and Corporation for National Service (Eds.), *Expanding Boundaries: Serving and Learning* (pp. 2-6). Washington, DC: Corporation for National Service.

Gentry, W. A., Weber, T. J., & Sadri, G. (2007). *Empathy in the Workplace: A Tool for Effective Leadership*. Center for Creative Leadership. Retrieved from: http://www.ccl.org/Leadership/pdf/research/EmpathyInTheWorkplace.pdf

GlaxoSmithKline (2013). *Our Commitment to Fighting Malaria*. Retrieved from http://uk.gsk.com/media/300090/Malaria_factsheet_finalv2.pdf

Godfrey, P. C. (2000). A moral argument for service-learning in management education. In P. C. Godfrey, & E. T. Grasso, (Eds.), *Working for the Common Good: Concepts and Models for Service-Learning in Management* (pp. 21-42). Washington, DC: American Association for Higher Education.

Govekar, M. A., & Rishi, M. (2007). Service learning: Bringing real-world education into the B- school classroom. *Journal of Education for Business*, 1-10.

Gruenfeld, E. (2010). Thinking creatively is thinking critically. *New Directions for Youth Development*, 125, 71-83.

Hatcher, J. A., Bringle, R. G., & Muthiah, R. (2004). Designing effective reflection: What matters to service-learning? *Michigan Journal of Community Service Learning*, 11(1), 38-46.

Hofstein, A. & Lunetta, V. N. (2004). The laboratory in science education: Foundations for the twenty-first century. *Science Education*, 88, 28-54.

IBM (2009). *IBM Corporate Citizenship in Romania*. Retrieved from: https://www.ibm.com/ibm/responsibility/downloads/profiles/Profile_Romania.pdf

IBM (2011). *IBM's Corporate Service Corps: A New Model for Global Leadership Development*. Retrieved from: http://www.ibm.com/ibm/responsibility/corporateservicecorps/press/2011_16.html

Jacoby, B. (2003). Fundamentals of service-learning partnerships. *Building Partnerships for Service-Learning*, 1-19.

Jorge, E. (2003). Outcomes for community partners in an unmediated service-learning program. *Michigan Journal of Community Service Learning*, 10(1), 28-38.

Karns, G. (2005). An update of marketing student perceptions of learning activities: Structure, preferences and effectiveness. *Journal of Marketing Education*, 27(2), 163-171.

Kennedy, M., Fisher, M. B. & Ennis, R. H. (1991). Critical thinking: Literature review and needed research. Educational values and cognitive instruction: *Implications for Reform*, 11-40.

Kohls, J. (1996). Student experiences with service learning in a business ethics course. *Journal of Business Ethics*, 15(1), 45-57.

Kolenko, T. A., Porter, G., Wheatley, W., & Colby, M. (1996). A critique of service learning projects in management education: Pedagogical foundations, barriers and guidelines. *Journal of Business Ethics*, 15(1), 133-142.

Korngold, A. (2012). *International Corporate Volunteering: Experiential Learning Advances Diversity and Communications*. Fast Company. Retrieved from: http://www.fastcompany.com/1834193/international-corporate-volunteering-experiential-learning-advances-diversity-and-communicate

Laditka, S. B., & Houck, M. M. (2006). Student-developed case studies: An experiential approach for teaching ethics in management. *Journal of Business Ethics*, 64(2), 157-167.

Lauzen, M. M. (2014). *Boxed In: Employment of Behind-The-Scenes and On-Screen Women in 2013–2014 Prime-time Television*. Retrieved from: http://womenintvfilm.sdsu.edu/files/2013-14_Boxed_In_Report.pdf

Lundeberg, M. A. (1997). You guys are overreacting: Teaching prospective teachers about subtle gender bias. *Journal of Teacher Education*, 48(1), 55.

McGoldrick, K. (1998). Service-learning in economics: A detailed application. *The Journal of Economic Education*, 29(4), 365-376.

Mezirow, J. (1990). How critical reflection triggers transformative learning. *Fostering Critical Reflection in Adulthood*, 1-20.

Morgan, W., & Streb, M. (2001). Building citizenship: How student voice in service-learning develops civic values. *Social Science Quarterly*, 82(1), 154-169.

Norris, M.E. (in press). Fostering student credibility through sustainable engagement initiatives: The Service-, Operative-, and Lecture-Learning (SOLL) Model. *Journal of Service-Learning in Higher Education*.

Norris, M.E. (2014). Embracing humanism in international business education: An application of the Service, Operative, and Lecture Learning (SOLL) model. In N. Lupton and M. Pirson (Eds.), *Humanistic Management in the Era of Globalization* (pp. 213-228). Basingstoke, UK: Palgrave Macmillan.

PepsiCo (2015). *Community Service & Volunteering*. Retrieved from: http://www.pepsico.com/purpose/global-citizenship/community-service-and-volunteering

Petty, R. E., & Cacioppo, J. T. (1996). *Attitudes and Persuasion: Classic and Contemporary Approaches*. Boulder, CO: Westview Press.

Pithers, R. & Soden, R. (2000). Critical thinking in education: A review. *Educational Research*, 42, 237-249.

Pless, N. M., Maak, T., & Stahl, G. K. (2011). Developing responsible global leaders through international service learning programs: The Ulysses experience at PricewaterhouseCoopers. *Academy of Management Learning & Education*, 10, 237-260.

Rodgers, C. (2002). Defining reflection: Another look at John Dewey and reflective thinking. *The Teachers College Record*, 104(4), 842-866.

Sandberg, S. (2013). *Lean in: Women, Work, and the Will to Lead*. New York, NY: Knopf.

Schön, D. A. (1983). *The Reflective Practitioner: How Professionals Think in Action*. New York: Basic Books.

Schutz, A., & Gere, A. R. (1998). Service learning and English studies: Rethinking "public" service. *College English*, 60(2), 129-149.

Senge, P.M. (1990). *The Fifth Discipline: The Art & Practice of the Learning Organization*. New York: Doubleday/Currency.

Statistics Canada (2012). *Labour Force Survey Estimates (LFS), by National Occupational Classification for Statistics (NOC-S) and Sex, Unadjusted for Seasonality*. Retrieved from: http://www5.statcan.gc.ca/cansim/a26?lang=eng&retrLang=eng&id=2820009&paSer=&

Stone, P. (2007). *Opting Out? Why Women Really Quit Careers and Head Home*. Berkeley, CA: University of California Press.

Stone, P. (2013). *Gender & Work: Challenging Conventional Wisdom*. Boston, MA: Harvard Business School.

Tate, R. (2013, August 21). Google couldn't kill 20 percent time even if it wanted to. *Wired Business*. Retrieved from http://www.wired.com/2013/08/20-percent-time-will-never-die/

Meghan E. Norris holds a PhD in Social/Personality Psychology from Queen's University and has published on topics including social and consumer behaviour, biased information processing, social influence and the benefits of engagement. She has won both teaching and research awards and her work has been published in academic journals including the *Journal of Consumer Psychology*, *Social and Personality Psychology Compass* and the *Journal of Service-Learning in Higher Education* in addition to other industry and academic outlets. Her academic work has been supported by grants from the Social Sciences and Humanities Research Council of Canada, The Nova Scotia Gaming Foundation and other public and private organizations. Dr Norris is committed to applying evidence-based principles to conduct and apply research that has tangible benefits for individuals and the community. Demonstrating this, in addition to applied consulting work, she has held multiple academic appointments internationally and regularly teaches university courses in the fields of psychology and consumer science.

Katelynn Carter-Rogers is a recent Master of Science graduate from Saint Mary's University in Halifax, Nova Scotia. She has published on topics including facial perception, decision-making, first impressions, competitive behaviour, and test derogation. Katelynn is an independent consultant with an ongoing academic affiliation with the Social Attitudes Psychology Laboratory at Saint Mary's University. Her primary areas of expertise are social psychological factors influencing eyewitness identification, first impression, and social attitudes.

Part IV
Long-standing traditions being challenged to promote gender equality in the workplace

11

Gender equality in the US Military
Women are still fighting the culture wars

Patricia K. Gleich
University of West Florida, USA

The US Military has, since its inception, operated as an institution in society, formally framed by policy and law that first proscribed women's open service and then maintained a gendered, two-tiered system. Although the past century has seen policy changes, expressly after the Women's Armed Services Integration Act of 1948, only after the demise of conscription and the introduction of the All-Volunteer Force (AVF) in the mid-1970s have policies regarding women's service opportunities changed substantially. After decades of women's successful service, command achievements, medals for courage in combat and exemplary performance, the US Military has finally announced it intends to remove that two-tiered system, despite strong resistance from some military leaders. This chapter discusses the role that policy changes, cultural barriers and resistance have played in the societal understanding of women's roles and service, and, in the lives and careers of women who were part of a qualitative research study, exploring their lived experiences as careerists in the US Military between 1960 and 2010.

Achieving gender equality in the US Military continues to be a perpetual process manifested through the interaction between progressive policy changes and slower cultural changes reflecting the attitude, actions and power of both those who support and those who resist change. In 2013, the Secretary of the US Department of Defense announced a commitment to making the US Military more gender neutral, by opening all positions formerly closed to women through rescission of the Direct Combat Exclusion Rule (DCER) and provided guidance on the management of the implementation process (Office of the Assistant Secretary of Defense, 2013). The official standard for gender-neutrality means that all members of the Armed Forces serving in a military career designator must meet the same performance outcome-based standards (Kamarck, 2015, p. 17). This announcement came two years after recommendations that supported such policy changes contained in the Military Leadership Diversity Commission's report, *From Representation to Inclusion: Diversity Leadership for the 21st Century Military* (Military Leadership Diversity Commission, 2011). During the intervening two years debate intensified on the question of whether gender neutrality is actually achievable, or even advisable (Fredenburg, 2015). The queries and the resistance come from various voices in the military and from some in the general public, primarily based on persistent ideological understandings of women's appropriate roles and abilities, and on gendered stereotypes (Brownson, 2014; Koeszegi *et al.*, 2014). Specifically, questions continue about the reality of gender neutral minimum physical standards and the overall effect of the presence of women on men and the social dynamics of units, as well as performance levels, readiness and effectiveness of combat units (Egnell, 2013).

The purpose of this chapter is to view and discuss the question of and progress toward gender equality in the US Military using a historical framework, lived experiences of women who have served in the US Military, formal and permanent policies related to service for women, positions through analysis within a contemporary social context. The social context, which shapes and interacts with the policy changes, at times leading change and at other times resisting it, provides a structure and a lens for analysing and for understanding the ongoing process and resistance that has characterized the long movement towards expanded opportunity for women in the US Military. Although **gender neutrality** and **gender equality** are at times used interchangeably in discussions of gender inclusion in a workforce, *gender neutrality* refers to equal standards and *gender equality* refers to equal standards and opportunities (Johnson, 2015). Throughout this chapter the term *gender neutrality* will be used primarily to define the minimum process goal—removing gender as a measurable criterion for entry to all occupational classifications—as this is the terminology utilized by the policy-makers. However, *gender equality*, a more inclusive term that considers both the measurable aspects of equal opportunity and the cultural barriers to that equal opportunity—one that leaves open the possibility that the culture of the organization may need to change in order for it to become more gender equal—will also be included in the discussion (Egnell, 2013).

If one is to study gender in the military contemporaneously and comprehensively, one must look at a number of dimensions, including those connected to culture. Unlike civilian employers who operate under mandates to promote and provide equal opportunity within the workplace, the US Military has historically had policies limiting positions and promotional opportunities open to women— formalized gender-based rules (Enloe, 2000; Hasday, 2008). Although the number and type of positions open to women have increased over the past 67 years, since women have been allowed to become legitimate and permanent military personnel, positions labelled **direct ground combat** and in what is commonly known as the **elite communities**, such as Navy Seals, Army Rangers and some Special Operations billets, remain closed to women (National Women's Law Center, 2015).

The US Military sets physical standards for entry into all occupational classes and there exists a common belief that women are not capable of meeting many of the standards in occupations restricted to them, thus to allow women to enter these fields—in the minds of some—is synonymous with a lowering of those standards (Brownson, 2014). The US Department of Defense has stated repeatedly that no standards will be lowered; the goal is *gender neutrality*, the use of measurable physical standards that are the same for both men and women. Culture-based assumptions about capabilities of women underlie disbelief and omit two important considerations. First, are physical standards realistic or can they be set artificially high in order to make women's achievement of them exceedingly difficult (Goodell, 2010)? And, second, standards alone do not address the cultural barriers that have kept women from applying in numbers equal to men for positions in desirable fields that have been open to them for at least two decades (Brownson, 2014). If one is to look comprehensively at gender equality in the US Military, one must go beyond absolute standards and include rates of participation by men and women in the various communities or occupational specialities and possible barriers (King, 2015).

Assurances from the Secretary of Defense that standards will remain intact have not forestalled debate on any facet of the issue of women in the military and analysis. Reports and discussions in government and in the military continue, highlighting the differing ideological views on women's roles in the military and demonstrating the unrelenting interaction between policy change and cultural resistance or adaptation to, and acceptance of, this paradigm shift (Barrett, 2001; Bensahel *et al.*, 2015). If an insurmountable barrier to total integration and inclusion of women exists, the mind-sets and stereotypes that cannot go beyond the image of *fighting men* and who adjudicate women less physically capable, regardless of what they demonstrate through performance in training, will likely be that barrier (Van Orst, 2015).

Women in the US Military face obstacles common to all women who enter other male-dominated fields or occupations in the private sector, but they do not have the protection of laws that require equal treatment and provide a means to redress treatment when it is not equal to men in the workplace. Although men and women serving in equal positions are to be treated with equity, the historical policies and practice of closing certain positions to women in a male-dominated military have maintained the position that women do not fit into the culture of certain military communities (Koeszegi *et al.*, 2014). Yet, there is a need for qualified personnel and public opinion on women serving in all facets of the military, including combat, seems to be slowly shifting towards acceptance (Dimock *et al.*, 2013). However, legal attempts to expose and challenge remaining discriminatory occupational restrictions on women in the US Military generally and in the service academies (the primary training ground for leaders) have found that the Department of Defense and the individual academies are being facile in resisting the release of data that would substantiate or refute claims of bias as potentially an unreasonable burden and expense (Sussman, 2015).

Exploring how the US Military reflects the interaction between cultural values, policy and culture change is integral to understanding the experiences of women who have served in the military throughout history, and most especially in the last 60 years. Women in the military must be viewed as women in society, but, within a smaller and socially connected unit or institution of society apportioned by gender and, at times, rigorously guarded (Moskos, 1990; Carreiras, 2006). Although women have served in the US Military since before the country proclaimed its independence in 1776, only in the last 60 years have women experienced limited legitimacy in their position and have women enjoyed visibility in their roles.

Women's service history in the US Military

The experience and understanding of women in society and the military is best viewed through a chronology of their service in the US Military, framed by policy, as seen in Table 11.1.

Table 11.1 **Chronology of US Military policies on women's service**

Source: compiled from Blanton (1993); Burrelli (2013); DoD Personnel, Workforce Reports & Publications (August 2015); Ebbert and Hall (1999); Kamarck (2015); Manning (2013); Rutgers Institute for Women's Learning (2010).

Dates	Policy title/change and action	Type of service/change
1776–1900	Before formal policies—Women were "employed" or volunteered, masqueraded as men or otherwise served invisibly.	Cooks, nurses, signal corps, during the US Civil War 6,000 nurses served in military hospitals and near battlefields as volunteers or contract employees, served on hospital ships
1901–1908	Establishment of Nurse Corps; Army (1901) Navy (1908)	First women in the US Military "officially". Status, pay and benefits were not equal to men
1909–1921	National Defense Act of 1916	Created Reserve Officer Training Corps and National Guard—Women serve as clerks and nurses and in Europe in communications and driving ambulances and in the US as shore battery personnel and submarine watchers. Yeomanettes, women serve in Navy

Dates	Policy title/change and action	Type of service/change
1922–1942	1942 -P.L. 689; 56 Stat. 730. P. L. 554, 56 Stat. 278	Congress creates women's service branches as temporary and as non-combatant service; women are official, if temporary members of the armed forces. 500,000 women volunteer for service, nurses, clerks, aircraft mechanics, aircraft pilots, trainers, ambulance drivers, flight nurses and cryptographers
1945–1948	P. L. 625; 62 Stat. 356; "Women's Armed Services Integration Act of 1948	Allowed women to become permanent, regular members of the US Military. Set a cap of 2%, allowed only one officer above O-5. Exclusionary language included mandate that women were not allowed on ships in combat or airplanes in combat
1949–1972	1951—The Defense Advisory Committee on Women in the Services (DACOWITS) was established; 1967—P.L. 90-130;81 Stat. 374	During the Korean War, female reservists were involuntarily recalled to active duty for first time. More than 120,000 women serve, many as battlefield nurses. Increased numbers of women enlisted or were commissioned after the 2% ceiling was eliminated in 1967. Women, 265,000, served during the Vietnam War, 12,000 volunteered to serve as battlefield nurses, flight nurses, air traffic controllers, communications specialists, intelligence officers, clerks and in other capacities in different branches of the armed services in the combat area.
1973–1979	Equal Rights Amendment passes 92nd Congress and is signed by President Richard Nixon. (Adoption of the Amendment failed ultimately because it was not ratified by the required majority of states.)	Conscription ends. All Volunteer Force actively recruits women; the age requirement for without parental consent now same as men; ROTC Units, Service Academies and US Coast Guard open to women; mandatory separation due to pregnancy ended; women serve on non-combatant ships; Navy trains first women aviators; Congress directs Secretary of Defense to submit a definition of the term "combat" and recommendations for expanding job classifications for female members of the armed forces
1980–1992	1988—Department of Defense adopted a "risk rule" pertaining to women and combat. 1991—P.L. 102-190; 105 Stat. 1365; 1659 et seq.	Excluded women from non-combat units or missions if the risks of exposure to direct combat, hostile fire, or capture were equal to or greater than the risks in the combat units they supported. Women are deployed in Grenada, Panama and in the Persian Gulf. A number were killed or captured but the many women who served bravely and competently were acknowledged by Congress and military leadership

Dates	Policy title/change and action	Type of service/change
1993–2004	1993—P.L. 103-160; 107 Stat. 1659 et seq; Repeal of risk rule and promulgation of new 1994 Direct Ground Combat Definition and Assignment Rule	Repealed the prohibition on women serving on combatant vessels and aircraft; required Secretary of Defense to ensure occupational performance standards were gender-neutral; required Secretary of Defense to notify Congressional Armed Services Committees 90 days before any policy changes concerning the assignment of women to ground combat roles; required the Secretary of Defense to notify committees 30 days prior to opening any "combatant unit, class of combatant vessel, or type of combat platform" to women
2005–2008	CRS Report RL32476 issued, P.L. 109; t. 3251; National Defense Authorization Act F Y 2006	Identified co-location in combat, Rand report found that DOD was not complying with law as hundreds of women had received Combat Action Badges for service in Iraq and Afghanistan
2009–2012	Duncan Hunter National Defense Authorization Act for Fiscal Year 2009, P.L. 110-417; 122 Stat. 4476 established the Military Leadership Diversity Commission (recommendations released in 2011)	Commission called for elimination of all combat exclusion policies for women and the creation of a "level playing field" for all qualified service members. Called for "barrier analysis" to reveal demographic diversity patterns. In 2012 the DOD advised congress that it was eliminating the co-location policy and allowing women to be assigned to occupational specialities that engage in direct combat. The DOD opened 14,325 additional positions to women; Women (officers) began serving on submarines
2013–2015	Rescission of Direct Combat Exclusion Rule	Secretary of Defense announces openings for women to serve in previously restricted occupations—combat arms occupational specialities and non-combat specialities assigned to combat units. Gender neutrality to be implemented by 2016

Evidence of the results of more recent changes in military policy and the increase in numbers of women serving can be seen if one looks at the demographics of the female veteran population. According to a 2014 report, approximately 9% of all veterans are women with this percentage expected to double by 2014 (National Center for Veterans Analysis and Statistics, October, 2013). The median age of female veterans in 2012 was 48 and the median age of male veterans was 64. This younger female veteran population is indicative of a large group with more recent service, the largest female cohort being those with post 9/11 service (National Center for Veterans Analysis and Statistics, June, 2015).

Yet, in spite of rising percentages of women in the US Military, the proportion of those women who are officers has hovered between 16 and 17%, with the percentage of women in each rank decreasing as the rank rises. As of June 2015, of the 906 flag officer billets [Generals and Admirals] 61 or 6.7% are filled by women (DoD Personnel, Workforce Reports & Publications, August, 2015). Women are also under-represented in desirable areas of the military. According to Stephanie P. Miller (2011), who headed the Women's Office of Policy for the US Navy, though the US Navy typically promotes the statistic that 16% of officers are women, it fails to mention that almost half of those women are in healthcare occupations. In aviation, considered by most an elite community in both the US Navy and the US Air Force, and open to women for more than two decades, the participation rate for women has not risen above 6.5%, while in the US Marines women make up less than 8% of the total force and less than 7% of the officers (Office of the Assistant Secretary of Defense for Readiness & Force Management, June, 2014). Low numbers of women in fields that have long been open to them might require a different type of explanation, one that explores how masculine culture shapes the US Military (Brown, 2012b).

Military culture and appropriate *work/roles* for women

Progress towards increased inclusion of women in all positions of the US Military continues to be shaped by society's views of appropriate and legitimate roles for women in general society. At the core of the ongoing debate is the degree to which women are to be involved in offensive manoeuvres (combat) and positions that carry risk (Enloe, 2000). Traditionally, roles for women in military service divide into two groups: one group epitomizing what might be viewed as more historical and traditional women's roles, i.e. nursing, clerical or other administrative support or supply; and a second set of roles for women who served outside of the expected roles, either secretly or unofficially in the early days of service and more recently as co-located personnel in combat arenas. The meaning of *degree of risk*, regulated by policy, defies uniform interpretation because women have long served in positions of risk due to their proximity to the battlefield (Sterner, 1996). Working as medical or administrative personnel, or more recently when attached to combat units, women have served with, but not officially a part of, combat units. They have travelled with the combat units, experienced the same danger as the men in the units, were wounded and some killed by arms fire or explosive devices, yet since they were not officially part of a combat unit the cultural meaning of their service has been different from that of men (Kamarck, 2015).

Women in the military are understood, in part, through social roles that are often anchored in institutions of society and, at times, in the myths that are connected to those institutions (Greenwood *et al.*, 2008). Social domains are not simply structures; they are interactive systems possessing both borders and fluidity (Lizardo, 2010). Men have been encouraged and expected to enter and operate freely in a public domain, as they passively occupy a private domain at home but leave that habitat for their primary activity, to go to school, to work or to war (Morgan, 1994). Expectations for men's capabilities and performance have traditionally been made on public domain activities, thus men's self-image and roles are defined there (Kimmel, 1993). Historically, women's roles have been viewed as located in what is labelled as the private domain, encompassing the family and home, and primarily shaped by the needs of the family: *the home front* (Risman, 2004). When women go out into the public domain, they may encounter resistance and traditional role expectations designed to constrain their forays out of the private domain (Hochschild and Machung, 2012).

Roles represent the descriptive, containing the expectations of what each gender group does or can do, and the injunctive, containing the information of what each gender group should do (Eagly and Karau, 2002). Because of the dual function performed by gender roles, in addition to stereotypical beliefs about an individual's behaviours and personal qualities, the expectations also equate behaviours and personal qualities with particular gender roles, influencing the perception that someone is or is not behaving commensurate with their gender group or operating in a sphere that is open only to a particular gender role. This can result in the defining of *real* masculinity by its distance from those rejected as not being sufficiently masculine (Connell, 2005). To blend in then, to attain legitimacy in one's role, women must both *perform* (do) and *be* (fit). Thus, for women in the US Military to be viewed and treated as equal with men, they would be required to perform satisfactorily and be deemed as appropriately belonging. Performance is, to a degree, within the control of an individual woman, but, fitting the legitimate image for a position in the military and when that image is firm in the minds of others, is not within her control.

As women's roles in society have expanded and in view of policy changes proactive for women, it might seem that decades would have brought women closer to equity in the US Military. Yet, this has not happened, in part because the culture of the military has remained male dominated and at times has been tolerant of behaviour that exhibits male privilege through sexual misconduct against women in an effort to reinforce the borders between private and public domains (Goldstein, 2001; Carwford, 2014). Recent dismissals of US Military commanders seem to signal an amelioration of the environments that were hostile to women and tolerant of sexual misdeeds (Barry, 2014; Stachowitsch, 2013). According to Fred Stone, a recently retired US Air Force Colonel and faculty member at the University of Utah, there were 18 flag officers and 255 commanders at the rank of Lieutenant Colonel and higher removed for personal conduct between 2005 and 2013. Forty per cent of the removals were for violations for "sexual offenses, such as adultery, harassment, and sexual assault" (Stone, 2015).

Culture as a barrier to change

The US Military is a cultural institution operating through a system of formal and informal policies and procedures. Its norms are long-established and often very traditional (Cafornio, 2006). In the US Military, change at the institutional level is accomplished through a progression of policies, implementation of procedures stemming from the policies, and leader commitment to the policies and procedures. Command decision-making authority is robust, and commitment along the chain of command of the military often reflects the degree to which individuals believe change is permanent or inevitable (Ingram *et al.*, 2007). In the US Military, the elements of culture that reinforce the masculine or male images include the language, the standards and interpretation of those standards, the representative stories told and retold, and the heroes. Social messages are contained in who is represented and in who is absent (Brown, 2012a).

Cultural change within an institution such as the US Military involves modification of both the material and non-material dimensions. Material aspects of culture typically change more easily—uniforms, appearance, equipment—than the non-material aspects of culture—the values, beliefs, standards, attitudes and norms (Barrett, 2001). Non-material culture, defining and constraining behaviours and serving as the rules or the insider knowledge, created the cultural climate that for decades greeted women as they entered the US Military. In society and reflected in the US Military, numerical dominance provides the opportunity for the dominant group to compound the majority effect with the construction of symbolic hierarchies (Risman, 2004). Once hierarchies are constructed, group members situate themselves at the top and establish a norm or ideal based on attributes of their master status, effectively blocking entry of others or the expansion of roles (Hinojosa, 2010; Koeszegi *et al.*, 2014).

While the military, as an institution, has slowly modified policies that excluded women over the past 60 years (as seen in Table 11.1), language, an element of culture that can be used to reinforce gender, has changed more slowly (Holm, 1992). Use of the phrase *fighting man* in the US Military code of conduct continued until 1988, 40 years after women became "official" (Federal Register, 1988), and the arched stone portal to the US Air Force Academy entreated in two-foot high letters, *Bring Me Men*, until 2003, 27 years after the first class of women entered the Academy. The entreaty was removed only after findings of ongoing sexual misconduct forced change to a number of policies (Schemo, 2010). When one gender group is privileged by virtue of the language used, those who are not included in that group are not only seen as secondary, they may be invisible (Coates, 2004).

Language has also been used to connect male characteristics and male bodies to the ideal soldier. The lower status of women has been emphasized through feminized language to shame men viewed as weak and suggestive female images to sexualize and objectify women (Duncanson, 2009). Continuing linguistic practices reinforce the belief that soldiers should embody what Boon (2005) calls the **hero figure**, a construct of Western culture, representing the ultimate in masculinity; providing a platform for affiliation and emulation; and demeaning male soldiers who do not exemplify this norm (Boon, 2005). Thus, when men who are deemed weak and non-masculine are humiliated, taunted and called girls or worse, the stereotype of the masculine male is reinforced, and the negative position of women is bolstered (Hinojosa, 2010). These embodied images are also conveyed as arguments to restrict women from certain positions in the military based on perceived physical shortcomings (King, 2015).

The use of images antithetical towards women has continued until recent years, in spite of service branch efforts to increase the numbers of women serving (Burke, 2004). A website that promotes itself as the Aircraft Resource Center features a H-53 helicopter, flown during the Iraq War, proudly displaying silhouettes of nude women depicted as part of the personalized camouflage, though such art has been long banned (Faith, 2008). Similarly, a commander (during 2011–2013) of the then all-male Blue Angels, the Navy's public demonstration squadron, was reassigned and then given a letter of reprimand. The captain was removed from his command after investigation of charges that he had failed to stop obvious and repeated instances of sexual harassment, had condoned widespread lewd practices within the squadron, permitted crew photographers to video close-up images of female spectators' breasts at airshows which were then played in the wardroom, allowed pornographic photos in aeroplane cockpits and created an environment hostile to women (Crites, 2014).

When women are invisible, or are seen as unsuitable and unable to perform, to allow them to operate in key positions becomes at least a mistake or at most simply unthinkable. The scenario is then used to mischaracterize women as a threat to the effectiveness of the military, proliferating fear of the consequences of women in service (Milko, 1992). Women have been both excluded from the role of "fighting man" or warrior—viewed as the only authentic military role—and absent from the images of warrior—even for children's toys (Meyer, 1998; McCall, 2011). While women have been portrayed as warriors of ancient times and are seen as such in more recent popular culture, through movies and video games, it would be difficult to measure any positive effect of this influence on the thinking of US Military decision-makers (Emad, 2006; King, 2015).

Military masculinity

The exploration of roles and expectations for men and women and "normalcy" has a decades-long history in the US Military. An article published by Daniel Brown in 1958 while he was a psychologist at the US Air Force Academy reviewed his research in identifying "inverted personalities"—women who articulated a preference for what was then believed to be masculine interests (Brown, 1958). While this line of demarcation between the role expectations for men and women has been mitigated somewhat since 1958, in more recent studies of perceptions related to gender and leadership capabilities held by men, women continue to be viewed as lacking the same measure of leadership characteristics as men—in the Boyce study, even after exposure to female leaders in the military (Boyce and Herd, 2003; Koch *et al.*, 2015). To understand this, one must continue to look at the way roles are gendered (delimited by sex) and the stereotypes connected to the gendered roles. There is a substantial body of work exploring the relationship between masculinity, military service or soldiering, and the role of warrior. How then are gendered stereotypes so deeply imbedded in thinking that examples of women as effective military leaders are seen as exceptions to the rule that women cannot lead? Sandra Bem (1994) wrote of "gender polarizing" as an extreme way that sex roles are understood. Sex roles are not merely different for men and women; they are set as oppositional, requiring a paradigm shift in order to view women as able to legitimately and effectively operate in positions that have been traditionally filled by men in the US Military (Bem, 1994).

Morgan discusses this connection among men and the exclusion of women when he notes that "military experiences separate men from women while binding men to men ... a separation that reaches deep into a man's sense of identity and self" (Morgan, 1994, p. 166). He notes that one of the constructions emanating from this dialectic of men separated from women is the common use of sexual aggression and shaming in training and bonding of soldiers (as cited in Morgan, 1994). Labelling those men who do not meet certain standards of masculinity as "girly", or "sissy" or "fags" strengthens the male and masculine connection while degrading and detaching the feminine. Goldstein also observes that enemies, subordinates and non-soldiers are feminized in an all-male environment, and connoted negatively as he notes, "The absence of actual females [in military settings] frees up the gender category [male] to encode domination" (Goldstein, 2001, p. 356).

Karen Dunivin, a military sociologist and at the time a Colonel in the USAF, wrote in 1997 of a construct that underlies the understandings many have related to women in the military. Her construct—which she explained as a model of interaction—demonstrates the power of the traditional and gendered role beliefs infused in what she called the evolving CMW (combat-masculine-warrior) paradigm, an exclusionary model, dominated by male-centred language and based on historical and traditional expectations for men's and women's roles—constraining the capacity for change (Dunivin, 1997).

Linda Grant De Pauw discussed roles attributed to women: the victim, the instigator (the adversative of the victim) and the camp follower. Absent is a female warrior, except for one who can muster an androgynous image and pass as a man, though passing also risks the penalty of discovery and shaming (De Pauw, 1998). Hinojosa (2010) observed that the military and war may be one of the most salient linkages between hegemonic masculinity and men's bodies, and it has historically supported the *boundedness* of military life, creating an environment for the production and representation of a masculine norm. Brown (2012a) describes this situation and writes of representations of women in army recruitment images as vehicles that at once include and separate. Brown's content research found that while images of women may currently be positioned as engaged in work in contemporary advertisements, typically rather than being shown in action or participating in overt activities that reflect a wartime environment as the men are, women were portrayed behind desks or tables, in a marching line or in fatigues doing calisthenics (Brown, 2012b).

If one views the acceptable gender role types of women in Western society and the characteristics associated with the occupant of those roles, the limits of the roles emerge. One finds role opportunity for the mother (image/role) who is both organized and nurturing as well as selfless to the point of martyrdom and virtually saintly. One finds too, the vulnerable and weak victim (image/role), who is insufficient to protect herself and whose very weakness may prompt gallant and danger-laden male behaviour—saving the damsel in distress. The final image permitted for women and reinforced by early efforts in the US Military to shield troops from women of *doubtful character* who may cause moral injury (Horton, 2014) is the self-centred and distrusted aggressor, the harlot, cast as temptress, a potential threat to males by stealing or controlling their masculinity, which threatens their cohesion with fracturing rivalry or, to their wives, by alienating the affection of their man (De Pauw, 1998).

The male role of warrior is portrayed and understood as having interchangeable characteristics with the honourable and daring hero (Barrett and Sarbin, 2008; Titunik, 2008). In lieu of a female warrior role, the traditional private domain roles open to or, importantly, attributed to women, would seem to explicate the arguments limiting the roles of women in the military. The historical role of victim placed in a warrior situation would require potentially self-sacrificing protection by a heroic male; one of the fears expressed by those who oppose opening additional positions to women is that of male soldiers protecting female soldiers at all costs. The historical role of nurturer may adapt to a nursing function, especially one that portrays the nurse as a mother substitute for young soldiers (male) who need tender comfort and consolation, or it may transfer from a supportive mother figure to an efficient administrative support person, taking care of the private needs of the male warrior and freeing him for battle (Boldry *et al.*, 2001; Eagly and Karau, 2002).

The sole traditional role that includes self-interest, strength, cunning and aggression, prized characteristics among males, is the harlot—distrusted, unvirtuous and stained; devilishly desirable to many males but causing competition within the group and a threat to the camaraderie of the male unit members. She may also, because of self-interest, not be depended upon to act in concert with or on behalf of the group, thus not promoting group unity cohesion (Connell, 2005; Egnell, 2013).

Absent is a historical or traditional role for women that includes the characteristics that make the male warrior a capable, trusted and revered image—the assurance that he will do his utmost, using his considerable power and he will prevail in competition against his foe. For the female warrior to be understood and accepted there must be a role for women that allows them to be not only capable, but also legitimate. As long as women who perform in the roles previously labelled as male are seen as exceptions, women as a group will not be viewed as dependably and predictably capable.

Utilizing role portrayals written in commonly understood descriptive characteristics traditionally attributed to men and women (Stachowitsch, 2012), it is possible to depict graphically the role positions and traditionally understood characteristics related to the warrior. These stereotypical characteristics are displayed in Figure 11.1.

Figure 11.1 **Gender roles and characteristics. The historically and typically understood male and female roles and characteristics are displayed in relation to compatibility or perceived compatibility with the role of warrior**

Source: Gleich (2014).

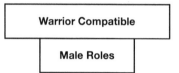

Warrior Compatible

Male Roles

Hero Role	**Masculine, Man**
Selfless, Patriotic, Risk-taker, Valiant, Strong, Confident, Competitive, Dominant, Masculine, Daring, Brave, Protector, Noble, Other-centred	Strong, Brave, Conqueror, Tough, Protective, Stoic, Confident, Intimidating, Competitive, Dominant, Aggressive, Unemotional

Warrior Incompatible

Female Roles

Mother/Angel Role	**Victim Role**	**Harlot Role**
Merciful, Selfless, Caring, Sacrificial, Kind, Strong, Agreeable, Resilient, Competent, Supportive, Relational, Cooperative, Diplomatic, Nurturing, Emotional, Peacemaker, Other-centred	Innocent, Passive, Powerless, Protected, Vulnerable, Weak, Passive, Ineffectual, Submissive, Unsure, Frail, Emotional, Helpless, Exposed	Corrupting, Wicked, Tainted, Booty, Spoiled, Strong, Hardy, Selfish, Dominant, Manipulative Private, Alluring, Confident, Calculating, Achieving, Emasculating, Damaging, Debauching, Self-centred

While the male and hero roles are compatible (almost interchangeable) with the role and characteristics of the warrior, the traditional roles assigned to women and the characteristics that are attributed to those roles are not compatible with an image of a female warrior.

Women's lived experience in US Military culture

The interaction in the military between policy and culture is also apparent in the lived experiences of women who served in the military during the time of policy change in the US Military. A qualitative research study of the time period 1960 through 2010 obtained personal narratives from 35 women who served in the US Military for a minimum of 20 years during the study time period (Gleich, 2014). Throughout their tenure of service, the two-tiered position classification system framed their service and their opportunities. The study participants included both women who followed careers more traditionally assigned to women and others whose ambitions took them in the direction of positions or specialities that were seen as men's domains. Experiences of both groups, while largely positive, were dissimilar. Those who followed traditional career paths found less resistance to their ambitions and fewer barriers to success. The women in the study who labelled themselves as successful, though not always supported by achievement through rank, were those who after entering formerly male-dominated domains were not disheartened by encounters with a resistive culture imposed by individuals who placed barriers or attempted to deter them by adversarial or obstructive actions.

The study participants utilized several different routes or combinations of strategies in order to effectively manage military culture and have a successful career.

- Those women who challenged male-dominated occupations found it necessary to exhibit extreme capability and tenacity and to prove themselves both worthy and appropriate for their job continually and repeatedly throughout their careers.

- Women who worked in careers and occupations that were female-role typed and/or female dominated, such as nursing or administration, avoided the threat to masculine domains and could thrive and succeed without resistance or ridicule.

- Some women were able to capitalize on high-placed male-members who lent their support and influence, at times mentoring them as well, and, importantly, giving them the benefit of their own networks and early notice of opportunities and promotional prospects.

- Most women were able to find a level of camaraderie and support that nourished them, though this often meant allowing themselves to be viewed and treated as an exception to their gender when working in male-dominated jobs.

- Success was often articulated as women having found and used an inner strength that allowed them to persevere and surmount the obstacles placed before them. Interestingly, while for some this was a source of pride, others noted this extra effort added stress and pressure to their lives.

For many highly capable women, the result of a military culture that did not accept them was a premature retirement—leaving a military service they loved because they had become frustrated with, and felt repeatedly damaged by, promotional inequities and decisions that were or appeared to be based on gendered thinking and male preference. As one study participant stated, "I loved the Navy— loved flying, but I left because I was tired of the humiliation in seeing less capable men get the promotions I had earned" (Gleich, 2014, p. 130). Officers repeatedly indicated that they knew they would not be promoted beyond a mid-range rank and this left them less motivated to achieve in a military organization that affords status and rewards success with advance in rank.

While the women of the study cohort understood they were entering a two-tiered system with policies and rules based on gender, they expected policy changes would necessarily open opportunities. They did not anticipate encountering resistance to policy change from a military culture that did not welcome them and the effect this would have on their sense of self and on their careers.

Reconciling policy and culture and moving towards equality

According to Barrett (2001), policy changes in the military have never been universally accepted by those who are directed with enforcing them, creating resistance to change and sham enforcement. Some argue that policy changes are forcing social engineering through the military—a contentious topic discussed with vigour since the days of the Second World War (Moore and Webb, 2000). An individual still quoted from 1941 and remembered for little else, Col. Eugene Householder was a 1907 graduate of the US Military Academy at West Point. He delineated the purpose of the military in a way that precluded policies promoting inclusion, "The Army is not a sociological laboratory. Experimenting with Army policy, especially in a time of war, would pose a danger to efficiency, discipline, and morale, and would result in ultimate defeat" (Katznelson, 2006, p. 272; Waldman and Lekawa, 2013).

Dunivin (1997) wrote hopefully after Desert Storm (1990–1991) that women's roles in the military were shifting from an ambiguous or minimally active soldier to an active participant in a war. She expected abandonment of rules prohibiting women from being assigned to combat—given the excellent service of 40,000 women who served, died, were wounded and captured during that conflict (Dunivin, 1997).

The 2013 announcement of the rescission of the DCER affirmed that all positions would be opened to women by January 2016, ending a three-year transition period. The stated intent of this policy change is: "that no individual who wants to serve her or his country should be forbidden from competing for or serving in any military capacity solely because of gender" (Office of the Assistant Secretary of Defense, 2013, p. 2). Ostensibly this means male gender as a requirement for positions closed to women will be eliminated and both men and women will be required to demonstrate an appropriate and identical level of physical fitness. If this minimal goal can be achieved, it will be important for women who plan on a military career, both insuring expanded career opportunities because more types of work will be open to women and improving promotional opportunities, historically better after service in combat occupations, barred to women (Asch *et al.*, 2012).

A June 2015 report on the progress made towards reaching this goal reveals that women are now eligible for 95% of US Military occupations, but many direct combat positions remain closed to them, despite numbers of women who have qualified for them (Van Orst, 2015). The Van Orst (2015) report also indicated that the utmost care was being exercised in maintaining physical standards, personnel safety, and the safety and security of the nation.

The National Women's Law Center has raised concerns that integration of women is not going according to schedule, that nebulous cultural studies might be used to demonstrate the women are a detriment to force cohesion, and that there is little transparency in the process at the service branch level (National Women's Law Center, 2015).

The US Air Force has taken the lead in bringing more women into that branch with an announced goal of increasing the percentage of officers who are women from the current 20% to 30% over the next year and has plans to eliminate the last 1% of positions currently closed to women (Office of the Secretary of the Air Force, 2015).

The US Navy retains 2% of billets closed to women, but has increased recruitment goals for enlisted women to 25% and is in the process of out-fitting all new ships as well as retro-fitting existing craft berthing (Office of Women's Policy, 2015). The Navy has also assigned female enlisted personnel to submarines—joining the 100 female officers already serving on submarines (Faram, 2015). In a move to be more hospitable to women service personnel, both the Navy and the Air Force have announced plans to triple maternity leave to 18 weeks and to defer deployment until one year after the birth of a baby (Losey, 2015). The US Army and Marines have not announced recruitment goals for women.

At the time of writing of this chapter, the overall percentage of women serving in the US Military stands at 15.5% or about one in seven (Kamarck, 2015). One other marker of change is the slowly rising percentage of women who are officers and within that group, the incremental increase in senior officers who are women. Currently, 17% of officers are women (DoD Personnel, Workforce Reports & Publications, August, 2015).

While roles for women in the US Military have expanded, the question that addresses the needed changes to military culture—women's place and role in the military—is not yet settled. The persistence of questions of fitness and legitimacy of women in certain roles continues to shape the rate of implementation of policies beneficial to women's career choices and provides barriers to increases in the numbers of women entering elite occupations or communities.

The definitive question of equality for women in the military is not yet fully answered, but the degree of movement in that direction will be clarified as the US Military branches submit to the Secretary of Defense and make public their plans to fully implement the policy decision of 2013 (Kamarck, 2015). Ultimately the US Congress will receive the Department of Defense recommendations for gender neutrality, readiness and other priorities for the US Military, and the next steps will be taken after January 2016.

Note: In late 2015 the US Marine Corps asked to be exempted from the rule to integrate women (Baldor, 2015). However, on 9 March 2016, Ashton Carter, US Secretary of Defense announced that plans to implement the full integration of women into all branches of the US Military had been approved and that all branches "may now execute your plans to open all previously-closed positions, occupations, specialties, career fields and branches to women" (Office of the Secretary of Defense, 2016).

Yet, the dogged question remains; will culture change to conform to policy?

References

Asch, B., Miller, T. & Malchiodi (2012). *A New Look at Gender and Minority Differences in Officer Career Progression in the Military*. Santa Monica, CA: Rand Corporation.

Baldor, L. (2015, September 19). Marine commandant recommends women be banned from some combat jobs. *Marine Corps Times*.

Barrett, F. (2001). The organizational construction of hegemonic masculinities: The case of the US Navy. In: S. Whitehead & F. Barrett, (eds.), *The Masculinities Reader*. Malden, MA: Blackwell Publishers, Inc.

Barrett, F. & Sarbin, T. (2008). Honor as a moral category: A historical-linguistic analysis. *Theory & Psychology*, 18(1), 5-25.

Barry, J. L. (2014. A few good (wo)men: Gender inclusion in the United States Military. *Journal of International Affairs, Columbia University*, 18 November.

Bem, S. (1994). *The Lenses of Gender: Transforming the Debate* (1st ed.). New Haven, CT: Yale University Press.

Bensahel, N., Barno, D., Kidder, K. & Sayler, K. (2015). *Battlefields and Boardrooms: Women's Leadership in the Military and the Private Sector*. Washington: DC: Center for a New American Society.

Blanton, D. (1993). Women soldiers of the Civil War. *Prologue Magazine*, 25(1).

Boldry, J., Wood, W. & Kashy, D. (2001). Gender stereotypes and the evaluation of men and women in military training. *Journal of Social Issues*, 57(4), 689-705.

Boon, K. (2005). Heroes, metanarratives and the paradox of masculinity in contemporary western culture. *The Journal of Men's Studies*, 13(3), 301-312.

Boyce, L. & Herd, A. (2003). The relationship between gender role stereotypes and requisite military leadership characteristics. *Sex Roles*, 49(7/8), 365-378.

Brown, D. (1958). Sex-Role Development in a changing culture. *Psychological Bulletin*, 55(4), 232-242.

Brown, M. (2012a). A woman in the army is still a woman: Representations of women in US military recruiting advertisements for the all volunteer force. *Journal of Women, Politics & Policy*, 33(2), 151-175.

Brown, M. (2012b). *Enlisting Masculinity: The Construction of Gender in the US Military Recruiting Advertising during the All-Volunteer Force*. New York: Oxford University Press.

Brownson, C. (2014). The battle for equivalency: Female US Marines discuss sexuality, physical fitness and military leadership. *Armed Forces 7 Society*, 40(4), 765-788.

Burke, C. (2004). *Camp All-American, Hanoi Jane and the High-and-Tight: Gender, Folklore and Changing Military Culture*. Boston, MA: Beacon Press.

Burrelli, D. (2013). *Women in Combat: Issues for Congress*. Washington, DC: Congressional Research Service.

Cafornio, G. (2006). Some historical notes. In G. Cafornio (ed.), *Handbook of the Sociology of the Military* (pp. 7-27). New York: Springer.

Carreiras, H. (2006). *Gender and the Military: Women of the Armed Forces of Western Democracies*. New York: Routledge.

Carwford, M. (2014). A culture of hypermasculinity is driving sexual assault in the military. *Huffington Post*, 14, 4.

Coates, J. (2004). *Women, Men and Language: A Sociolinguistic Account of Gender Differences in Language* (3rd ed.). Abingdon, UK: Routledge.

Connell, R. (2005). *Masculinities* (2nd ed.). Berkeley, CA: University of California Press.

Crites, R. (2014). *Command Investigation into the Facts and Circumstances Surrounding Possible Violations of the Department of the Navy Policies on Equal Opportunity and Sexual Harassment by the Former Commanding Officer of the U.S. Navy Flight Demonstration Squadron between July 2010 and November 2012*. Pearl Harbor, HI: Department of the Navy.

De Pauw, L. (1998). *Battle Cries and Lullabies: Women in War from Prehistory to the Present*. Norman, OK: University of Oklahoma Press.

Dimock, M., Doherty, C. & Tyson, A. (2013). *Broad Support for Combat Roles for Women*, Washington, DC: The Pew Research Center for The People and The Press.

DoD Personnel, Workforce Reports & Publications (2015, August). *Active Duty Military Personnel by Service by Rank/Grade*. Retrieved from https://www.dmdc.osd.mil/appj/dwp/dwp_reports.jsp

Duncanson, C. (2009). Forces for good? Narratives of military masculinities on peacekeeping operations. *Feminist Journal of Politics*, 11(1), 63-80.

Dunivin, K. (1997). *Military Culture: A Paradigm Shift?* Maxwell Air Force Base: The Maxwell Papers.

Eagly, A. & Karau, S. (2002). Role congruity theory of prejudice toward female leaders. *Psychological Review*, 109(3), 573-598.

Ebbert, J. & Hall, M. (1999). *Crossed Currents: Navy Women in a Century of Change* (3rd ed.). Lincoln, NE: Potomac Books, an Imprint of the University of Nebraska Press.

Egnell, R. (2013). Women in battle: Gender perspectives and fighting. *Parameters*, 43(2), 33-41.

Emad, M. C. (2006). Reading wonder woman's body: Mythologies of gender and nation. *Journal of Popular Culture*, 39(6), 954-984.

Enloe, C. (2000). *Maneuvers*. Berkeley, CA: University of California Press.

Faith, J. (2008). *USMC CH-53*. Aircraft Resource Center. Retrieved from http://www.aircraftresourcecenter.com/AWA1/301-400/walk385_CH-53/walk385.htm

Faram, M. (2015). More enlisted women sought for sub duty by 2016. *Navy Times*, 19 August.

Federal Register (1988). *Executive Order 10631: Code of conduct for members of the Armed Forces of the United States as amended by EO 12633*. Federal Register. Retrieved from http://www.archives.gov/federal-register/codification/executive-order/10631.html

Fredenburg, M. (2015). Putting women in the military is a worse idea than you'd think. *National Review*, July.

Gleich, P. (2014). *Culture Change in the Military and Society Viewed through the Life Course of a Select Group of Women Military Careerists Born between 1940 and 1960*, Ann Arbor: ProQuest.

Goldstein, J. (2001). *War and Gender: How Gender Shapes the War System*. Cambridge: Cambridge University Press.

Goodell, M. (2010). Physical-strength rationales for de jure exclusion of women from military combat positions. *Seattle University Law review*, 34, 17-50.

Greenwood, R., Oliver, C., Sahlin, K. & Suddaby, R. (2008). *The SAGE Handbook of Organizational Institutionalism*. Thousand Oaks, CA: Sage.

Hasday, J. (2008). *Fighting Women: The Military Sex and Extrajudicial Constitutional Challenge*. Retrieved from http://scholarship.law.georgetown.edu/

Hinojosa, R. (2010). Doing hegemony: Military, men and constructing a hegemonic masculinity. *The Journal of Men's Studies*, Spring, 18(2), 179-194.

Hochschild, A. & Machung, A. (2012). *The Second Shift* (Revised ed.). New York: Penguin Group.

Holm, J. (1992). *Women in the Military: An Unfinished Revolution* (2nd ed.). Novato, CA: Presidio Press.

Horton, H. (2014). Gendered bodies and the U.S. Military: Exploring the institutionalized regulation of bodies, MA Dissertation, University of New Orleans.

Ingram, H., Schmeider, A. & Deleon, P. (2007). Social Construction and policy design. In: P. Sabatier (ed.) *Theories for the Policy Process* (2nd ed.) (pp. 93-128). Boulder, CO: Westview Press.

Johnson, R. (2015). Why is it so hard to explain gender inequality? Down So Long: The puzzling persistence of gender inequality. In: *Down So Long: The puzzling persistence of gender inequality* (pp. 1-28) s.l. (unpublished manuscript).

Kamarck, K. (2015). *Women in Combat: Issues for Congress*. Washington, DC: Congressional Research Services.

Katznelson, I. (2006). *When Affirmative Action was White: An Untold History of Racial Inequality in Twentieth-Century America* (Reprint ed.). New York: W.W. Norton and Company.

King, A. (2015). Women warriors: Female accession to ground combat. *Armed Forces & Society*, 41(2), 279-387.

Koch, A., D'Mello, S. & Sackett, P. (2015). A meta-analysis of gender stereotypes and bias in experimental simulation of employment decision making. *Journal of Applied Psychology*, 100(1), 128-161.

Koeszegi, S., Zedlacher, W. & Hudribusch, R. (2014). The war against the female soldier? The effects of masculine culture on workplace aggression. *Armed Forces & Society*, 40(2), 226-251.

Lizardo, O. (2010). Beyond the antinomies of structure: Levi-Strauss, Giddens, Bourdieu, and Sewell. *Theory and Society*, 39(6), 651-688.

Losey, S. (2015). New Air Force rules give new moms longer break from deployments. *Air Force Times*, 8, 7.

Manning, L. (2013). *Women in the Military: Where They Stand* (8th ed.). Washington, DC: Women's Research and Education Institute.

McCall, J. (2011). *Woman or Warrior? How Believable Feminist Shapes Warrior Women*. Las Vegas, NV: UNLV University Libraries/Theses/Dissertations/Professional Papers.

Meyer, L. (1998). *Creating G.I. Jane*. New York: Columbia University Press.

Military Leadership Diversity Commission (2011. From representation to inclusion: Diversity leadership for the 21st-century military. Arlington, VA: US Government.

Milko, J. (1992). Beyond the Persian Gulf crisis: Expending the role of servicewomen in the United States Military. *American University Law Review*, Summer 14.

Miller, S. (2011). *Today's Women and Tomorrow's Navy Organization*. Anne Arundel Community College (ed.). Arnold, MD: Office of Women's Policy, US Navy.

Moore, B. & Webb, S. (2000). Perceptions of equal opportunity among women and minority army personnel. *Sociological Inquiry*, 70(2), 215-239.

Morgan, D. (1994). Chapter 9, Theatre of war: Combat, the military and masculinities. In: M. Kaufman & H. Brod, (eds.) *Theorizing Masculinities* (pp. 165-182). Thousand Oaks, CA: Sage.

Moskos, C. (1990). *Army Women*. Retrieved from http://www.theatlantic.com/magazine/archive/1990/08/army-women/6156/

National Center for Veterans Analysis and Statistics, June, 2015. *Profile of Veterans: 2012 Data from the American Community Survey*. Washington, DC: U.S. Department of Veterans Affairs.

National Center for Veterans Analysis and Statistics (2013, October). *Projected Veteran Populations*. Washington, DC: Department of Veterans Affairs.

National Women's Law Center (2015). Integration of women into ground combat: Status report, Washington, DC.

Office of the Assistant Secretary of Defense for Readiness & Force Management (2014, June). *Defense Manpower Requirements Reports, FY 2015*, Washington, DC: U.S. Department of Defense.

Office of the Assistant Secretary of Defense (2013). Subject: Elimination of the 1994 Direct Combat Definition and Assignment Rule. *Memorandum for Secretaries of the Military Departments Acting Under Secretary of Defense for Personnel and Readiness Chiefs of the Military Services*, 24 1.

Office of the Secretary of Defense (2016, March). *Approval of Final Implementation Plans for the Full Integration of Women into the Armed Forces*. Washington, DC: US Department of Defense.

Office of the Secretary of the Air Force (2015). Air Force secretary announces bold moves to boost women, minorities. *Air Force Times*, 4 March.

Office of Women's Policy (2015). *Navy Personnel Command*. Retrieved from http://www.pub lic.navy.mil/bupers-npc/organization/bupers/WomensPolicy/Pages/default.aspx

Risman, B. (2004). Gender as a social structure: theory wrestling with activism. *Gender and Society*, 18(4), 429-450.

Rutgers Institute for Women's Learning (2010). *Women's Leadership Fact Sheet: Women in the U.S. Military Services*. Retrieved from http://iwl.rutgers.edu/documents/njwomen count/Women%20in%20Military%202009%20Final.pdf

Schemo, D. (2010). *Skies to Conquer: A Year Inside the Air Force Academy*. Hoboken, NJ: John Wiley and Sons.

Stachowitsch, S. (2012). Professional soldier, weak victim, patriotic heroine. Gender ideologies in debates on women's military integration in the U.S. *International Feminist Journal of Politics*, 14(2), 157-176.

Stachowitsch, S. (2013). Feminism and the current debates on women in combat. *E-International Relations*, 19 February.

Sterner, D. (1996). *In and Out of Harm's Way: A History of the Navy Nurse Corps*. Seattle, WA: Peanut Butter Publishing.

Stone, F. (2015). *Why the military's solution to bad leadership isn't going to fix anything*. Task & Purpose. Retrieved from http://taskandpurpose.com/ why-the-militarys-solution-to-bad-leadership-isnt-going-to-fix-anything/

Sussman, P. (2015). Yale Law Clinic accuses military academies of gender discrimination. *Connecticut Law Tribune*.

Titunik, R. F. (2008). The myth of the macho military. *Polity*, 40, 137-163.

Van Orst, J. (2015). *Official Provides Update on Combat Jobs for Women*. US Department of Defense. Retrieved from http://www.defense.gov/news/newsarticle.aspx?id=128680

Waldman, H. & Lekawa, S. (2013). A force to be reckoned with. *Washington University Political Review*, 12 4.

Patricia Gleich holds a doctorate in Social Science, teaching sociology and engaging in qualitative gender-related research at the University of West Florida. Her dissertation study investigated the effect of social change on the status, perceptions and acceptance of women in the US Military, particularly the consequences of resistive culture. Gleich is currently investigating the environment for and acceptance of legal same-sex marriage in the (US) southern states through the experiences of same-sex couples. Her previous work includes health and human service programme development and evaluation through state government and a national (US), non-profit human relations organization.

12

Women on corporate boards in Egypt
Time for change

Ghada Howaidy
American University in Cairo, Egypt

This chapter addresses women on boards in Egypt. It describes the local context with reference to global trends and recommends specific actions to improve gender equality on boards in Egypt that may be relevant to other emerging economies. The influence of traditional forces, both religious and military, and of change in the power structure in Egypt beginning in 2011, on the role of women in public life, is discussed as well as the gap between progressive laws and practice. Data compiled by the Egyptian Stock Exchange on 233 companies in 2013, showing that women hold 8.7% of board seats, are analysed and compared globally and regionally. Lessons learned are presented, including the experience of the Women on Boards programme in Egypt that seeks to disrupt existing patterns of gender bias. Continuous and persistent efforts to keep gender equality on the national agenda are needed for a change in mind-set and practice.

Gender equality is a complex issue. Its manifestations are global, systemic and political. But gender inequality is also local, organizational, cultural and personal. Such a multi-dimensional issue requires multiple interventions at different levels for a change in mind-set and practice to happen. This chapter addresses women on corporate boards in Egypt. It describes the local context with reference to global trends and recommends specific actions to improve gender equality on boards in Egypt that may be relevant to other emerging economies. Egypt, a country of 90 million people, has witnessed social and political turmoil beginning in January 2011. Like many other countries, Egypt is at the crossroads of the debate of whether or not to legislate a quota for women on corporate boards, and if so, how? Lessons learned from the experience of other countries as well as an understanding of the dynamics of such major change in the local context provide valuable insights for fostering gender equality. Also, major change can be considered as a continuous state of "becoming" that is made up of small wins rather than an end state to be reached.

Gender issues in the Egyptian context

While Egyptian women obtained the right to vote in 1956, and Egypt had its first female minister in 1962, in 2015 there were only four women in the 35-member cabinet. In addition, the percentage of women in Parliament went down from 12.5% in 2010 to 2.0% in 2011 (ECWR, 2012, p. 5). One of the plausible views in explaining the retreat of women from public life in Egypt is offered by Dawoud (2012). She suggests that many of the rights obtained by women in recent decades have been associated with the authoritarian regime of former president Mubarak. President Mubarak ruled from 1981 to 2011; his wife headed the National Council for Women, and his son was widely believed to have been groomed to succeed his father as president. The Mubarak regime is considered one of the factors that triggered the January 2011 uprising in Egypt. Dawoud (2012, p. 160) also argues that:

> Even though Egyptian women actively participated in the 25th of January revolution [2011], they did not gain more rights in post-revolutionary Egypt. On the contrary, a backlash against women's rights emerged in the form of attempts and/or concrete steps to repeal the laws pertaining to women that were introduced or amended by the Mubarak regime.

Dawoud goes on to explain that in her view this backlash took place mainly because of "… the identity of the key decision makers concerning women's rights under the Mubarak regime" (*Ibid*). In other words, the laws were rescinded because they were associated with Mubarak's wife who had led the process for putting these laws in place. It should be noted that many other laws passed during the Mubarak regime were not rescinded as a result of the power shift in 2011. It is clear, however, that those who did assume power during that period were in favour of a more limited and traditional role for women in public life.

After the uprising of January 2011 that ousted former president Mubarak after 30 years in office, Egypt was ruled by the Supreme Council of the Armed Forces until June 2012. This was followed by the Muslim Brotherhood candidate Mohamed Morsi who won the presidential election and assumed office for one year until he was ousted by a second popular uprising in June 2013. At that time, the head of the constitutional court became interim president for one year until the former minister of defence was elected as president in 2014.

The Egyptian Constitution of 2014 states in articles (11) and (180), respectively, that the state will ensure that women have equal rights and reserves 25% of local council seats for women. However, in practice the public discourse in post-2011 Egypt is becoming more heroic and masculinized, with the all-male military poised as a role model for efficiency and patriotism. This view was captured in a newspaper article entitled "Do you really love justice?" The writer, Reem Saad, argues that the small group of youth who created a movement against military trials for civilians in Egypt is struggling to put this issue on the public agenda. She adds that this group is not only resisting the injustice of the state in this respect, but more importantly it is up against a society that by and large blesses such actions and considers them the main way to realize control and consequently in their view security. This line of thought, Saad adds, considers justice itself, as well as rights activists, as soft and unmanly, in contrast to the macho image of all that is military that is portrayed in the media. The masculinized and heroic image includes characteristics like speed and decisiveness and ignores what the writer argues the public consider as "girly details" such as due process and rights (Saad, 2013). This analysis seems plausible especially when seen in the light of statements in the Egyptian media, such as "Egypt needs a man to put it in order", that appeared to be preparing the public for the necessity of having a president with a military background.

The relevance (and threat) of this public discourse is that it reinforces the association of the seemingly desired heroic leadership with masculine characteristics (Fletcher, 2004). Such statements nurture gender bias and ensure that gender equality will not be at the forefront of national development efforts in practice. So while equal rights for women can be mentioned in Egypt's Constitution, in practice it can be postponed under the guise of expediency of security. Such are the arguments used in times of social and political upheaval.

Women on corporate boards in Egypt

Research conducted in different parts of the world makes the business case for gender equality in terms of economic growth, sustainability, improved inclusive decision-making and better governance in general (Adams and Ferreira, 2009; McKinsey & Company 2015; Stephenson, 2004).[1] Women in decision-making positions are said to bring a gender-sensitive perspective to the table, which may not be obvious as issues are discussed with the assumption that what works for men works for women, or the impact on women is the same on men. The presence of women on corporate boards also has been correlated with less disruption: "Companies with a higher percentage of WOB [Women on Board] tend to be involved in fewer governance related controversies, including fraud, accounting, bribery and corruption-related controversies, in the last three years" (MSCI, 2014, p. 9).

---

1 See also Catalyst website (www.catalyst.org) which provides research, tools and events that make the business case in support of diversity and inclusion.

Terjesen *et al.* (2009) argue that women on boards should not only be about the bottom line. They suggest that such studies are about "… exploring a link between gender diversity and performance, not establishing causality" (p. 326).

> After a new male director is appointed, if there is a change in shareholder value either in the immediate or longer term, this would be unlikely to be attributed to his male gender—so why should we expect a female appointee to add directly to the corporate bottom line? (Terjesen *et al.*, 2009, p. 330).

They therefore conclude that research: "… shows that gender diversity on corporate boards contributes to more effective corporate governance through a variety of board processes, some of which do not show up as a direct influence on the firm's bottom line" (Terjersen *et al.*, 2009, p. 334).

A report by the African Development Bank claims that there is overall lack of familiarity with the concept of how greater gender diversity in management teams actually leads to better business outcomes on the African continent, including in Egypt (AfDB, 2015, pp. 8-9). Many of the barriers that hinder women's access to boards in Africa generally exist in Egypt. For example, women who work in the corporate sector are in most cases from a privileged background. Corporate board appointments are largely through informal processes, and term limits for existing board members (mostly male) are rarely in place (AfDB, 2015, pp. 44-47). This view is echoed in Terjesen *et al.* (2009, p. 324) where research on women directors in the Middle East reveals for example, "…that the majority of Jordan's women directors are connected to the controlling or founding family, signaling the importance of '*wasta*' ('connections')", rather than institutionalized practice.

According to unpublished data compiled in December 2013 by the Egyptian Stock Exchange, and obtained with permission by the author, women held 8.7% of total board seats on 233 listed companies. Forty-eight per cent of the companies had no women on their boards. Table 12.1 shows the percentage of companies by number of women on their boards. Only 7% of the companies have more than three women directors, which is widely considered to be the "critical mass" that normalizes the presence and voice of women on boards (Terjesen *et al.*, 2009, p. 322). One company, Maridive & Oil Services, had six women board members who made up 35% of the board (EGX, 2013).

Table 12.1 **Number of women on corporate boards in Egypt, 2013**
Source: EGX (2013).

Number of women on the board	Percentage of companies (n = 233)
0	48.4%
1	31.4%
2	12.4%
3	5.2%
4 or more	2.6%

Table 12.2 shows the relation between board size and the percentage of women on the board. The total number of board members in the 233 companies was 2,204, ranging from 3 to 24 members in each company; the average was nine board directors. Approximately two-thirds (64.8%) of women directors served in companies whose board sizes ranged from 6 to 15 members, while the highest percentage of women directors (17.1%) was in companies with fewer than five directors.

Table 12.2 **Women on Egyptian corporate boards, by board size, 2013**
Source: EGX (2013).

Number of directors	Percentage of companies (n = 233)	Percentage of directors that are women	Percentage of total women directors (n = 193)
Less than 5	23.2	17.1	18.2
Between 6 and 10	40.1	8.0	33.4
Between 11 and 15	24.0	0.9	31.4
Between 16 and 20	9.4	7.7	14.5
More than 20	3.3	0.8	2.5

Insights on women corporate directors in Egypt are also available from broader based surveys conducted by GMI Ratings and the African Development Bank. These sources include far fewer Egyptian companies; however, they do provide meaningful regional and global comparisons. The 2013 GMI survey of 6,000 companies in 45 countries, for example, includes seven Egyptian companies. The GMI survey encompasses MSCI Emerging Markets Index companies with over $1 billion in free-float market capitalization (GMI Ratings, 2013). That survey shows Egyptian company boards comprised 4.4% women on average, compared with 7.4% on the boards in companies in Emerging Market countries, and 11.8% on the boards of all companies in the survey (see Table 12.3.) The number of companies included in the GMI Survey from the Middle East and Africa is 112, with 15.5% women directors.

Table 12.3 **Global comparisons of corporate directors, by gender, 2013**
Source: GMI Ratings (2013).

Number of female directors	All global companies surveyed Average (n = 5,977)	Emerging markets average (n = 851)	Egyptian companies average (n = 7)
1	63.0%	46%	43%
At least 3	13.0%	7.4%	0.0%
Overall average of female directors	11.8%	7.4%	4.4%

Further data are provided by the African Development Bank's 2015 report on women directors in 12 African countries (AfDB, 2015). This report shows that women comprise 12.7% of the corporate directors in the 307 listed companies in the study. The companies included in the report are blue-chip index or all-share index in some cases. Egypt, which has 20 companies in the report, is placed ninth with 8.2% women directors. Kenya and South Africa had the highest share of women directors, with 19.8% and 17.4%, respectively (see Table 12.4). Côte d'Ivoire and Morocco had the lowest percentage of women directors, at 5.1% and 5.9%, respectively.

Table 12.4 **Women corporate directors in African countries, 2013**
Source: African Development Bank (2015).

Country	Percentage of women directors	Number of companies
Kenya	19.8	20
South Africa	17.4	40
Botswana	16.9	22
Zambia	15.9	21
Ghana	15.7	34
Tanzania	14.3	11
Uganda	12.9	8
Nigeria	11.5	50
Egypt	**8.2**	**20**
Tunisia	7.9	20
Morocco	5.9	25
Côte d'Ivoire	5.1	36

The African Development Bank report highlights that the African continent "… comes third after the US and Europe, and first among other emerging regions in terms of women's representation on boardrooms of top listed companies" (AfDB, 2015, p. 3). The report also highlights that the countries with the greatest representation of women directors, Kenya and South Africa, have government mandates for women on boards of state-owned companies. Further, in the private sector, Kenya, Morocco, Malawi, Nigeria and South Africa have "…integrated gender diversity into principles of good corporate governance" (AfDB, 2015, p. 10). The AfDB report also points to a number of barriers to increased women's representation on corporate boards in Africa. These include cultural issues, such as "old-boy" networks, structural issues such as the lack of transparency in board nominations, and governmental issues related to weak regulatory enforcement (*Ibid.*, p. 15).

Lessons learned

Lessons learned from international experiences of improving gender equality on boards (MSCI, 2014; AfDB 2015) point to the importance of legislation that required quotas that are enforced, with sanctions, in order to institutionalize gender diversity on boards. As mentioned above, some African countries, such as Kenya and South Africa, have mandated women's representation on state-owned company boards (AfDB, 2015, p. 10). Similar legislation for government-owned companies is being considered in Brazil (MSCI, 2014, p. 5). The AfDB report also highlights cross-border influence from European multinational companies that require their subsidiaries to have targets of 30–35% women for their executive boards, such as Orange in France and Barclays in the UK (AfDB, 2015, p. 34).

As mentioned above, some research suggests that companies with more women in decision-making positions perform better and score higher in terms of corporate governance. Research also shows that boards with at least three women: "… are significantly more active in promoting non-financial performance measures such as customer satisfaction, employee satisfaction, and gender representation, as well as considering measures of innovation and corporate social responsibility" (Terjesen *et al.*, 2009, p. 329).

It is therefore important to position interventions aimed at increasing the number of women on boards within the framework of corporate governance and not only as a gender equality issue. This positioning has the added advantage of associating and aligning women's leadership and presence with the purpose of the company.

Leaders of companies with all-male boards often claim they cannot find qualified women candidates (MSCI, 2014; The Boston Club, 2014). A personal interview by the author with a senior executive in a consulting firm working with leading family businesses in Egypt highlights this issue. In particular, he described the "ideal candidate" for board membership as someone who had board experience; understood the role of a board; had experience in bigger size businesses to help the company grow; had what it takes to turn around a business; had exposure horizontally across organizational functions; and had international experience. "Unfortunately we cannot find qualified women", he said.

The same excuse of not finding qualified candidates is echoed in the MSCI 2014 report and has led to the creation of databases such as the Diverse Directors Database in the United States, the Women's Exchange Network in Canada, and the Global Board Ready Women's database in Europe. In addition, movements emerged that seek to increase women's representation on boards such as the 30% Coalition and the 2020 Women on Boards Campaign (MSCI, 2014, p. 3). These efforts are important steps in the process of change and they can be considered small wins that make a difference. The next section of this chapter describes a similar small win in Egypt.

The Women on Boards programme in Egypt

The American University in Cairo School of Business initiated a pilot Women on Boards programme in 2014, together with the Egyptian Corporate Responsibility Center (ECRC) which is a joint project between the United Nations Development Programme in Egypt and the government's Industrial Modernization Center. This was done with a consortium including the Women and Memory Forum and the Women in Business Committee of the American Chamber of Commerce in Egypt. Partners in the training component of the programme also included the International Finance Corporation (IFC) and Ashridge School of Business in the United Kingdom. Inspired by the UN's Women's Empowerment Principles, the programme mission is:

> To improve the gender balance of corporate boards in Egypt and the Middle East and North Africa region by sensitizing male board members to gender issues, qualifying women from different corporate sectors and outside the corporate mainstream to be appointed to corporate boards, and advocating for policy and legislative changes that institutionalize gender diversity on corporate boards.

The Women on Boards project in Egypt includes a number of components such as:

- Training on corporate governance, leadership and board competences for women
- Creation of a database of qualified board-ready women
- Research on the dynamics of board creation in Egypt
- Awareness raising for existing boards on the value of gender equality
- A policy whitepaper for the introduction of a quota for women on boards

The pilot phase of the project has been completed with the creation of the consortium, delivery of one training programme for 13 participants, and increased visibility of the project in Egypt and the region through presentations at different conferences, including the UN Global Compact and Principles for Responsible Management Education (PRME) meetings. In addition, a four minute video was created with testimonials from the inaugural programme participants.

The Egyptian Women On Board database of board-ready women will build on the experience of the Women and Memory Forum in creating a database of professional women called "Who Is She in Egypt?"[2] Currently the project is in the institutionalization phase and is actively fundraising in order to establish a project management unit to scale the project and explore the potential for regional replication.

2 See http://www.wmf.org.eg/en/ for further information.

More generally, women (and men) in Egypt need to be vigilant in identifying opportunities to foster greater gender equality on corporate boards. Working for gender equality *is* change, meaning that the small everyday actions we do and conversations we have are the way in which we practise change towards greater gender equality. This is a slightly different way of seeing change, in the sense that we do not wait for an end product of a process to tick a box that "change" has happened, but rather we consider that the process itself with all its details is the change (Shaw, 2002). As we become aware and conscious of why gender equality is important for each one of us personally and reflect on our own practice to see if there are things we can do better to support greater gender equality, we actually practise that change. In addition, we each have a sphere of influence in our social, professional and political lives. In each of these spheres, having conversations about gender bias, naming it, discussing its manifestations, and innovating solutions for it in a specific, local context, is change.

Second generation gender bias is subtle. It occurs by gendering work, reward systems, organization cultures and career paths to fit men's lifestyles, so they become the standards by which women are measured. For example, "…to be perceived as being of high ability, a woman must provide more evidence than would her male counterpart" (Biernat and Kobynowicz, 1997 quoted in Terjersen *et al.*, 2009, p. 322). Recommendations to overcome such bias include raising the awareness of both men and women about the existence of this bias and naming it so we can talk about it. We also need to provide coaching support to women as they assume leadership roles so they can internalize this transformation in identity, and ground women's sense of leadership so that the common purpose, rather than their gender, becomes the focus (Groysberg and Bell, 2013). This is what the Women on Boards programme in Egypt is trying to accomplish.

Conclusion

This chapter is about the practice of change. The understanding of change presented here is one that is informed by the notion of continuous "becoming" rather than thinking of change as an end point to be reached (Tsoukas and Chia, 2002). Egypt lags behind global and regional averages for women directors with only 8.7% representation of women on corporate boards. The Women on Boards initiative described above was initiated as a reaction to the status of women on corporate boards in Egypt. In the context of political and social volatility which has characterized Egypt since 2011, there is a need for such action that represents key steps; small wins that move us forward.

International initiatives such as the UN's Women's Empowerment Principles are important enablers in the process of change but definitely not sufficient in themselves. They are enablers for local activists as benchmarks and reference points as well as platforms for networking and support. However, government actions may have different political considerations locally and internationally. Therefore, persistence and multiple interventions that accumulate small wins may be a more pragmatic path for change. Such a path will undoubtedly entail setbacks and failures but it may also keep gender equality on the agenda and disrupt existing patterns of bias.

Further research is needed to dig deeper and analyse the dynamics of board composition in Egypt. This could show whether women are on the board as family members in family-owned businesses, as investors, as independent directors, as representatives of institutional shareholders, or as directors of subsidiaries of international companies operating in Egypt. In the latter case, as mentioned above, European companies, for example, may be complying with their home country regulations regarding board composition with respect to the number of women directors. Such research could shed light on the most effective interventions that could disrupt biased patterns and hopefully make a difference in gender equality on boards in the specific context of Egypt.

References

Adams, R.B., & Ferreira, B. (2009). Women in the boardroom and their impact on governance and performance. *Journal of Financial Economics*, 94, 2, 291-309.

African Development Bank Group (AfDB), Quality Assurance and Results Department, Gender and Social Development Monitoring Division (2015). *Where are the Women: Inclusive Boardrooms in Africa's top listed companies?* Retrieved from http://www.afdb.org/fileadmin/uploads/afdb/Documents/Publications/Where_are_the_Women_Inclusive_Boardrooms_in_Africa%E2%80%99s_top-listed_companies.pdf

The Boston Club (2014). *"No More Excuses". The 2014 Census of Women Directors and Executive Officers of Massachusetts Public Companies* Retrieved from http://www.thebostonclub.com/index.php/download_file/view/483/99/

Dawoud, A. (2012). Why women are losing rights in post-revolutionary Egypt. *Journal of International Women's Studies*, 13(5), 160-169.

The Egyptian Center for Women's Rights (ECWR) (2012). *Report on Egyptian Women Conditions in 2012: Women: Get Out to the Streets*. Egypt: Egyptian Center for Women's Rights. Retrieved from http://ecwronline.org/pdf/reports/2013/egyptian_women_conditions_in2012.pdf

The Egyptian Stock Exchange (EGX) (2013). "Board Composition of 233 Companies". Unpublished report.

Fletcher, J.K. (2004). The paradox of post heroic leadership: An essay on gender, power, and transformational change. *Leadership Quarterly*, 15(5), 647-661.

GMI Ratings (2013, April). *GMI Ratings' 2013 Women on Boards Survey*. Retrieved from http://www.calstrs.com/sites/main/files/file-attachments/gmiratings_wob_042013-1.pdf

Groysberg, B., & Bell, D. (2013). Dysfunction in the boardroom. *Harvard Business Review*, 91(6), 88-97.

McKinsey & Company (2015). *Women Matter: The Business and Economic Case for Gender Diversity*. Retrieved from http://www.mckinsey.com/features/women_matter

MSCI Inc. (2014, November). *Governance Issue Report: 2014 Survey of Women on Boards*. New York: MSCI Inc.

Saad, R. (2013, September 29). Do you really love justice? (in Arabic) *El Shorouk* [homepage of *El Shorouk* newspaper]. Retrieved from www.shorouknews.com

Shaw, P. (2002). *Changing Conversations in Organizations: A Complexity Approach to Change.* London: Routledge.

Stephenson, C. (2004). Leveraging diversity to maximum advantage: The business case for appointing more women to boards. *Ivey Business Journal*, Sept/Oct 2004. Retrieved from http://iveybusinessjournal.com/publication/leveraging-diversity-to-maximum-advantage-the-business-case-for-appointing-more-women-to-boards/

Terjesen, S., Sealy, R. & Singh, V. (2009). Women directors on corporate boards: A review and research agenda. *Corporate Governance: An International Review*, 17(3), 320-337.

Tsoukas, H. & Chia, R. (2002). On organizational becoming: Rethinking organizational change. *Organizational Science*, 13(5), 567-582.

Ghada Howaidy is executive director of strategic alignment at the American University in Cairo (AUC) School of Business. She has an MA in Middle East Studies from AUC and an MSc in public management from the London School of Economics and Political Science, as well as executive training at Harvard Business School. In 2015 she completed the Ashridge Doctorate in Organizational Change.

13

Mann Deshi Bank and Udyogini

Successfully collaborating to empower women*

Smita Shukla
University of Mumbai, India

Women in India are often treated as second-class citizens. Gender bias and discrimination are rampant in Indian society. Work being done by Mann Deshi Udyogini, a unique business school for rural women, is significant. No background education or degree is required to enrol for the business management courses being offered by this business school that works hand-in-hand with Mann Deshi Mahila Sahakari Bank. Mann Deshi Udyogini provides skill training while the bank provides financing to women so that they can run successful microenterprises. The chapter highlights success stories of Mann Deshi Udyogini. It also highlights the work being done by Mann Deshi Bank and Mann Deshi

* The author acknowledges the support of the following people in developing this chapter: Mrs Chetna Gala Sinha, Chairman of Mann Deshi Bank; Mrs Rekha Kulkarni, Chief Executive Officer of Mann Deshi Bank; Mrs Vanita Shinde, Chief Administrative Officer of Mann Deshi Bank; Mrs Madhuri Torane, in charge of Mann Deshi Udyogini activities; Ms Shaheen, a trainer at Mann Deshi Udyogini; Miss Shobha Raut; Mrs Vanita Pise; Mrs Surekha Vijay Kale; and Mr Shivaji Maruti Yadav. The chapter is based on first-hand interviews and interactions with the above-mentioned members and clients of Mann Deshi Bank, Mann Deshi Udyogini and Mann Deshi Foundation.

Foundation in building gender capabilities for strengthening female participation in rural India.

Vanita Pise, a beneficiary of Mann Deshi Udyogini support, says that Mann Deshi has given her "*Hunar, Hisab and Himmat*"; that is, "skill, financial strength and courage". This statement highlights the work being done by Mann Deshi Udyogini, Mann Deshi Bank and Mann Deshi Foundation, together known as the "Mann Deshi Group". The contributions of these institutions are remarkable in light of the fact that in India gender bias favouring males is widespread in urban and especially rural areas.

According to the 2011 Census of India there are only 943 females per 1,000 males in India. Indian states such as Haryana, Punjab that are infamous for gender bias favouring males have less than 850 females per 1,000 males. In spite of strong legislation the practice of sex selective abortions is still prevalent in India. The National Family Health Survey (NFHS-3, International Institute for Population Sciences (IIPS) and Macro International, 2007) highlights that only 26% of women in rural areas participate in decision making for obtaining healthcare for themselves; 7.6% of women participate in decisions regarding major household expenses; and only 10% of women are able to decide on visiting their family and relatives. For urban areas these figures are 29.7%, 10.4% and 12.2%, respectively. Females in India are often treated as a burden on the family. They are frequently deprived of education, food and healthy living conditions by members of their own families. In addition they are married off early and are then dependent on their husbands in matters of finance as well as power to make decisions for the wellbeing of their families.

The institutions of the Mann Deshi Group are relentlessly working to empower rural women with the skills and financial strength needed for fighting and creating their place in male-dominated Indian society.

Mann Deshi Foundation and its founder

Mann Deshi Foundation is a non-governmental organization that has been instrumental in setting up both the Mann Deshi Udyogini and the Mann Deshi Mahila Sahakari Bank. Mann Deshi Foundation has empowered over 300,000 women and girls over the years.[1] The Foundation's founder is Mrs Chetna Gala Sinha.

Chetna holds a Master's degree in Economics from the University of Mumbai. Right from her student days at the university, she got involved in social activities and initiatives. She derived her inspiration from Jayaprakash Narayan (also known as JP), a well-known political leader and social reformer (1902–1979). JP had participated in the freedom movement of India and had worked along with well-known political leaders such as Mahatma Gandhi and Jawaharlal Nehru. By the 1970s JP

---

1 Mann Deshi Foundation, About Us, http://www.manndeshifoundation.org/

was disillusioned with the government, which he felt was not doing enough to empower the poor and downtrodden. He thus gave a call for "Total Revolution" in India. Chetna in the early 1970s joined a student wing of the Janata Party, a political party formed under the guidance of JP, where she actively raised and supported the issues of slum dwellers in Mumbai.

Chetna married a like-minded classmate from the University of Mumbai and moved to live in her husband's ancestral village, Mhaswad, located around 300 km away from the megacity of Mumbai.

In Mhaswad, along with her husband, Chetna worked on issues and problems related to farmers and rural women. She was also involved in providing women in the area with "Panchayati Raj" training, the concept of local self-government at the village and district level promoted by the Government of India. Chetna was keen on ensuring higher participation of women in Panchayati Raj institutions from Mhaswad and nearby areas. Women, thus, often used to approach Chetna with their day-to-day issues and problems. This is how the Mann Deshi Foundation took shape in 1996. The Foundation continues to work actively for the development of poor and vulnerable women in and around the Mhaswad area.

Chetna has been awarded numerous awards and recognitions as a result of her work. To name a few: the Harvard University Bridge-Builder Award; the Ashoka Change Makers Innovation Award; the CII-Bharti Woman Exemplar Award; the Microfinance Process Excellence Award; the Jankidevi Bajaj Award for Rural Entrepreneurship; and India's Social Entrepreneur of the Year Award.[2] She was named the Social Entrepreneur of the Year by the Schwab Foundation. She has also been a World Fellow at Yale University and is an Ashoka Fellow for life. Mann Deshi institutions have also been awarded several national and international honours.

The Mann Deshi Foundation initiated a community radio station known as "Mann Deshi Tarang Vahini 90.4". Through its creative programming, the community radio is empowering women to improve their lifestyles and those of their families. The community radio programmes focus on improving family health, diet, water conservation, cleanliness and financial literacy. The community radio also runs regular competitions engaging women and children.

The Mann Deshi Foundation is also running skill development programmes for women in the city centres of Satara and Pune in association with the NSDC (National Skill Development Corporation) India. The skill development programmes which Mann Deshi is offering are based on its surveys of industry requirements in and around the region. After women are trained they are placed in firms through the Mann Deshi Employment Bureau in these city centres. Most of the women joining the NSDC skill training programme are, however, encouraged to start their own micro-ventures.

---

2 http://www.manndeshibank.com/Bank_Staff.html?page=sixth-page

Mann Deshi Mahila Sahakari Bank

Chetna states that, in 1993, a woman interested in opening a savings account in a bank approached her and told her that the bank was refusing to open an account for her. Chetna approached the bank and several other banks on the woman's behalf. All of the banks informed Chetna that they were not in a position to open an account for the woman as she was extremely poor and thus was not a viable client. This provoked Chetna to consider establishing a bank for rural women in the region. Ela Ben Bhatt, founder of SEWA (Self-Employed Women's Association) encouraged Chetna to do so and introduced her to the Friends of Women's World Banking in India organization that then guided her through the basics of initiating a cooperative bank. Chetna then approached the Registrar of Co-operatives in Maharashtra who further assisted her in completing the proposal and required documentation. A minimum of ten members were needed to promote the cooperative bank, so Chetna encouraged several rural women from the Mhaswad region to join in as promoting members of the proposed cooperative bank. Chetna was not keen on establishment of a regular commercial bank. She wanted to establish a cooperative bank as it is an institution which is owned by its members and is generally the culmination of shared interests, problems and aspirations. Under the cooperative model it is also possible to secure equal rights for all members, based on the "one member, one vote" concept.

Once the Registrar approved her proposal she approached the Reserve Bank of India (Central Bank of India) for a banking licence. However, her application was rejected on the grounds that all the promoting members were illiterate and had put their thumb impressions on the proposal, thus the application was not fit for granting a banking licence. Though Chetna was discouraged by the Reserve Bank of India's refusal to grant the licence, the women in the group were not. They told Chetna that they would learn to read and write and then approach Reserve Bank of India again. With remarkable determination the women attended literacy classes organized by the Mann Deshi Foundation and in less than six months they were ready to approach the Reserve Bank of India again for the banking licence. This time Chetna took 17 women members to meet with officers at the Reserve Bank of India. In spite of their rural background the women confidently interacted with the senior officers of the Bank regarding a requirement of the women's cooperative bank in the region. The women also challenged the officers to a competition in calculating interest of any principal amount stating that they would be able to do the calculation faster than the officers at the Central Bank. The women succeeded in this challenge and the banking licence was granted for the Mann Deshi Mahila Sahakari Bank.

Chetna recalls that in spite of having the licence it was not easy to initiate operations of the bank. For instance, they encountered political resistance from the individuals who themselves had failed to get banking licences in the past. Getting a place to rent for the bank's office was also difficult on account of this resistance. In addition, the promoters of the bank encountered some cultural and social resistance. Most of the men sarcastically commented on the capability of females in handling finances. Their view was that women cannot handle finance. In spite of all of these issues Mann Deshi Mahila Sahakari Bank started its operations on 11 August 1997 becoming the first regulated cooperative bank in India managed by and for women.

Mann Deshi Bank continues successfully operating as a microfinance bank and is arranging micro-lending facilities for women in rural areas. The Bank is also a pioneer in terms of initiating concepts such as "door step banking", daily and weekly savings products and the issuance of smart cards. Banking products and processes at Mann Deshi Bank are designed in such formats that women can hold greater control over the cash they earn. Chetna says all the innovations of the Bank are based on requirements of its customers. For instance, poor women customers had conveyed to the Bank that it was not possible for them to do banking by visiting a branch of the Bank as it meant loss of time in terms of earning their livelihood. Women also wanted to save on a daily and weekly basis with the Bank as they were not keen on keeping their earnings at their home. The women felt that they lost control over their money if it was maintained at home as the men in the family felt that they could determine expenditures. Further, women also feared that men in their family could squander the money on liquor. Mann Deshi Bank thus developed products and processes that suited the requirements of its female customers.

According to the November 2014 Newsletter of the Rural Financial Institutions Programme (RFIP) Mann Deshi Bank has recently initiated a weekly market cash credit product for micro-entrepreneurs. This product was initiated on the recommendation of Germany's GIZ (Deutsche Gesellschaft for Internationale Zusammenarbeit) and India's NABARD (National Bank of Agriculture and Rural Development) under the RFIP. There was a need for the cash credit product as many of the women were small vendors who purchased goods on credit from wholesalers who charged daily interest up to 1.4%. Now through this product the Bank is infusing liquidity in the micro-businesses and is bringing down the financial cost of business.

Mann Deshi Bank has been very successful in ensuring inclusion of the names of women in property papers and documents. At the time of granting a bank loan, Mann Deshi Bank asks the husband to submit in writing on a Stamp Paper[3] an acknowledgment that his wife has been developing and expanding his property and hence should be treated as a co-owner. Further, the Bank gives an interest subsidy on loans when property papers are in the woman's name.

Mann Deshi Bank was also instrumental in introducing government regulation by the Revenue Department of the Government of Maharashtra whereby the

---

3 Stamp papers are printed by the Government of India's Security Printing Press and are used for documenting transfer of property, commercial agreements and the granting of power of attorney.

names of women can be included on household property documents on the basis of simple submission to the Gram Panchayat.[4]

All of the above have resulted in the positive inclusion of the names of women as owners of household property.

Mann Deshi Udyogini

Mann Deshi Udyogini is a business school established in 2006 with the idea that a woman cannot be empowered only on the basis of monetary support. For complete empowerment women also need to be provided with training in skills to run successful microenterprises. The Udyogini, thus, operates hand-in-hand with Mann Deshi Mahila Sahakari Bank. Moreover training centres of Mann Deshi Udyogini are co-located with Mann Deshi Bank's branches .The only exception to this is Mann Deshi Udyogini's branch in Hubli, Karnataka. Currently Mann Deshi Udyogini is offering courses from seven centres located at Mhaswad, Dahiwadi, Vaduj, Satara, Pune, Lonand and Hubli. In addition, the Udyogini has three extremely innovative Mobile Business Schools that essentially bring the business schools to the doorsteps of the beneficiaries. More specifically, buses have been converted into mobile classrooms that travel from village to village of rural Maharashtra for imparting skills training to rural women.

The students at Udyogini are rural women in an average age bracket of 18 to 50. The women who receive training from the Udyogini come from varied backgrounds including; farmers, goat and sheep herders, vegetable vendors, potters, spice makers and basket weavers. No background education or degree is required to enrol for the simple business management courses being offered by Udyogini. Mann Deshi Bank provides finance while Mann Deshi Udyogini provides training in skills to women so that they can run successful microenterprises.

The courses offered by Mann Deshi Udyogini have three important components: training in technical skills; training to build financial literacy and marketing skills; and training for confidence building. Technical training accounts for over 60% of course components. Examples of courses include: basic computer skills, bag making, stitching, dress designing, beauty parlour training, English language training, food processing training and goat rearing. The duration of the courses, which range from basic to advanced, is from one day to around three months.

Udyogini also offers an MBA programme. Under this programme select women entrepreneurs from rural areas are introduced to mentors who guide them for a period of 12 months. Based on a Needs Assessment Survey, the participants are provided with training in areas including: working capital management, supply chain management, and marketing skills. The curriculum of the modules has been

---

4 Local government body at a village level.

designed in collaboration with Mann Deshi Udyogini's staff and microfinance institutions such as Accion Microfinance. After 12 months a Mann Deshi Udyojika[5] certificate is awarded to the participants. Udyojika is also linked with Yashwantrao Chavan Maharashtra Open University, a renowned open university in India located near the city of Nashik in Maharashtra. The female entrepreneurs who overcome major individual challenges and exhibit outstanding growth during the programme are recognized and honoured upon its completion.

Transforming life through Mann Deshi Udyogini: some success stories

Mann Deshi Udyogini has successfully transformed the lives of many females in the rural areas in and around the Mhaswad region in Satara. It has helped women to create space for themselves in an otherwise male-dominated Indian society. Examples of some of the success stories highlight the effectiveness of the programmes are given below.

Surekha Vijay Kalel

Surekha Vijay Kalel is a farmer and goat herder. She studied up to the 12th standard[6] but could not continue her studies after getting married. She was provided with training in a goat-rearing course at Udyogini. On account of her enthusiasm and positive learning attitude she was further supported by the Udyogini in undergoing training in a course on artificial insemination of goats. She now earns additional income from the goat insemination service she provides. She is also a banking correspondent of Mann Deshi Bank promoting its recurring deposit scheme. In addition she is a trainer for other females interested in goat rearing and artificial insemination courses. Surekha states that Mann Deshi is the reason she has been able to improve her family income substantially. She is now respected by her family, in-laws and society at large.

Vanita Pise

Vanita Pise also has a remarkable success story. Vanita's family had suffered the failure of the family business. Consequently, she had to take a loan from Mann Deshi Bank to start a business of rearing buffaloes and selling milk to support her family. Through Mann Deshi Bank she became involved in a self-help group through which she got the idea of making paper cups to cater to a local requirement of the village.

5 "Udyojika" means "woman entrepreneur".
6 Grade 12 or higher secondary school.

She used a loan from Mann Deshi Bank to buy a paper cup making machine. She then completed the business and marketing training programme offered by Mann Deshi Udyogini. Through the programme, Vanita was able to identify a wholesaler in Satara who agreed to supply her with the required paper and also promised to procure ready cups from her. Very soon she started producing around 5,000 cups a day and made a handsome profit. Encouraged by her success she bought some more paper cup making machines for herself and some other members of her self-help group. She started supplying raw material to other members of her self-help group and started taking commissions for selling their products. Suddenly, her supplier of paper for paper cups backed out from the arrangement. With sheer courage and determination Vanita developed a new supply chain for raw material and finished products. Her efforts were recognized and in 2006 she was awarded with the CII-Bharti Women Exemplar Award given to her by then Prime Minister of India, Dr Manmohan Singh. Vanita Pise's life has transformed since then. She is often invited to speak by reputed institutions across the world. She was also invited by the Reserve Bank of India to interact with its board of directors. She was inducted onto the Board of Directors of Mann Deshi Mahila Sahakari Bank. On account of her success she is often consulted on issues women face in the area by local politicians, including the members of the Legislative Assembly and the Member of Parliament from her region. Vanita's monthly income has improved significantly and now she earns around 30,000 rupees per month. Her children are now pursuing reputed technical courses in city-based institutions.

Shobha Raut

Shobha Raut's story is also very inspiring. Shobha suffered from polio when she was less than a year old. In spite of her disability she completed her Bachelor's degree in Commerce. She approached Mann Deshi Bank for a job but was rejected on account of her physical disability as the job required a considerable amount of field work related to its doorstep banking format. She thus accepted another clerical job near Satara. However, following an accident she had to relocate to Mhaswad. Shobha was provided with a loan of 15,000 rupees by the Mann Deshi Bank and also received training at the Mann Deshi Udyogini on running a microenterprise. She now successfully runs a grocery and a ladieswear shop at Mhaswad. She procures her products from Satara, Pune and Mumbai and sells them in Mhaswad. To expand her business further she took another loan from the Bank. She is currently repaying that loan. Shobha is supporting her father and mother. She has also financed the engineering education of her brother. Her father has pledged his property in her name.

Some more success stories:

- **Shabana Isak Kazi** runs a successful tailoring business from her house. She learned tailoring at Mann Deshi Udyogini and was subsequently provided with a loan by the Mann Deshi Bank for purchasing a sewing machine. She supports her family and has been able to fund new construction for her house.

- **Baby Balaso Lohar** is a 45-year-old who never attended school. The untimely death of her husband forced her to work as a housemaid for a year. Thanks to training provided by Mann Deshi Udyogini and a loan from Mann Deshi Bank she now sells snacks and various wares from a mobile cart and successfully supports her family.

- **Hafiza Firoz Tamboli** is a photographer and also runs a beauty parlour. She acquired her training and a loan from Mann Deshi Udyogini and Mann Deshi Bank. She is now running both her ventures successfully and her income has increased substantially.

- **Anita Bharat Kumbhar**, a potter by caste, is successfully running her pottery business as a result of the training and support provided by Mann Deshi Udyogini and Mann Deshi Bank. Anita attended the Udyojika MBA programme at Udyogini. She also prepares products catering for festival requirements in the region. Her stall at the Mann Deshi Marketing Fair consistently receives very good public response. Anita now successfully supports her family and is educating her kids.

- **Kanchan Kundan Bhagwat** married early and was not able to continue her studies. She undertook training in preparing snacks at Mann Deshi Udyogini; she was further supported by Mann Deshi Bank. She now employs several other women in her ready-made snacks business and her snacks are in great demand even in the city centres like Satara and Pune.

- **Malan Mane** is an illiterate woman. In the past she somehow managed her family by making traditional cane baskets. She, too, was supported by Mann Deshi Udyogini as well as Mann Deshi Bank. She now makes different types of cane baskets and products. She has been able to substantially enhance her income.

Other initiatives of Mann Deshi Udyogini

Mann Deshi Udyogini also runs a toll-free helpline number for women micro-entrepreneurs. The helpline was initiated after an unfortunate incident in which a woman tea vendor trained at Mann Deshi Udyojika was arrested by police as she was using subsidized cooking gas instead of a commercial gas cylinder. Mann Deshi Udyogini was able to secure her bail and convinced the authorities that the woman was not at fault as she was not aware that domestic cooking gas cannot be used for commercial operations. The helpline number enables women entrepreneurs to reach the Foundation for help in various cases of distress.

Mann Deshi Udyogini has also initiated a Chamber of Commerce for the rural women entrepreneurs. The aim of the Chamber of Commerce is to further the initiatives of its participants.

Lessons learned

The Mann Deshi Group highlights that the involvement of stakeholders is essential for real change. The Mann Deshi Foundation has focused on building trust and confidence of women participants. The Foundation has also encouraged community involvement through its community radio station.

The successful Mann Deshi model operates on two support pillars: Mann Deshi Bank and Mann Deshi Udyogini. The Bank provides the financial support and the Udyogini business school hones skills. Mann Deshi Bank operates in a cooperative format in order to ensure active participation of women as promoting members. The Bank also has been very sensitive to the requirements of borrowers and has created innovative items such as the weekly cash credit product to support women vendors. The Bank is further empowering women by encouraging inclusion of their names in the property papers. The Bank does this by subsidizing interest costs on loans for such cases. Efforts of Udyogini on the other hand have ensured that productive assets and capabilities are created so that women borrowers are easily able to repay the bank loans. Udyogini also provides continuous support to women in distress through its toll-free helpline.

The Mann Deshi Foundation's passion to bring change in the status of women by using the support of the Bank and Udyogini has resulted in multiple success stories of women's empowerment.

Summing up

Mann Deshi Foundation, Mann Deshi Bank and Mann Deshi Udyogini have been able to create a significant difference in the lives of women associated with the initiatives of these institutions. The success of Mann Deshi Udyogini can be seen in the fact that it has generated more than 140,000 women business school graduates since 2006. Sixty per cent of these women graduates have either started, or are running, their own businesses. Most of them used support from Mann Deshi Bank to start and scale their business.

The Mann Deshi institutions have evoked considerable global interest. Interns from top business schools around the world, including Harvard Business School and Columbia University, frequently visit and work with institutions promoted by the Mann Deshi group.

As Chetna Gala Sinha notes, a remarkable change which she has been able to observe is that the women who are active in Mann Deshi group institutions are now being selected by politicians to enter local elections. Moreover, Chetna notes that another major impact of the Mann Deshi group's work has been a change in the attitude of society at large. People who used to believe that women could not handle finance are now taking women seriously and are, in fact, seeking their advice.

References

International Institute for Population Sciences (IIPS) and Macro International (2007). *National Family Health Survey (NFHS-3), 2005-06, India: Key Findings*. Mumbai: IIPS. Retrieved from http://cbhidghs.nic.in/writereaddata/linkimages/NFHS-3%20key%20 Findings5456434051.pdf

Rural Financial Institutions Programme (2014, November). Newsletter. Retrieved from https://www.giz.de/en/downloads/giz2014-en-rfip-newsletter-november.pdf

Smita Shukla is Associate Professor in the area of Finance and Economics at Alkesh Dinesh Mody Institute for Financial and Management Studies, University of Mumbai. She holds Master's degrees in both Economics and Management and a doctorate degree in Management.

Conclusions

Kathryn Haynes
University of Hull, UK

Patricia M. Flynn
Bentley University, USA

Maureen A. Kilgour
University of Winnipeg, Canada

As noted in the Introduction, this book is the second in a two-book series on Gender Equality as a Challenge for Business and Management Education in association with Greenleaf Publishing and PRME (Principles for Responsible Management Education). These edited volumes arose out of the work of the PRME Working Group on Gender Equality, whose mission is to bring together academics and employers to provide support and resources for integrating gender issues and awareness into management education and the business world.

This book addresses issues of gender equality across a wide range of businesses, organizations and cultural environments worldwide. It provides a number of lessons on overcoming challenges to gender equality in the workplace. These are summarized at the end of this chapter, along with suggested areas for further research. In addition to providing useful case studies, including examples of best practices and unique perspectives on gender equality in non-traditional workplaces such as the Church of England and the US Military, this book addresses factors beyond the workplace that can help foster greater gender equality at work. In particular, it calls attention to: the influence that leaders within organizations can and do have in tackling gender issues; innovations that address gender inequality in a range of settings from the corporate board room to the coffee fields; and long-standing traditions that are being challenged to promote gender equality in the workplace.

Factors beyond the workplace that influence gender equality

It is evident from the wide range of subject matter contained in the chapters in this volume that gender equality, or inequality, in organizations does not stand alone within the organization, but interacts with wider societal issues and contexts outside the organization. Part III of this text provides examples of such issues, including the need for respect for women; security and safety; empowerment and the ability to work; and opportunities to develop skills. These challenges occur for women in all parts of the world, developing and developed, though they may differ in different contexts. In Chapter 7, for instance, external factors affecting gender equality in the global coffee industry include control over assets, availability of time, physical mobility and personal safety. Physical mobility is also relevant, as seen in Chapter 8, in the context of Australian transport systems that enable women's active participation in the workforce. Similarly, personal safety both in the home and in the workplace is a central factor in promoting gender equality, as addressed by the initiatives against domestic abuse seen in Chapter 9.

The interaction of family life and caring responsibilities is another area where factors beyond the workplace influence gender issues within. In most societies it is still women who bear the brunt of caring responsibilities, despite the increasing involvement of men in some cultures and contexts. In addressing deep-seated societal and organizational challenges, the influence of men in promoting gender equality is a critical factor. Gender equality issues affect everyone and require collaboration and the support of men and women; whether the topic is violence, safe societies or workplace equality.

Leadership to address gender equality

This book provides examples of how organizations have addressed some of these wider cultural issues. Yet organizations do not simply reflect society; they also influence and change society and wider cultural norms. The impact of strong organizational leadership in challenging gender inequalities in whatever form they take is so important.

The book also includes chapters that highlight the different forms of leadership in organizations working to overturn inequitable societal norms and stereotypes, and provide new opportunities and solutions to address gender equality. A board of directors in a company can exert a strong influence on the promotion of policies and practices, including those which can have positive effects on gender inequality both within the organization and beyond in its sphere of influence. This is clearly seen in Chapter 1, which examines the board of a high-tech company that, contrary to the norm, has been gender balanced since 1997. This company strives to promote values such as customer orientation, leadership and profitability as well as interpersonal values of enjoyment, a sustainable work–life balance, respect for diversity, mutual trust and equality of opportunities. The implicit goal is to disrupt any gendered subtext within the organization. Similarly, Chapter 12 addresses the leadership role played by corporate boards in tackling gender inequality.

In Chapter 4 we see how the influence of a CEO committed to gender equality, in this case Gay Gaddis of T3, can work from a values-based perspective, through investment in programmes to support parents in her organization. This case is an example of leadership on gender equality coming from the CEO level. However, leadership in challenging gender inequality can take other forms as well. For example, it may not be expected that the general legal counsel within an organization would be a driver for action on gender equality, but Chapter 3 discusses the transformational role that lawyers can play in reducing gender inequality in the workplace. The work of such lawyers can go well beyond legal compliance into best practices and the promotion of gender equality within the organization.

Leadership can be a very personal and gendered challenge for those undertaking such responsibilities. In Chapter 6, for example, we read the account of a Church of England priest in negotiating her own leadership style in a traditionally masculine context, where women leaders have been and remain in the minority.

Each of these role models of leadership on gender equality demonstrates the importance of the drive and commitment of women to bring about organizational and societal change and to promote and support the leadership opportunities for other women. This leadership may be informal or formal, in one small area or across the organization, and may be expressed in different ways or styles. But interventions like those discussed in this book promote broader awareness of the need for gender equality and its benefits for men as well as women, for organizations and for society at large.

Innovations to address gender inequality

Strong leadership is also a factor in fostering innovations to address gender inequality; and many of the leadership examples in these chapters drive organizational innovation. In Chapter 4, innovative working practices that facilitate caring for infants while maintaining a career are implemented by a committed CEO. The arrangement demonstrates that creative thinking from employers and employees working together can invent new ways to deal with both career and family responsibilities and bring about social, financial, business and emotional benefits. Similarly, in Chapter 5, further innovations in working practices through the use of a job-sharing arrangement in higher education not only enable individuals to benefit from senior management and leadership development opportunities, but also bring benefits to employers and organizations. For example, childcare and work have to, in some way, be integrated to drive both economic and social well-being; this integration is important in moving towards equality of opportunity for women and men. When this occurs through organizational innovation and when such practices influence how employees, organizations and societies view caring responsibilities, wider societal change can occur.

Innovations can take place in other ways as well, not just through leadership but though creative thinking about reducing gender inequality. Chapter 8 illustrates how applying an innovative approach to transport mobility brings about improved opportunities for women in the workplace at the same time as issues relating to women and their caring responsibilities are addressed. In Chapter 10, service-learning engagements result in a number of positive outcomes for students, communities and organizations, including an increased sense of self-efficacy, increased political engagement, reduction of stereotypes and increased capacity for diversity. There is an opportunity to extend this pedagogy in a very meaningful way to address gender equality within the workplace. Chapter 13 illustrates the innovative benefits of new business models and collaborative arrangements. In this case, Mann Deshi Udyogini, a unique business school for rural women, partners with a bank, creating opportunities where no background education or degree is required to enrol in the business management courses.

Challenging long-standing gendered traditions

Ultimately, this interaction of organizational and societal change enables a shift in gendered attitudes which are necessary prerequisites to the promotion of a more gender equal world. However, as we have seen, some traditions remain deeply rooted and difficult to alter. Nonetheless, initiatives and interventions can have a reformist effect and promote incremental change. For example, in Part IV of this book, we see the beginnings of change in three very varied geographical and cultural areas of the world, where long-standing gendered traditions have prevailed over many decades or even centuries. Chapter 11 addresses the US Military where policy changes have opened up previously denied roles for women. It remains to be seen how these will affect cultural barriers and resistance. Chapter 12 highlights the religious and military traditions that influence the opportunities for women to serve on corporate boards in Egypt, demonstrating that change can occur in small steps. Chapter 13 illustrates the challenge to long-held beliefs about women and opportunities for empowerment of rural women in India provided by the collaboration of a business school and a bank. All three of these chapters highlight the benefits of interventions and policy shifts in addressing long-standing gendered traditions.

Lessons learned

Numerous lessons can be drawn from the case studies, innovations and best practices highlighted in the chapters of this book. These include:

Women in organizational leadership:

- Having a critical mass of women in top management, an influential female leader or a female CEO can be instrumental in fostering an organization's ability to address and promote gender equality (Chapters 1, 3 and 4).

- Women leaders may have to overcome gendered stereotypes of embodied leadership in order to lead authentically and resiliently. Organizations can crucially support this through specific reference to and valuing of women's experience in cultural change (Chapter 6).

Value-driven organizations:

- Organizations that foster equality practices and narratives from their inception and/or embed them in their values are well-placed to drive change, since resistance is less likely (Chapters 1 and 4).

- Creating shared value between employees and companies supports the empowerment of women, especially in developing contexts (Chapters 2 and 13).

Practices to improve gender equality:

- Innovative employment practices and flexible work can support women's career development (Chapters 4 and 5).

- Safety and mobility initiatives support women's employment opportunities (Chapters 7 and 8).

Business and economic issues:

- Business growth can create an environment in which gender equality initiatives can thrive (although we must address gender equality even in times of economic slowdown or recession) (Chapter 1).

- Economic empowerment and access to credit are important factors in socially empowering women (Chapters 2 and 13).

- Skills development for both women and men facilitates opportunity and cultural change, reducing stereotypes (Chapters 10 and 13).

Wider societal issues:

- Factors internal and external to the organization interact to cause and perpetuate gender inequality, hence both need to be addressed (Chapters 3, 7, 8, 9 and 10).

- In the face of long-standing traditions that prolong gender inequality, incremental steps support shifting perceptions and change (Chapters 6, 11, 12 and 13).

These are important lessons that can be applied and addressed in a number of contexts in a variety of ways. Yet there is a continued need for further work to address the challenge of gender inequality in the workplace. This may take the form of changing organizational practice through the recognition that gender equality brings about business benefits. We would also argue, however, that as well as the business case for gender equality there is also an ethical imperative in the interest of social justice for all.

Areas for further research

As individuals and organizations strive to challenge gender inequality and to promote equality, there is also a case for further research on these issues. This could take the form of the following:

- Field research to increase understanding of the effects of gender inequality or equality
- Case studies of interventions within organizations
- Monitoring and evaluation of the implementation of equality practices and policies
- Deeper and richer understanding of the societal context within which organizations challenge gender inequality
- Personal accounts and narratives of individual leaders or workers to inspire or challenge
- More detailed exploration of the interaction of roles both within and outside the workplace
- The influence of men and male leaders on gender equality and inequality

Numerous obstacles remain in the goal to achieve gender equality for women at work. Despite enormous challenges, many of the workers, employers, leaders, managers, business leaders and policy-makers highlighted in these pages offer guidance and inspiration for others in tackling gender inequalities. The outcomes of continued and persistent interventions, proactive policies, organizational commitments and cross-sector partnerships can be highly beneficial for the entire workforce, the business world and, of course, society at large.

About the editors

Patricia M. Flynn, PhD, is trustee professor of economics and management at Bentley University, USA, where she served as Dean of the McCallum Graduate School of Business for ten years. Her numerous publications focus on corporate governance, women in business and technology-based economic development. She is co-chair of the PRME Working Group on Gender Equality, and co-editor of the two related books in the PRME/Greenleaf Series on Gender Equality in  Management Education. In 2016, she was the inaugural recipient of the Distinguished Woman Leader in Business Education award given by the Women Administrators in Management Education at AACSB-International; the award now bears her name.

Kathryn Haynes, PhD, is Dean of the Faculty of Business, Law and Politics at Hull University, UK, and a Fellow of the Institute of Chartered Accountants in England and Wales. Her research, which has been funded by grants from the Economic and Social Research Council (ESRC) in the United Kingdom, centres on issues of gender and social responsibility in relation to the professions; the body and embodiment within organizations; identity; and sustainability. She is a co-chair of the PRME Working Group on Gender Equality.

Maureen A. Kilgour, PhD, is a professor in the Faculty of Business and Economics at the University of Winnipeg in Canada. She is a member of the UN Women's Empowerment Principles Leadership Group, founder and co-chair of the PRME Working Group on Gender Equality and co-editor of three Greenleaf Publishing books (two in the PRME series and one on Gender and CSR). Her research focuses on business and human rights, global governance and CSR. She has worked in policy development, advocacy and as a consultant for numerous organizations in the areas of industrial relations, human rights and gender equality.

For Product Safety Concerns and Information please contact our EU
representative GPSR@taylorandfrancis.com
Taylor & Francis Verlag GmbH, Kaufingerstraße 24, 80331 München, Germany

www.ingramcontent.com/pod-product-compliance
Ingram Content Group UK Ltd.
Pitfield, Milton Keynes, MK11 3LW, UK
UKHW021828240425
457818UK00006B/118